RADIO'S 100 MEN OF SCIENCE

GUGLIELMO MARCONI

RADIO'S
100
MEN OF SCIENCE

Biographical Narratives of
Pathfinders in
Electronics and Television

ORRIN E. DUNLAP, Jr.

Essay Index Reprint Series

BOOKS FOR LIBRARIES PRESS
FREEPORT, NEW YORK

INTERNATIONAL STANDARD BOOK NUMBER:

0-8369-1916-5

LIBRARY OF CONGRESS CATALOG CARD NUMBER:

70-128235

PRINTED IN THE UNITED STATES OF AMERICA

CONTENTS

PART I
PIONEERS OF ELECTRICITY

PART II

PIONEERS OF THE RADIO AGE

CONTENTS

CONTENTS

APPRECIATION

Many of the radio pioneers have read their "careerographs" as presented here, and to them the author expresses sincere appreciation for their interest and for the time taken from their busy days to make the stories authentic as a historic record. From Marconi, Branly, Fleming, De Forest, Armstrong, Zworykin and others much of the information came to the author first-hand. For the story of those who have passed on, as Faraday remarked "to the glorious hope," the author has consulted their writings and scientific papers.

To those authors who across the years biographically recorded the work and pictured the personalities of the front-rank men in electrical discovery, the author is extremely grateful, for he has drawn upon their observations and linked them with the men of science who followed to make radio. One of the most helpful sources of information was the splendidly written little book, *Pioneers of Electricity*, by J. Munro, published in 1890—on the threshold of wireless, when the world little suspected what the men of science were planning for the generations ahead.

Many thanks are due George Clark, a veteran of wireless, for his friendly interest and helpfulness in the search for dates and data. Also, to Hazel C. Souhami for the careful typing of the manuscript —a painstaking process. To Louise L. Dunlap for her thoughtful reading and editing of the manuscript, and for many excellent suggestions which added immeasurably to the completeness and inspirational value of the story, the author is most grateful.

PREFACE

To have met and talked with radio pioneers and to have corresponded with others adds to the pleasure of recounting their scientific missions in life—their contributions to communication and to civilization. From their brains sprang great industries with employment for millions of people, new comforts, conveniences and services. In one year the American public has spent $130,000,000 for electric light bulbs, and in that same period American industry has expended more than $300,000,000 in research. Thomas A. Edison, it has been estimated, created fifteen billions of dollars of wealth that might never have existed had it not been for his genius. Marconi's invention of wireless begot billions too.

Memory recalls these impressions of several personalities:

Marconi—reserved, modest, punctual and neat; always the diplomat moving within a small circle of his own choice, keeping his thoughts and observations much to himself, wondering when he might find a few leisure hours.

De Forest—restless, enthusiastic; in his shirt sleeves testing some new idea in a maze of wires, oblivious to those waiting for him at the doorway; a tenacious fighter, a good letter writer—a man who enjoyed the strife of life.

Zworykin—quiet, daring, a wizard in electronics, telling of new wonders in television and no more excited about it than when relating his experience of being lost in the fog, skimming New York Harbor while flying his own land plane; a scientist with a good sense of humor. Ask him if he ever dreamed about electrons and he would answer, "I sleep soundly!"

Pupin—immigrant to inventor and teacher, introducing Marconi at a meeting of the Institute of Radio Engineers, humorously telling him that the crowd had gathered not so much to hear what he had to say as to see his boyish smile; enthusiastically discussing television, superbly confident of its future and suggesting that "televisioner" might be a parallel term for radio listener.

Alexanderson—a hard worker, friendly but never a prophet; rushing hither and yon across open fields in the Mohawk Valley which were covered with a web of his antennas; a family man, a father sitting at home showing his children how television pictures are plucked from the air.

Tesla—tall, mysterious octogenarian, seemingly disappointed with much of the past, looking with a cynical eye on the future, in his frock coat delivering a sermonlike talk on the ether, on light, on transmission of power by wireless, and on immortality.

John Hays Hammond, Jr.—seagoing Yale man turned scientist, sitting in a turret-shaped room in his medieval castle overlooking Gloucester Harbor, revealing the details of a television "eye" for airplanes and talking about radio-controlled torpedoes; a good host on board his laboratory schooner, the *Odysseus III*, using for his cabin a once-secret chamber below decks.

Edison—tireless, endowed with fine simplicities, broadcasting in an improvised glass studio in Madison Square Garden, throwing up his hands over his head as if surrendering to the mystery of it all, then smiling bashfully like a boy caught talking to himself as he hurried away from the microphone to sit alongside Mrs. Edison and his cronies, Henry Ford and Harvey Firestone.

Sir Robert Watson-Watt—England's radar expert, visiting Radio City as the head of a distinguished British Scientific Commission. Flanked by admirals, generals, wing commanders and other officers resplendent in their gold braid and starred uniforms, the short, spectacled Sir Robert appearing more as the typical professor than as a warrior of science who had done so much to save Britain from being blitzed to defeat. Extremely friendly, radiating a quick sense of humor, most gracious in manner, thanking his host for "that amazing spectacle—a most delightful luncheon served on one of New York's wartime, meatless Tuesdays."

. . . .

The selection of scientists and pathfinders for a place in this book necessarily includes the pioneers in electricity, for they were the trail blazers of radio. There is only one Faraday, one Edison, Morse, Bell, Marconi, or De Forest. Science is a marathon that never ends; as leaders in the race drop out new ones come in to set the pace. Marconi won first prize in wireless, but his death did not signal the end of the race in radio any more than the telephone stopped development with Bell, the telegraph with Morse, or the airplane with Wright.

Progress goes on. Contemporaries are running far beyond Marconi. Time has yet to measure their pace and to deal out the prizes. So a number of them are listed here because they show promise; they are running a good race.

Inventors have their own individual styles as do artists, authors, composers and song writers. There are two classes of inventors—those who create systems and those who invent devices. Maxwell and Marconi were systemic. They dealt with a broad general field, or association of things into vast functional aggregations. Edison and De Forest were device inventors, whose achievements greatly stimulated systemic developments—Edison, electric lighting, the phonograph and the motion picture; De Forest, broadcasting.

If, from radio's 100 pioneers in science, the most outstanding were to be listed, according to their contributions to the advance of the art, the "Big Ten" would be: Faraday, Henry, Maxwell, Hertz, Marconi, Fessenden, Fleming, De Forest, Armstrong and Zworykin.

While "science moves, but slowly creeping on from point to point," the men named in this book have played important parts to effect in radio a radical change or entire change; they have reconstructed or rebuilt on new lines. They drove stakes along the pathways of progress; they erected mileposts. They built stairways, not merely steps, from floor to floor in the mighty and towering structure of radio. Each man was a pioneer in his particular field—an originator of a new device or a new method which went beyond merely skilled technique and exerted a profound influence on one or more of the arts. Their charm was and is in their simplicity; their fame in electricity, radio and electronics.

Study of their lives reveals that most of them had poetical minds; they thirsted for knowledge from early youth right up to the closing days of their lives. Entranced by the beauties and mysteries of Nature, they reverently watched for unexpected hints from it, and were forever cross-examining the universe to learn Nature's secrets. Most of them responded to the thrill of the sunset, the lightning, birds, mountains, forests and the sea.

Curiosity and persistence, versatility and imagination, marked their characters; hard work and study, simplicity and faith, marked their days and nights. Their love of Nature was closely linked with a devout spirit. Almost all in their study of science and Nature found evidence of a Supreme Architect of the universe—in the words of Oersted:

> The universe is a manifestation of an Infinite Reason,
> and the laws of Nature are the thoughts of God.

New York, 1944   O. E. D. JR.

The Genesis of Radio

Radio is the creation of a long line of scientists whose work goes back more than 100 years. In the beginning they discovered mysterious sparks and strange electrical effects, but years passed before they were able to interpret the practical significance of the electric spark.

In 1867 Maxwell calculated existence of an all-pervading medium —the ether—through which light, heat and electric waves traveled. Without knowing it, the scientific world was on the threshold of wireless. Hertz then produced electric waves and demonstrated that they would at least cross a room, thereby proving Maxwell's mathematics were correct. Branly next invented the coherer to detect the invisible impulses. Marconi linked all three ideas to give to the world his new system of signaling. Thus, in 1896 wireless telegraphy was born.

From Maxwell's discovery to Marconi's, twenty years had passed —a twinkling as science measures time. But wireless had been on the way long before Maxwell. Its beginning goes back to the discovery of "electrum" by Thales of Miletus, and from his day on across the centuries Nature dropped many a clue that led to wireless. Each discoverer and inventor in turn received inspiration from predecessors and contemporaries. Even Edison is said to have remarked, "I begin where the other fellow left off."

Contending that the discoveries of science are the discoveries of the laws of Nature, and like Nature do not go by leaps, Justice Frankfurter of the United States Supreme Court observed that even Newton and Einstein, Harvey and Darwin, built on the past and on their predecessors.[1]

[1] Marconi Wireless Telegraph Company of America *vs.* United States, June 21, 1943, Justice Felix Frankfurter dissenting in part.

1

Seldom indeed has a great discoverer or inventor wandered lonely as a cloud [said Justice Frankfurter]. Great inventions have always been parts of an evolution, the culmination at a particular moment of an antecedent process. So true is this that the history of thought records striking coincidental discoveries—showing that the new insight first declared to the world by a particular individual was "in the air" and ripe for discovery and disclosure.

The real question is how significant a jump is the new disclosure from the old knowledge. Reconstruction by hindsight, making obvious something that was not at all obvious to superior minds until someone pointed it out—this is too often a tempting exercise for astute minds. The result is to remove the opportunity of obtaining what Congress has seen fit to make available.

The inescapable fact is that Marconi in his basic patent hit upon something that had eluded the best brains of the time working on the problem of wireless communication—Clerk Maxwell and Sir Oliver Lodge and Nikola Tesla. Genius is a word that ought to be reserved for the rarest of gifts. I am not qualified to say whether Marconi was a genius. Certainly the great eminence of Clerk Maxwell and Sir Oliver Lodge and Nikola Tesla in the field in which Marconi was working is not questioned. They were, I suppose, men of genius. The fact is that they did not have the "flash" that begot the idea in Marconi which he gave to the world through the invention embodying the idea.

Discovery after discovery, invention after invention, has been heralded as revolutionary, yet looking back across the years, each appears as but a step—some, of course, more important than others in the evolution of a miraculous system of communication: radio.

Ideas and instruments which seem momentous at the time of their conception are worn thin by the years. Where are the feeble sparks that sputtered the messages of Marconi's triumph in the nineties; the famous sparks that were the voices of such ships as the *Titanic* and *Lusitania*? Where are the crystal detectors that transformed electric impulses from the air back into sound? Where are the powerful arcs that whistled history-making code dispatches and casualty lists across the Atlantic during the World War from 1914 to 1918?

For the passing moment, all those historic devices were given front-page importance, yet none was imbedded deeply enough in the foundation of radio science to withstand the onslaught of progress. Each in turn was discarded to make way for new instruments, which in a short time would meet the same fate.

Many a man across the century contributed a revolutionary idea, theory or instrument; yet when fitted to the wheel of communication it became but one of the cogs of progress. The world and the heavens have been the laboratory of radio as men of many nations experimented on land and sea, on deserts and on mountains, to learn the secrets of Nature in which wireless is wrapped.

The most significant developments, the biggest steps in the evolution of radio, have been born out of tiny clues which scientific minds wrested from Nature. Mathematics and scientific calculations started the old order of things tumbling, as an inquisitive mind reached into the emptiness of incommunicable space to show to those of a more practical frame of mind the pattern of the instruments needed to put a skin of unseen waves around the globe.

The pre-Marconi men, who believed that they had found clues for electric communication without wires, generally did so by accident. While experimenting in the field of electricity, they observed that its effects were not necessarily bound to a wire. More or less mystified, they groped around "wireless" through induction, conduction (current leakage) and electrostatic coupling. These influences led them astray from the real clue. Preece and Lodge, for instance, were entranced by magnetic induction, Morse by conduction and Dolbear by electrostatic effects. They failed to recognize the fact that radiation was the great clue to wireless.

Marconi grasped that idea, and made electromagnetic radiation a practical method of wireless communication. The pre-Marconi men pursued will-o'-the-wisps, but they clung to the idea that some system of wireless signaling lurked in the cards dealt by science to the world. Those who followed Marconi improved upon what his practical mind achieved.

The driving forces of radio—electromagnetic waves, electrons, wavelengths and sound itself—have been elusive, unseen and puzzling. By studying the faint glow of electrical effects, by unraveling the mystery of tiny sparks, by watching and listening to simple things—even an insignificant cricketlike click or some peculiar magnetic action—man has pieced together the science of a new pattern of international communications: radio and television.

Thousands of patents demonstrate that radio is by no means the conception of a single mind. Man did not make the "ether." He did not invent electricity, magnetism or electrons. They have existed since the creation of the world. But man had to fashion the tools to enliven and harness these forces with which the earth and the air are endowed. The disagreement on theories, the continuous stream of new instruments, the quick obsolescence of apparatus, the continual cropping up of new ideas are proof that the riddle of radio is endless. Research leads man on, but no one ever completes the unfinished symphony of science.

Naturally, some men are pre-eminent in the scientific cavalcade. The timeliness of their entrance upon the stage of science, their persistence, initiative, financial resources, economic affiliations, courage and ability to keep everlastingly at it were the factors which gained recognition for them, for their discoveries and for their machines. Behind each one who has helped to envelop the earth with invisible messages, music, voices and pictures have marched the reserves—the promoters, financiers, statesmen, businessmen, legal specialists, industrialists, opportunists and showmen.

Also supporting the pioneers of science were the thousands of indefatigable experimenters and helpers, who toiled behind the scenes to nurture the germ of a big idea and to make it work. Some paved the way for discovery. Others fitted the key of invention to the lock of practical usefulness. Such men worked for Edison and for Marconi. Their patient toil from day to day, the joy they won from seeing a dream come true, is all a part of the romance of radio. The most humble of these is saluted when an S O S is answered, or when man snaps a simple switch and picks up music from a far corner of the earth.

Today radio, no longer confined to sending and receiving messages, enlists men from many fields of science. The radioman in the latest sense of the word may be a specialist in electron optics, photography, thermionic emission, chemistry, lenses, acoustics, plastics and metallurgy, or he may be an expert in power-supply devices, fluorescent materials, magnetism or electron multipliers. Men from all these fields work in the modern radio laboratories.

The roll call of radio's leaders in science reveals that the master minds of wireless were born in the nineteenth century. Fame was achieved through simple, comparatively crude tools; they had no radio-electron tubes, no microphones, no electronic "eyes." Knowledge of the "ether" was scant. Electrons were a great mystery. Nevertheless, in the mauve decade, men triumphed in wireless.

The roaring 1840's produced Edison, Bell, Fleming and Branly. In the fifties Lodge, Pupin, Thomson and Tesla were born. The sixties called up Fessenden and Steinmetz. In the seventies came Marconi, De Forest, Alexanderson and Rutherford. The eighties brought Hull, Hammond, Langmuir, Arnold and Zworykin; the gay nineties, Armstrong, Beverage, Watt and others.

But where are the master minds of the twentieth century? More than forty years have passed. Too early? Scarcely is that the explanation, for Marconi was in his teens when he scored, and only twenty-seven when he sent the first signal across the Atlantic.

This may lead some to believe that the day is gone when an individual can triumph alone; that never again will a man's name be attached to his invention as Marconi, Edison, Morse, and Bell.

Since their pioneering days invention has become more complex; it calls for team play by experts in numerous fields, who concentrate their talents and skills to achieve the ultimate result. Such co-operative research assures success more quickly; it saves time and eliminates the necessity of a lone inventor groping in fields foreign to his knowledge and capabilities. The splendidly equipped laboratory makes available the tools, resources and experiences so vital to invention.

The modern inventor is not pictured as impoverished and forlorn, fighting without food and funds for recognition and support of his ideas. In contrast with the inventor of the past he works in an atmosphere conducive to clear thinking. He enjoys freedom from worry regarding the necessities of life; he has a security in his adventure in science and in the future that many of the pioneers missed through disappointment and sorrow. Even Morse waged such a struggle; his whole energies were called upon to extricate himself from the confusion and hardship in which he was unhappily placed. He, like many other inventors, had to devote time to the defense of his invention against those who would pirate.

By no means does the modern blending of individuals and individual efforts in well-organized laboratories mean that gone forever is the attic, cellar, woodshed or garage workshop. Neither has the drama and romance been stripped from invention. So long as there is incentive, as there is in America; so long as young minds have an aptitude for science and are schooled along that line, there will be no end of opportunity. Ideas may well be born in humble surroundings, on a farm for that matter, far away from any great laboratory. The day has not gone when the best-equipped laboratories in the world will bow to the genius of a lone inventor—to patient, plodding perseverance.

Since the turn of the century radio has been in a period of transition, a period of development and assimilation—and in war.

It may be expected that after the gains of the prewar and war periods are consolidated, the period of assimilation will end. Radio never will be stagnant. There will come a day in the postwar era when new wonders will appear and with them new wizards. Certainly, during the remainder of the twentieth century, new master minds will come forward. They are active in the field today, but it is difficult to appraise their work in relation to the future. Then, too, their achievements in the late thirties and early forties have been secrets of war.

Geniuses of tomorrow may be but boys today. Radio will call upon them for the fresh ideas they can contribute. Powerful are the tools they will have to work with compared with those of their predecessors. Youth today has the radio-electron tube; Marconi had but the coherer.

Nothing is new in radio for long. What is new today is old tomorrow. Unlike the surface of the earth the ethereal spectrum is still unexplored. The new frontiers of the world are the far-flung frontiers of science. The realm of the microwave is a wide-open and mysterious empery across which will be blazed the trails of the future of radio. No barrier is there to block the alert young man enthusiastically interested, with an aptitude for science and an ardor for work. For him radio-electronics is a field that will be forever new and unlimited as the lives and achievements of radio's men of science attest.

Limitless in its scope, infinite in its opportunities, the future of radio is as unfathomed and uncharted as the boundless space in which it performs. Its past is as if measured by seconds, and its wonders are as if worked within a passing moment compared to the vastness of its future and the miracles to be expected in the years to come.

"We are living in a generation that has given science the green light," said David Sarnoff, President of the Radio Corporation of America, to the research and engineering staff of RCA.[2] We are fortunate to live and work in a country that has come to look upon change and invention, new methods and new services, as an inherent part of American culture and civilization, rather than something to deny or to obstruct or to prevent.

We happen to be living at a time when the world is determined to move forward. We are not likely to go back to the methods of yesterday. We must not stand in the way of change. Our aims should be to help direct change along useful lines and to strike the happy balance between those who would destroy everything, because they belonged to yesterday, and those who would try anything because it had not been tried before. That is the balance where experience and integrity count most. . . .

The services of radio are many—many more than we can comprehend even with our daily contact with the art. Anything that can make a sound, or a mark on a piece of paper, or control some device at a distance, and transmit sound and sight through space, lends itself to a multiplicity of uses depending upon the needs of the time and upon the opportunities of the moment.

New inventions are geared to the times and to the generations in which people live. There was the Steam Age, then the Electrical Age, and later came

[2] March 12, 1941.

the Radio Age. Now I think we are on the eve of a new age—the Electronic Age. Just as electricity *electrified* industries and life in general, so these developments that you gentlemen are producing with tubes and circuits will *electronize* industries and create the Electronic Age.

It is not the invention of yesterday, but the research of tomorrow, that will chart the future of radio and determine its destiny. . . . The advances of the next fifty years will make those of the last fifty pale into insignificance.

In the infinitesimal electron is found the great promise of radio's future; the electron is to radio what a second is to time and what time is to the future. It has been called the cornerstone of a billion-dollar wartime industry traveling on a meteoric path brilliant with prospects.

Oddly enough, to pick up the electron stream and trace back to its source leads to ancient Greece. The science of electronics has trickled down through the ages. Scientists, grasping the electron's significance, have invented devices to harness its magic and power. As a result, the stream has broadened into a mighty river, which produces electrical power as it flows through the great man-made generator—the electron tube!

PART I

PIONEERS OF ELECTRICITY

Thales of Miletus

PATRIARCH OF ELECTRICIANS

BORN: 640 B.C.
Greece

DIED: 548 B.C.
Greece

THALES OF MILETUS, philosopher, astronomer and mathematician, also won title to "the Patriarch of Electricians" through his observations of the phenomena of frictional electricity and magnetism. Entranced by the magic power of amber when rubbed by silk, and by the attractive property of the lodestone, Thales, according to the classic authors, thought that possibly a "soul" or spirit dwelt within them. Otherwise, how could it be explained that tiny straws and feathers would leap to the excited amber?

The strange phenomenon of amber acquiring an electrical charge by friction later suggested the word "electricity," for the Greeks had a word for amber; they called it "elektron" from the Greek for sun-god, because amber had a sunny luster. The lodestone, also classed with amber because of its attractive property, was obtained at Heraclea in Lydia, hence was called the Heraclean stone. Its later name, magnet, came from Magnesia on the Meander, or from Magnesia ad Sipylum, where it was also found as magnetite.

Diogenes Laertius relates that Thales was active in politics before he became a philosopher whose mental training was stimulated by the mysterious elektron sparks. Aristotle, Plutarch and Herodotus wrote about him, for his fame extended through all Hellas. One story has it that Thales was of Phoenician descent, belonging to the clan of Thelidae, while another describes him as "a native Milesian of noble birth."

Recognized as the father of Grecian geometry, astronomy and philosophy, Thales, according to Plutarch, knew that the earth was globular; he defined the magnitude of the sun as being 720 times as great as the moon, and predicted the solar eclipse. He also taught

11

that water was the elemental fluid and material source of all things. Several theorems are attributed to him, for example, "a circle is bisected by its diameter." But it was his familiarity with the simple phenomenon of frictional electricity in amber—a fossil resin—that gave him seniority among electronic scientists.

Thales' predictions appear to have created profound impressions among the Greeks; he shook their faith in omens and stimulated an interest in natural science and the forces of Nature. At the age of ninety-two, while a spectator at the Milesian games, he died, overcome with the heat. Demophilus remarked, "To those who run in the stadium the prize is in the end of the race; to those who labor in wisdom the reward is in old age."

From Plutarch it is learned that Thales by his own wish was buried in a neglected part of the Milesian fields, which he had predicted would become the marketplace. But not so, for the site was buried under the silt of the Meander, which partially filled up the Latmian Gulf. An inscription on the tomb of Thales reminded the passer-by of ancient Greece that although it was lowly, the fame of Thales ascended to the skies. His statue, erected by the Milesians, carried these words: "Miletus, fairest of Ionian cities, gave birth to Thales, great astronomer, wisest of mortals in all kinds of knowledge."

Centuries later, "elektron" flowing through the arteries of telegraph, telephone and radio would become the life blood of communications. Electrons would "paint" television pictures, and the electron tube would beat as the heart of a new science—*electronics*.

William Gilbert

SUPREME EXPERIMENTER OF HIS DAY

BORN: *May 24, 1544*
Colchester, England

DIED: *November 30, 1603*
Colchester, England

WILLIAM GILBERT, or as he spelled it, Gilberd, is remembered as the most distinguished man of science during the reign of Queen

Elizabeth—"the scientific star of Elizabeth's glorious reign, and one of the first experimentalists that England ever produced."

William was the eldest of Hierom Gilberd's sons; he studied at both Cambridge and Oxford. From St. John's College, Cambridge, which he entered in 1558, he took his A.B. degree, and later became mathematical examiner of the College. In 1569 he achieved his degree of M.D., and in 1600 was appointed Physician to the Court of Queen Elizabeth.

Gilbert's tomb in the chancel near the Church of Holy Trinity, in Colchester, bears a Latin inscription that he composed a book concerning the magnet. It was that celebrated treatise *Of the Magnet and Magnetic Bodies, and that Great Magnet the Earth*, published in 1600 which is described as "the treasury of Gilbert's fame." It reported on his many experiments in electricity and magnetism, and his renowned discovery that the earth itself is a huge globular magnet; he explained that this accounted not only for the direction of the magnetic needle pointing north and south, but also for the dipping of the needle. Also in his *De Magnete* treatise Gilbert used the term "electric" (after the Greek word elektron) to describe the attraction of amber and other bodies for certain light objects, when subject to friction. More than 2,000 years had passed since Thales of Miletus, and little new had been added to the science of electrified amber and the lodestone, but Gilbert took it up and opened the way into the future.

In the Middle Ages fables of magic and witchcraft were linked with this strange force elektron, and that had a retarding effect. Gilbert discarded such ideas, appealed to rational thinking and "sifted the grain of electrical and magnetic phenomena from the chaff of medieval phantasy and legend; he laid the foundations of a true science."[1]

He discovered that many materials besides amber had the power to attract light things after being rubbed, while others did not. To prove it he held the particles excited by friction toward an "electroscope," which he invented. It was a straw pivoted like a compass

[1] *Pioneers of Electricity*, J. Munro, 1890

needle so that it indicated the approach of an electrically charged body. For example, he found glass, sealing wax, the diamond and other crystals to be electrics, while ivory, flint, marble, metals and the emerald were nonelectric. Scientists have since learned that all bodies are capable of becoming electric when "frictionized," if they are properly insulated.

Gilbert and the scientists of his time were unaware of another property, that of *conducting* electricity; neither did they know that metals as well as glass can be electrified by friction but they must be insulated from the hand, otherwise the electricity escapes to earth through the body of the experimenter. Gilbert noticed that dry weather and a north wind were favorable to his experiments, while moist weather and a south wind were detrimental. Apparently he did not recognize water as a conductor; neither did he suspect that moisture by condensing on the cold surface of the electrified rod or crystal enabled the electricity to escape to earth.

It is interesting to recall that before Gilbert's magnetic experiments the mariner's compass was in general use, in fact was known in Europe during the twelfth century and is reported to have originated in China by way of Arabia. The first European compass was a piece of lodestone floated in a cup of water so that it pointed approximately north and south. The pivoted needle came later, and also the graduated scale.

"The magnet is wonderful in innumerable experiments," said Gilbert, "and, as it were, a living force. . . . I think that the whole creation, all globes, all stars, and the glorious earth itself, are governed from the beginning by a proper and determinate life, and have their movements of self-preservation. Although there are not any organs in the stars, the sun, or the planets, which can be recognized by us, yet they live. If there be anything of which man can boast, assuredly it is life; and God Himself (by Whose will all things are ruled) is intelligence, is mind."

In tribute to Gilbert, Galileo said, "I extremely admire and envy the author of 'De Magnete.' I think him worthy of the greatest praise for the many new and true observations which he has made."

Bacon, however, is said to have characterized Gilbert's treatise as a "painstaking experimental book; an instance of extravagant speculation founded on insufficient data."

Gilbert bequeathed his books and instruments to the College of Physicians, but they were consumed in the great fire of 1666.

Described as stoical but not cynical, Gilbert was reserved but not morose. In his book *Worthies of England*, Thomas Fuller of London wrote in reference to Gilbert, in 1662, "The memory of this Doctor will never fall to the ground, which his incomparable book, 'De Magnete,' will support to eternity."

Otto Von Guericke

INVENTED A STATIC MACHINE

BORN: *November 20, 1602*
Magdeburg, Germany

DIED: *May 11, 1686*
Hamburg, Germany

OTTO VON GUERICKE, burgomaster of Magdeburg and philosopher, to establish proof of atmospheric pressure built an "electric" generating machine consisting of a globe of sulphur mounted on a shaft so it could be turned by a crank. As it rotated against a glove on the dry palm of the hand, the friction caused sufficient "electrification" to attract small particles. The device later became known as an electrostatic machine for it generated static electricity; it transformed mechanical work into electrical energy.

While experimenting with the machine, von Guericke was puzzled by the fact that after a short time the attracted particles were repelled. Unknown to him, a feather or light particles assumed a like charge to that of the sulphur ball, and when that occurred they were repelled because "like charges repel each other." Little did he realize that the tiny discharges of static he generated were of the same stuff as the electric bolts that leap during thunderstorms.

Stephen Gray, a Brother of the Charterhouse, predicted that means would be found for collecting larger quantities of "electric fire," which seemed to be of the same nature as lightning. Later discovery of the Leyden jar, or electric bottle for collecting electricity, fulfilled Gray's prophecy.

Von Guericke's primitive frictional machine was changed in later years by various experimenters, among them Sir Isaac Newton, S. A. Varley, W. T. B. Holtz and James Wimhurst, who so improved it in 1878 that it became known as a Wimhurst machine. In the process of evolution the frictional machines were superseded by "influence" machines. Operated by electrostatic induction to convert mechanical work into electrostatic energy, they made use of a small initial charge, replenished or reinforced accumulatively. These static machines helped many a physicist to pave the way for development of devices which some day would make wireless telegraphy practical.

Von Guericke also invented the air pump, and thereby contributed a most useful tool to research and to development of the vacuum tube. His friction-type electrostatic generator might well be called the first electrical machine.

Pieter Van Musschenbroek

DISCOVERED THE LEYDEN JAR

BORN: March 14, 1692
Leyden, Holland

DIED: September 9, 1761
Leyden, Holland

PIETER VAN MUSSCHENBROEK, physicist and professor at Leyden University, while attempting to confine or "store up" electricity by charging water in a bottle, discovered one of the main units of radio —the condenser.

A wire attached to an insulated conductor, kept charged by a frictional-electric machine, was dipped into the water. One day Cuneus, one of his pupils, held the bottle in his right hand while the water was connected by wire to the main conductor of the electric machine. Innocently, Cuneus withdrew the wire with his left hand and received such a violent shock that he dropped the jar. Musschenbroek, anxious to try it himself, received a livelier shock. He found that when the jar of water was on a table it could not be electrified, but when a hand was placed around the bottle, the phenomenon recurred. Seeking a substitute for the hand, he tried a metal coating and it did the trick.

The Leyden jar, as the bottle was named, became a scientific mystery. It remained for Benjamin Franklin to clear it up. He explained that when the inner coating or conductor, which corresponded to the water in the original Cuneus experiment, was positively charged, the outer coating (the hand of Cuneus) became negatively charged. When these were joined by a conductor as they were when Cuneus tried to move the wire away, the positive rushed to the negative, and caused the shock to the body.

In later years, further experiments revealed that a dry bottle with the lower part coated inside and out with tinfoil produced a more violent discharge. The bottle was still called a Leyden jar when wireless came into use and needed electrostatic condensers— the lungs of radio.[1]

Charles François Du Fay

RECOGNIZED TWO KINDS OF ELECTRICITY

BORN: September 4, 1698
France

DIED: July 16, 1739
France

CHARLES FRANÇOIS DU FAY, French savant and member of the French Academy of Sciences, discovered that sealing wax became electrified when rubbed with cat's fur and differed from an electrified

---

[1] Von Kleist of Germany is credited with the same discovery, working at the same time independently of Musschenbroek.

glass rod. He called one "resinous" and the other "vitreous." He recognized two kinds of electricity and noticed that like kinds repel each other; unlike attract. Later, Benjamin Franklin introduced the terms "positive" and "negative" electricity.

Du Fay found that metal wires or wet objects were the best conductors of electricity, although they were the most difficult to electrify. He is believed to have erected the first electric transmission line when he strung a thread across a quarter of a mile, suspended it on glass tubes (as insulators), wet the thread and conveyed impulses from one end to the other.

It was about this time that Stephen Gray, an Englishman, observed that the attracting power of amber, etc., for other bodies could be transferred by contact from one body to another, and transmitted from one part of certain bodies to all parts of it. Désaguliers (1736) called such bodies "conductors." Gray, however, is generally recorded as discoverer of the effect and differences of conductors and insulators. Bodies which conducted electricity better than others he called electrics; the others, nonelectrics.

Du Fay, in his *Fifth Mémoire* described the effect of his electric experiments on hot, compressed and rarefied air, the effect being produced by rubbing glass tubes with silk. He noted that a candle flame could not be electrified and that it was not attracted by an electrified body. He said:

This singularity merits a close examination, in which we will perhaps enter into the question of leakage; but of this we can assure ourselves, for the present, that this [phenomenon] is not due to the heat nor to the burning; for a red hot iron and a glowing coal, placed on the glass table, become electrified exceedingly.

Basing their work upon the findings of Stephen Gray and Du Fay, scientists in France and Germany started to improve the tools of electrical science and conducted numerous experiments. Among them were Abbé Jean Antoine Nollet of France, Johann H. Winckler and George M. Bose of Germany, Andreas Gordon of Scotland, von Kleist of Pomerania, John Canton of England and Tiberio Cavallo of Italy.

Benjamin Franklin

FOUND THE KEY TO STATIC

BORN: *January 17, 1706*   DIED: *April 17, 1790*
Boston, Mass.   *Philadelphia, Pa.*

BENJAMIN FRANKLIN, American statesman, printer, philosopher, scientist, writer and signer of the Declaration of Independence, grew up with a thirst for knowledge. In 1685 his father, Josiah, having joined the Nonconformists in England, emigrated to New England where he found religious freedom. Benjamin was Josiah's fifteenth child, his second wife, Abiah Folger, adding ten children to Josiah's first flock of seven.

Benjamin was sent to school at the age of eight in preparation for the ministry. Reading and writing he liked, but he failed in arithmetic. His passion was reading; his boyish love was for the sea. Schooling was cut short because of the family burdens upon his father, but Benjamin nourished his mind by reading good books. And his father "turned the table-talk on subjects likely to improve his children." Because of this Ben was always indifferent to the kind of food he ate.

He was apprenticed to the printing trade with his brother James. Ben's ingenuity and diligence substituted for the lack of fortune and education. He saved every possible cent to buy books. He became an expert printer and turned his attention to prose. When his brother started a newspaper, the New England *Courant*, Ben printed it. But there came a day when the brothers disagreed. Ben left Boston by sloop for New York, soon to move to Philadelphia to find work as a printer. He married Deborah Read, and in 1724 went to London. Two years later he returned to Philadelphia and in 1729 became editor and publisher of the Pennsylvania *Gazette*, which later became the *Saturday Evening Post*.

Ben had gone forth in the world with a proverb of Solomon which his father so often had repeated: "Seest thou a man diligent in his calling, he shall stand before kings." Ben never forgot it, as is indicated by a friend's remark: "I see him still at work when I go home from the club, and he is at work again before his neighbors are out of bed."

The day came when Solomon's proverb rang true for the diligent Franklin; he attended the coronation of George III. In 1778 he served as American ambassador to France, where his plain but venerable personality distinguished him among the powdered and laced courtiers of Versailles.

Franklin catalogued many rules to guide himself, for example, "Eat not to dullness; drink not to elevation." His *Poor Richard's Almanac*, widely read throughout the colonies, was a collection of wisdom, wit and useful hints, and from it he made a fortune. He found himself in public affairs and politics. Indicative of his versatility, in 1742 he invented an open stove. He later met a Dr. Spence from Scotland, whose experiments with electricity aroused his interest and led him into electrical researches. The flash of lightning was still a mystery, yet some electrical experiments seemed to indicate that electricity created by friction machines was of "the same nature as thunder and lightning."

"Of what use are these experiments?" asked an onlooker.

"Of what use is an infant?" replied Franklin, sensing the great future of electricity.

Apparently he suspected some such force as the electron, for in about 1749 he said, "The electrical matter consists of particles extremely subtile, since it can permeate common matter, even the densest metals, with such ease and freedom as not to receive any perceptible resistance."

Franklin invented the lightning rod—to ease the cloud by a slow discharge, or to carry off a sudden flash. He wrote to the Royal Society of London in 1750 suggesting that "electrical fire might be drawn silently out of a cloud before it came nigh enough to strike." In the summer of 1752, he set out "to draw down fire from the clouds." He made a kite with a wire projected from the upright stick, and to the end of the kite string he attached a length of silk ribbon for holding it, and a metal key from which to draw the sparks. One day there came a thunderstorm, and up went the kite while Franklin sought shelter in a shed. He noticed the floss on the twine bristling as if electrified, and as the kite string was moistened by the rain, it became a better conductor and yielded sparks to the key. Thus Franklin founded the study of static, or atmospheric electricity, and was cartooned as a new Prometheus; his fame as a scientist spread to Europe, for he had "snatched the lightning from heaven, and the sceptre from tyrants."

Franklin established the law of conservation of the electric charge and determined that there is a "positive" and a "negative" kind of electricity. His theories led later experimenters to discover that air could be substituted as the dielectric (insulating material) in place of glass in the construction of a Leyden jar or condenser.

Did this science have a future? Franklin was confident: "A turkey is to be killed for our dinner by an *electrical shock*, and roasted by the *electrical jack*, before a fire kindled by the *electrical bottle*, when the healths of all the famous electricians in England, Holland, France and Germany are to be drunk in *electrified bumpers* [glasses of wine] under the discharge of guns from the *electric battery*."

Despite all of his other activities, Franklin occupied himself with science at odd times, and "investigated a variety of matters." To him the scientific spirit of all things, even a grain of sand, was food for thought.

He was called the patron saint of the electrical sciences. Speaking of his researches in electricity, when that science was in its infancy, he said:

On some further experiments I have observed a phenomenon or two that I cannot at present account for, and am therefore become a little diffident of my hypothesis, and ashamed that I expressed myself in so positive a manner. In going on with these experiments, how many pretty systems do we build which we soon find ourselves obliged to destroy! If there is no other use discovered of electricity, this, however, is something considerable: that it may help to make a vain man humble.

At the age of eighty-two he remarked, "I have lived a long time and the longer I live the more convincing proofs I see of this truth, that God governs in the affairs of men. And if a sparrow cannot fall to the ground without His notice, is it probable that an empire can rise without His aid?"

In his last years Franklin suffered much pain, and he wrote to President Washington in 1789, "I should have died two years ago." But despite painful sufferings, his ever-curious and fertile mind was unimpaired until the last. Near the end, his daughter expressed hope that he might recover and live many years. "I hope not," replied Franklin, and when urged to shift his position that he might breathe easily he said, "A dying man can do nothing easy."

It was said that Franklin, in making his way through life, pursued his own advantage, but never at the cost of truth and honesty. "My rule," he explained, "is to go straight forward in doing what appears to me to be right, leaving the consequences to Providence."

Charles Augustin De Coulomb

APPLIED MATHEMATICS TO ELECTRICITY

BORN: June 14, 1736
Angoulême, France

DIED: August 23, 1796
Paris, France

CHARLES AUGUSTIN DE COULOMB, pioneer of experimental science in France, achieved fame through electrical and magnetic researches. In France, he was what Gilbert was in England two centuries earlier. Coulomb, described as "a mathematician and engineer with the love of definition and the habit of measurement," arrived at quantitative results, while Gilbert's were chiefly qualitative. He measured the force of attraction and repulsion between electrified bodies or magnetic poles and formulated the laws which governed them.

Coulomb was schooled at Paris, where he revealed an aptitude for mathematics, then entered the army as a military engineer. In 1779 he shared with van Swinden a prize offered by the Academy for the best design of a mariner's compass. He presented a paper at the Academy in 1784 on the elasticity of wires under a twisting stress. In these experiments he observed that a very feeble force was sufficient to twist a long thin wire through a large angle, and this led to the invention of his well-known torsion balance. Essentially it comprised a light needle suspended by a fine wire and protected from currents of air by a glass cover. A graduated scale indicated the turns of the counter-twist, and the rate of oscillation of the needle when deflected also enabled one to calculate the disturbing force.

This torsion balance found many uses, and Cavendish used it to determine the density of the earth by comparison with that of a ball of lead. Coulomb, however, made the most successful applications of his invention when he used it to measure the feeble force of frictional electricity and magnetism.

It will be recalled that Gilbert had used a pivoted needle to detect these forces, but he did not measure their intensity. Coulomb's needle was much more sensitive and could be deflected through a right angle by a rod of rubbed sealing wax held a yard away. He made the great discovery that electrical force obeyed the same law as the force of gravitation.

Presenting electrified bodies to the needle, which could itself be electrified, Coulomb discovered that the force of attraction or repulsion between two quantities of electricity was directly proportional to the quantities and inversely proportional to the square of the distance between them. In other words, if the distance between the bodies was doubled, trebled or quadrupled, the force they exerted in each other was respectively a fourth, a ninth or a sixteenth of what it had been.

Further, Coulomb proved that the force of attraction or repulsion between two magnetic poles is directly proportional to the strength of the poles. He showed that the poles were situated near but not quite at the end of a magnet. He was of the opinion that every magnet was made up of tiny particles, each a magnet, and he demonstrated that iron surrendered its magnetic virtue when heated to 700° centigrade—red hot.

All of these discoveries by Coulomb paved the way for other scientists to follow new lines of research. The International Congress of Electricians, in 1884 at Paris, recognizing the great importance of his scientific contributions, selected his name to designate the practical unit of electric quantity—a "coulomb."

Magnetism fascinated him to the end; just before his death he modified his opinion that the magnetic property was common to all bodies in some degree. He came to this conclusion by observing that a grain of iron could communicate magnetism to twenty pounds of another substance. As history records, Coulomb was the first to apply mathematics to the phenomenon of electricity; his experimental work was exact and profound.

Luigi Galvani

DISCOVERED ELECTRICITY FLOWS

BORN: September 9, 1737   DIED: December 9, 1798
    Bologna, Italy   Bologna, Italy

LUIGI GALVANI, Italian physiologist, by virtue of his discovery in electricity gave his name to galvanic current, galvanism and the galvanometer.

From the Galvani family had come several noted men of letters, but Luigi turned to theology in his studies at the University of

Bologna. There, at the age of twenty-three he fell in love with
Lucie Galeazzi, daughter of a professor. He changed from theology
to medicine, receiving his doctor's degree in 1762. His eloquent
lectures at the Institute of Bologna won him the professorship of
anatomy at his alma mater.

The story of Galvani and his discovery has several versions;
basically each is the same and each illustrates how a simple observation may lead to a great discovery. No matter whether intuition or
accident spotlights an invention, it might go unnoticed if the experimenter failed to have both eyes and ears open as well as mind.
Galvani proved this to be true, and his revealing tale is as follows:

The legs of frogs were skinned to make nourishing soup for
Madame Galvani, who was in delicate health. As they were lying
in Galvani's laboratory, an assistant happened to touch one of them
with a scalpel; greatly to his amazement the frog's leg convulsed.
At the same time sparks were being drawn from a near-by friction-
electric machine, and at every flash the leg twitched. Subsequently,
he noticed a similar twitching in frogs' legs hung on copper wires
from an iron railing. But in this instance no electric contrivance was
in action. Galvani also touched the nerve of the frog's leg with a
zinc rod and the muscle with a copper rod, then contacted both
metals. He concluded that he had discovered "animal electricity";
his announcement created a profound sensation in scientific circles,
as well as among the public. Perhaps, it was reasoned by some,
Galvani had solved the mystery of life—*electricity*. They substan-
tiated this conclusion by the fact that the dead frog's legs moved as
if alive.

Alessandro Volta challenged the theory of "animal electricity";
he refuted Galvani's hypothesis. What Galvani really discovered was
that electricity is a current; that it flows. Electricians learned to
recognize that galvanic electricity is that caused by two dissimilar
metals in contact. Volta, who took this clue from Galvani and built
the electric battery, always acknowledged with admiration his in-
debtedness to Galvani, although the latter believed Volta's interpreta-

tion of the frog's-legs experiment was. wrong, and he would never give up the idea that it was anything but "animál electricity." Time revealed how he held a great discovery between his hands and let it slip away through a misinterpretation. He clung to his mistaken theory until the end, concluding that perhaps even the brain itself was a source of "animal electricity."

Broken in heart and fortune, Galvani had sorrow heaped upon him in 1797 when his wife died; he returned to his brother's home, where a year later he passed away, little realizing that electricity would carry his name through the ages.

Alessandro Volta

INVENTED THE ELECTRIC BATTERY

BORN: February 18, 1745
Como, Italy

DIED: March 5, 1827
Como, Italy

ALESSANDRO GIUSEPPE VOLTA, Italian physicist, invented the voltaic cell, or battery, and in recognition of his achievement, the practical unit of electromotive force—the volt—was given his name.

Described as "a child of dull wit," he was unable to speak until four years old when he found his tongue and his intellect sharpened. Overjoyed, his father, a poor patrician, said, "I had a diamond in the house and did not know it." In school Alessandro was a leading student in rhetoric; he had a splendid memory. He played parts in school dramas, composed verses and wrote on the phenomena of chemistry.

After graduation from the Royal Seminary in Como, he devoted much time to the generation of electricity by chemical action. Appointed Rector of the Royal School in Como in 1774, he had new opportunities of research and the following year announced his discovery of the electrophorus, which he found by studying the insulating property of wood. Continuing the study of electricity he became interested in the condenser in 1778, and employed marble or varnished wood as the dielectric in preference to resin. In Volta's hands the condenser was a useful instrument for it enabled him to accumulate feeble charges of electricity until they could produce a strong effect.

Appointed professor of physics in the University of Pavia in 1779, Volta traveled widely, collecting equipment for his laboratory and talking with noted men of science. When in Paris, he showed Lavoisier and Laplace that electricity could be produced by the evaporation of water in a basin; he thought possibly he had discovered the source of atmospheric electricity. He wrote on "Meteorologia Electrica," which revealed that he had improved the electrometer for measuring electrical attraction.

Volta married Teresa Peregrini, a lady of noble birth, and they had three sons. It was about this time that Volta started on the work that made him immortal—the discovery of the voltaic "pile," or chemical source of electricity. He was convinced, as was Franklin, that electricity resided in all natural bodies in a state of equilibrium, and became active when that balance was disturbed, for instance by friction. His idea was to set it in motion by chemical action.

His compatriot Luigi Galvani supplied a good clue by his famous frogs'-legs experiment, which showed the existence of "animal electricity." Volta, however, challenged the theory of animal electricity for he believed the frog's legs were merely a delicate electroscope that detected the presence of electricity. He caught the idea that the electricity was generated by the *contact* of two dissimilar metals which had come into play during Galvani's experiment. Between Galvani and Volta a great controversy raged, but in the end it was said that Volta won, and that his victory opened a new realm of science. He had discovered a new method of generating electricity by the simple contact of two dissimilar bodies, without the aid of friction.

In building his first battery Volta used a series of cups containing a saline solution, in which plates of zinc and silver were dipped.

Each silver plate of a cup was connected with a wire to the zinc plate of the next cup, and the terminal plates of the series—zinc and silver—formed the poles of the battery, from which electricity flowed. His next battery, known as the "pile," comprised plates of zinc and copper laid one above the other, with moistened cloth between them. It was like a pile of coins. The electricity flowed from the terminal plates of copper and zinc, or the positive and negative poles of the battery.

Up to this time electricity caused by friction had shown great promise, but it did not flow in a continuous current easily controlled as did electricity from the battery.

When Napoleon entered Italy in 1796, Volta was sent as a deputy from Pavia to solicit protection. Bonaparte never forgot him, and in 1801 he summoned Volta to Paris to exhibit his battery before the Institute of France. Napoleon presented him with no end of honors in the years that followed; in fact, it was said that Napoleon's interest in Volta had something of affection.

Renown never turned Volta's head; he clung to the simple habits of his boyhood, for "an ardent love of home and science had purified his heart from worldly dross." In his last years he lived secluded from the world. He was buried with great pomp in the churchyard of Compora, and his first "pile" was preserved in the Palace of Brera, at Milan.

Those who knew Volta said that he was gifted with genius and was not denied the spirit of order and perseverance; he excelled as an experimenter because of sound reasoning, based upon clear observation of facts. He was not a theorist, nor was he a mathematician, but he left to the world a great engine of research—the battery.

André Marie Ampère

THE NEWTON OF ELECTRICITY

BORN: *January 22, 1775*
Lyons, France

DIED: *June 10, 1836*
Marseilles, France

ANDRÉ MARIE AMPÈRE, French physicist and mathematician, as a
child amazed his parents by his flair for figures. He no sooner
learned to read than he was into algebra, and at the age of twelve
borrowed books on calculus from the college in Lyons. The fact
that they were written in Latin did not stop André. There was no
school in the village of Polemieux where he lived, so it is recorded
that "Ampère had no teacher but his own genius." Later in life
he reckoned that he knew as much mathematics at eighteen as he
ever did; he had a retentive memory and read books on every
subject.

When his father perished by the guillotine in 1793—when Lyons
was taken by the army of the Convention—his farewell note to his
wife recalled that the books and instruments of geometry for André
had been their greatest expense, but advised her to regard it as wise
economy "since he has never had any other master than himself."[1]

"As to my son," he added, "there is nothing that I do not expect
of him."

For a long time, his father's death seemed to blight André's
existence; in fact, he confessed he was "without eyes or thought."
An interest in botany and poetry brought him out of the dust, as he
described it, but falling in love with Julie Carron really revived his
spirit. They moved to Bourg where he taught physics and chemistry
in the Central School. In 1803 he was appointed to the chair of
mathematics and astronomy in the lyceum at Lyons. Broken by the

---

[1] *Pioneers of Electricity*, J. Munro, 1890.

news of his wife's failing health, on June 7, 1804, in his diary he prophetically wrote: "This day has decided the rest of my life." On July 13, Julie was dead.

Ampère went to Paris as tutor at the Polytechnic School. He married again in 1806, and continued his work as a professor. He published numerous papers pertaining to mathematics, chemistry, natural history and physics.

September 11, 1820, was another day that decided the rest of his life. He learned of Oersted's discovery of the relation of electricity and magnetism.

Soon Ampère proved by a series of new experiments that all magnetic effects mentioned by Oersted could be produced by the electric current alone. He formulated a definite rule for finding the direction in which a compass needle turns when a wire conveying a current is held near it. Also he demonstrated the important fact that two parallel wires, carrying electric currents, attract each other when the currents flow in like directions, and repel each other when they flow in unlike or opposite directions. He proved that the force of attraction or repulsion is directly proportional to the strength of the currents, and inversely proportional to the square distance between them.

James Clerk Maxwell called him "the Newton of electricity."

Ampère showed that a spiral conductor, when fed by a current, behaved like a magnet; that it had a north and a south pole. He offered the theory that every atom in a magnet was magnetized by virtue of a circular electric current surrounding it. He went further to suggest that the earth's magnetism might be caused by currents circulating around it from west to east. It was in this discussion that he coined the term electrodynamics. His discoveries led to many developments based upon magnets, especially the electromagnet, the heart of the telegraph.

The power of his intellect was so vast and his tongue was so eloquent that Ampère was said to qualify as the absent-minded professor and as a long-winded talker. Someone remarked that his absence of mind to the outer world came from his presence of mind to the inner. His consciousness had the power of sharp forms and concentration that made him a great thinker. He had universality of mind, a fact which historians attribute to his lack of sustained effort in any particular direction, for he was generally wandering into fresh fields, working in fits and starts.

"Doubt," said Ampère, "is the greatest torment a man can endure on earth."

Ampère died at Marseilles while on quest of improved health, and it is reported that "his death was transmitted to Paris by the semaphore." Yet to come was the telegraph, telephone and radio for which he had helped to lay the groundwork. In appreciation of his contribution, the International Congress of Electricians adopted his name for the practical unit of electric current—the ampere.[2] He asked that these words be inscribed upon his tomb: Happy at Last!

Hans Christian Oersted

LIBERATED A MIGHTY FORCE

BORN: *August 14, 1777*
  Rudkjöbing, Denmark

DIED: *March 9, 1851*
  Copenhagen, Denmark

HANS CHRISTIAN OERSTED, Danish professor of physics, discovered that a wire carrying a current exerts a force upon a magnetized needle, that is, it produces a magnetic field; he discovered the relation between electricity and magnetism, and liberated a mighty force upon the world.

Having read of Benjamin Franklin's report that he had noticed a mysterious effect of electricity on a compass needle, Oersted experimented for twelve years or more to solve the riddle. While lecturing to a class in Copenhagen in the winter of 1819, according to one story, his attention was directed to the wavering of a compass needle when he chanced to put a wire parallel to the needle. Accord-

[2] An ampere will flow through one ohm when one volt is applied.

ing to another version, while he was demonstrating a fine platinum wire heated to a glow by the passage of a current through it, he noticed the needle of a compass underneath the wire began to swing as if influenced by another magnet.[1]

After the students departed he investigated further by using a stronger battery and larger wires. He succeeded in turning the first feeble impulse into an unmistakable deflection, thus proving that a current flowing in a wire produces a magnetic effect in a circular direction around the wire. He proved that an electric current gives rise to a circular magnetic field around the conductor through which it is passing, so that if a magnetic needle is brought near the conductor it will tend to set itself at a tangent to the circular field around it, that is, at right angles to the direction of the current. Here was the basis for determining magnetic lines of force—the foundation for great practical developments in the use of electricity—as well as for the development of measuring or indicating instruments.

Some said his discovery was an accident—the windfall of an experimenter—but others said accident or no accident Oersted discerned its true significance. As a result, the year 1820 was a happy one for him; his discovery was verified and honors were heaped upon him. Sir John Herschel, noted astronomer, remarked, "In science there was but one direction which the needle would take, when pointed toward the European continent, and that was towards Professor Oersted."

Oersted started scientists throughout the world thinking and experimenting along new lines. William Sturgeon, in England, was led to construct electromagnets comprising a spiral of bare wire wound upon an insulated iron core. Also, Sir Humphry Davy was inspired to the study of electromagnetism; he deducted that terrestrial magnetism might be caused by electric currents circulating in the earth, and that the aurora borealis might be caused by electrical discharge.

Oersted's discovery had cut a clear path into the future to develop-

[1] *Pioneers of Electricity*, J. Munro, 1890.

ments which made practical use of electricity, eventually the telegraph, electric light, telephone, transmission of electric power and
radio.

Oersted's parents had a large family; he and his brother Anders
were taught by an old German wigmaker and his Danish wife. Both
boys were eager to learn; their zeal for improvement never ceased.
Their thirst for knowledge led to borrowing every book within reach.
In 1793, they enrolled at the University of Copenhagen. Anders became one of Denmark's most distinguished jurists.

Hans, at the age of twenty, won a University medal for an essay
on "Limits of Poetry and Prose"; he passed his pharmaceutical
examination, following in the footsteps of his father, an apothecary.
That led him into chemistry and before long he was lecturing to
medical students at the University. Volta's discovery of the "pile"
led him to investigate the possible use of various acids and alkalis in
the battery. Then for several years he traveled widely throughout
Europe, finally, in 1806, obtaining the chair of physics at the University of Copenhagen. In 1814, he married; the Oersteds had seven
children—three boys, four girls.

As the years passed, Oersted pointed to the cultivation of science
as an exercise of religion, and he warned students:

It is only the conviction that while you devote yourselves to science you
are, at the same time, honoring God, that will enable you constantly to pre-
serve the courage and the power which your calling requires, and which you
will fruitlessly seek in incentives from without. . . . Many among you may
find honor which carries a name over the waves of time to distant races.
When you diffuse knowledge, you are instrumental in the consolidation of
God's kingdom on earth.

Students of Copenhagen laid a silver wreath upon his coffin on
March 16, 1851; the bells tolled and all Denmark was in mourning
for an ardent patriot who had once written to Goethe, "I am by birth,
memory and language bound to Denmark. It is there above all other
spots on earth that I should like my memory to be kept green and
my race flourish."

Denmark had lost, but would never forget, this "true man of science, who worked piously and purely at the discovery of truth in nature."

Georg Simon Ohm

FOUND A GOLDEN RULE FOR ELECTRICIANS

BORN: March 16, 1789   DIED: July 7, 1854
    Erlangen, Germany   Munich, Germany

GEORG SIMON OHM, German physicist, the eldest son of a locksmith, was also intended to be a locksmith, but having "learnt the value of knowledge" from a student of the Protestant University who lodged in the Ohms' home, Georg and his brother Martin took up mathematics and physics. Martin became a professor of mathematics in Berlin; Georg formulated the law which governs the flow of electric current and thereby immortalized the family name.

Georg was a natural-born teacher. In 1817 he instructed in mathematics at the Jesuit High School of Cologne. It was about this time that he learned how the "flux of heat" in a metal bar is directly proportional to the difference of temperature between its ends. Ohm set out to investigate what law regulated the flow of electricity in a conductor. He discovered that the electric current in a conductor is directly proportional to the difference of "potentials" between its ends. He showed that with the same difference of potentials, the current in different conductors is inversely proportional to the internal resistance of the conductor, or circuit. Thus he gave to the electrical world a golden rule—Ohm's law:

"A current flowing in any closed circuit is proportional to the force or voltage and inversely proportional to the resistance of the wire." The formula is written $I = E/R$.

The law was published in Berlin in 1827. Critics said Ohm was unworthy to teach physics; his law was absurd. Rebuffed, Ohm retired to private life. Ten years passed before scientists who had scoffed at him began to see the light; they began to support Ohm's law, and in 1841 he was recognized by the Royal Society of London.

Deeply touched by this tribute from Britain, his genius was stirred anew; he took to the study of molecular physics, wrote textbooks on physics and lectured. Overwork undermined his health, and as Dr. Lamont, of the Royal Observatory at Munich, remarked: "So ended the noiseless career of a simple, modest, and highly gifted man, who lived only for science."

Ever since 1861, the electrical world has called the practical unit of electrical resistance the ohm. In 1884, the Congress of Electricians, which met in Paris, made it internationally official.

Samuel F. B. Morse

INVENTOR OF THE TELEGRAPH

BORN: *April 27, 1791*   DIED: *April 2, 1872*
      Charlestown, Mass.   *New York City*

SAMUEL FINLEY BREESE MORSE invented the electric telegraph. Born with a genius for mechanics, he came from a long line of ancestors distinguished for intelligence, energy, original thinking, perseverance and unbending integrity.[1]

His father was the Rev. Jedidiah Morse, a militant orthodox clergyman, author and publisher. Morse's mother was the granddaughter of Dr. Samuel Finley, one of the early presidents of Princeton University.

At the age of four, Samuel revealed an aptitude for drawing and painting and at fourteen he was quite an accomplished artist. After attending grammar school at Andover, he went to Phillips Academy there, preparatory to entering Yale College, his father's alma mater. There he helped to support himself by painting portraits of professors

[1] *Life of S. F. B. Morse*, S. I. Prime, 1875.

and students for $5.00 apiece. Lectures on natural philosophy acquainted him with electricity, but when he was graduated from Yale in 1810, Morse put science aside and went to London to study art. Nevertheless, as he later remarked, his early interest in electricity contained "the crude seed which took root in my mind and grew up in form and ripened into the invention of the telegraph."

Meager finances plagued Morse for the next thirty years, forcing him to end his art work in London and return to America in 1816. He traveled through New England painting portraits for $15.00 apiece. His fame as a portrait painter spread, and his picture of President James Monroe hangs today in the City Hall at Charleston, South Carolina, where Morse resided for three years after his marriage to Lucretia P. Walker of Concord, New Hampshire in 1819.

Returning to New York from the South, Morse opened a studio and obtained an assignment from the City of New York to paint a portrait of General Lafayette who sat for the artist in the White House at Washington. While Morse was at work on this picture, Mrs. Morse died in New Haven, Connecticut. Because of slowness in communication, seven days passed after his wife's funeral before he received word of her death.

The painting of Lafayette, which now hangs in the New York City Hall, won recognition for Morse as one of the first-ranking American painters. With financial difficulties dispelled temporarily, he found time to revert to his old hobby—electricity. In 1829 he attended Columbia College to hear a series of lectures on the subject, but art still dominated his interest and in 1829 he returned to Europe to continue his art studies and to paint in famous galleries.

Sailing from Havre, France, on October 6, 1832, on board the packet ship *Sully*, Morse, one evening in the dining salon, met a group of men including Dr. Charles T. Jackson of Boston, who were discussing Ampère's experiments in electromagnetism. Dr. Jackson explained that the electromagnet "consists of a piece of iron bent in the shape of a horseshoe and wound with wire. When an electric current is sent through the wire the magnet will pick up a small bar of iron. Electricity travels instantly through the entire length of wire, and causes the magnet to act."

Could electricity be made to go over many miles of wire almost instantaneously? Dr. Jackson said "Yes," and Morse is said to have commented, "If the presence of electricity can be made visible in any part of the circuit, I see no reason why intelligence may not be transmitted instantaneously by electricity."

A great idea seemed at that very moment to take possession of Morse. He withdrew from the table and went out on deck to be alone with his thoughts. There, as he stared out over the deep, the telegraph was taking shape in his creative mind—eminently inventive and mechanical. He would transmit messages and record them at a distance! Morse was 41. His soul was aglow with discovery. He saw the telegraph from beginning to end, at the very beginning. If the electric spark in alphabetical form would travel ten miles without stopping, he saw no reason why he could not make it encircle the earth. Seldom had an inventor so completely grasped an invention at its inception.

There on shipboard he penciled sketches of the telegraph in his ever-present sketch book. And before the *Sully* docked in New York, he said to its Captain, "Well, if you should hear of the telegraph one of these days, as the wonder of the world, remember the discovery was made on board the good ship *Sully*."

Tele-graph—writing at a distance! That was the goal!

Upon returning to New York, Morse again confronted financial worries, and he was forced to paint for his living so that there was a lapse of three years before he could do anything about his electromagnetic telegraph idea. In 1825 he began work as Professor of the Literature of Arts of Design at the University of the City of New York.[2] As part of the fee, he was provided quarters in the university's building on Washington Square. During the winter of 1835-1836, he built his first telegraph instruments. He stretched 1700 feet of wire around his room at the university, and transmitted signals from the

2 Name changed to New York University in 1896.

sending instrument at one end to the receiving instrument at the other end of the wire.

Alfred Vail, a New York University graduate, was one of Morse's friends who was impressed with the "machine" and its possibilities. He convinced his father, Judge Stephen Vail, owner of the Speedwell Iron Works at Morristown, New Jersey, of the value of Morse's idea. Judge Vail advanced $2,000 and machine-shop facilities to build a set of telegraph instruments, although he was skeptical about the fantastic idea. On January 6, 1838, the young telegraphers invited him to write a message which they would send over three miles of wire stretched around the Morristown factory. Judge Vail wrote, "A patient waiter is no loser." He told Morse that if he could send the message and receive it at the other end of the wire he would believe that the telegraph was practical. The message came through all right and Judge Vail encouraged the two men to demonstrate the telegraph to the public. They went to New York University and on January 24, 1838, demonstrated to a group of New Yorkers, sending a message from one room to the other: "Attention, the Universe; By Kingdoms Right Wheel!" This humorous military command was inspired by the presence of General Thomas S. Cummings of the United States Army.

Two weeks later, Morse and Vail displayed their telegraph at the Franklin Institute in Philadelphia. Shortly afterwards permission was granted to demonstrate the telegraph in the Capitol at Washington before President Martin Van Buren and members of his cabinet. Ten miles of wire were strung around a room in the Capitol and the test was a success. Congressman F. O. J. Smith, Chairman of the Committee on Commerce, impressed by the idea, introduced a bill in Congress for construction of an experimental interurban line in 1838. Congressmen turned it down and Morse went to England to seek support but failed. Broke again, he returned to New York in 1840 and resumed teaching art.

Two years later Morse and his friends again went to Washington and installed a telegraph exhibit to exploit the invention. As a result a bill was introduced in the House of Representatives for an appropriation of $30,000 to build an experimental telegraph line from Washington to Baltimore. Congress acted favorably before the end of the session in 1843. Morse heard the good news from Annie Ellsworth, daughter of his friend, the United States Commissioner of Patents. President Tyler signed the bill, and Morse grateful for the good news promised Miss Ellsworth that she would have the honor of composing the first telegram. No time was lost in beginning construction of the line over the right-of-way obtained along the tracks of the Baltimore & Ohio Railroad.[3]

May 24, 1844, was selected as the day for the opening, with one terminal in the Capitol and the other in the Baltimore & Ohio Railroad station in Baltimore, where Vail was in charge. At the instrument in the Supreme Court chamber in the Capitol, a prominent crowd gathered, including Henry Clay and Dolly Madison, wife of James Madison, 4th President of the United States.

When Morse sat down at the telegraph key, Miss Ellsworth arrived with the message which she and her mother had selected, "What Hath God Wrought"—a Biblical quotation. Morse slowly tapped out the message. Vail received it in Baltimore and immediately sent it back to Washington, where it was received with great cheers. That was the beginning of the telegraph industry as a service to the public and it was heralded as having great possibilities for binding the young American nation of twenty-six States more closely together.

This success enabled Morse and his associates to raise enough money to extend the line to Philadelphia and New York. He licensed others to use the invention, and soon there were many small companies operating short telegraph lines in the East and Middle West offering limited service and charging separate rates. In 1851, Hiram Sibley and a group of businessmen at Rochester, N. Y., formed a company to build a line in the Mid-West. It became known as Western Union in 1856, because it represented a union of the western lines,

[3] Today more than 200,000 miles of pole lines are on railroad rights-of-way; trains were first dispatched by telegraphy in 1851.

with uniform rates and a uniform standard of service. In 1861, Western Union built the first continental telegraph line, mostly along railroad rights-of-way.

It is interesting to note that Morse did not start out with the idea of a manual transmitting key and an aural receiver, the forms accepted when the telegraph came into general use; instead he, as well as others who experimented with the telegraph, tried to design automatic machines.

Alfred N. Vail, Morse's co-worker, discovered that it was possible to read the messages by sound so that a pen or stylus was not necessary; a sound sufficed. Years later, however, with the advent of high-speed telegraphy and radio, the automatic recorders, handling more than 600 words a minute, came back, revealing that Morse's original idea of recording the messages was not far wrong.

When wireless came, it adopted the telegraph's ways; its key and its code. Later, however, the Continental Code, as used in telegraphy on the Continent of Europe, was adopted because it contained more dashes and no spaced-letters, hence less likely to be misunderstood or lost amidst static and interference. Therefore, in the United States the term International Morse or Continental Code signifies radio as distinguished from the Morse telegraph alphabet, although the latter is faster since it contains fewer dashes.

At the age of seventy-seven, the weight of years began to show upon Morse, yet his faculties were as sharp and vigorous as ever. But as he put it, he was "watching for the morning." And in 1868 he wrote to his grandson: "The nearer I approach the end of my pilgrimage, the clearer is the evidence of the divine origin of the Bible, the grandeur and sublimity of God's remedy for fallen men are more appreciated, and the future is illumined with hope and joy."

With all humility, when honors and praise were bestowed upon him, Morse would say " 'Not unto us, not unto us, but to God be all the glory.' Not what hath man, but 'What hath God wrought?' "

As he lay ill, among the physicians inspecting his lungs, one tapped upon his chest, and another remarked, "That is the way we doctors telegraph."

"Very good," said Morse. He had received his last message. The long, skilled fingers, which created electric messages annihilating time and space, were at rest; Morse's key was silent.

The telegraph sounders that ticked on April 2, 1872, tapped sad news—S. F. B. Morse had passed away in the dawn—a great, good heart had ceased to beat, but he left to his fellowmen the legacy of the telegraph which would click on and on as a pulse of the world.

Marking the Telegraph Centenary, *The New York Times* observed:[4]

When he devised his first instruments Morse knew nothing of the successful telegraphs that had been invented before him by Gauss, Steinheil and Wheatstone. Nor was the famous code attributed to Vail strikingly original. Like many another pioneer, Morse experimented in technical innocence, fortunately along lines that led to ultimate success and that brought him richly deserved honors. Who thinks of the chicanery, the patent suits, the frustration and poverty that embittered his early career and that were ultimately surmounted? For decades he has been looked upon as something less than the perfect hero painted in the standard biography and something finer than the grasping monopolist that Horace Greeley accused him of being. . . .

Today there are seven million miles of telegraph wire in the world—one-third of them in the United States. . . . Judged by its social effects the telegraph is one of the outstanding inventions. With it begins that shrinking of the planet which has been accelerated by radio and which is part of the technological unification of mankind.

Michael Faraday

COLUMBUS OF THE ELECTRICAL AGE

BORN: September 22, 1791
London, England

DIED: August 25, 1867
London, England

MICHAEL FARADAY, English chemist and physicist, was the third child of a blacksmith, James Faraday, who aimed to give his children the

[4] May 24, 1944.

three R's in day school. Early in life, Michael gained a reputation as a great questioner. At thirteen, he was an errand boy for a bookseller, who after a year advanced young Faraday to apprentice bookbinder. Surrounded by such books as Watt's *Improvement of the Mind* and Mrs. Marcet's *Conversations in Chemistry* and articles on electricity, Michael's thoughts turned to chemistry and simple electrical gadgets with which he experimented.

"Do not suppose that I was a very deep thinker, or was marked as a precocious person," said Faraday later in recalling the early years of his life. "I was a very lively, imaginative person who could believe the Arabian Nights as easily as the Encyclopedia, but facts were important to me and saved me. I could trust a fact and always cross-examine an assertion."

Faraday, at nineteen, attended lectures on natural philosophy; he made notes, illustrated them with his own drawings of the experiments, then bound them into book form. In 1812, Sir Humphry Davy lectured at the Royal Institution, and Mr. Riebau, the bookman for whom Faraday worked, took him to the lectures. Again he made notes and bound them.

Faraday became fascinated with science. He wrote to Sir Humphry Davy for a job at the Royal Institution. Davy advised him to stick to his trade; science was impecuniary. But Fate played a hand— three months later Davy's laboratory assistant was discharged and he offered the job to young Faraday, and thus Sir Humphry, as he later remarked, made the greatest of his discoveries.

Faraday went to work at the Royal Institution on March 1, 1813, his first assignment being to assist lecturers and to keep the apparatus polished. Soon he became Davy's experimental assistant. Ampère's experiments attracted his attention, and he also tried to make the magnetic needle rotate around a wire carrying a current. To his great delight it worked, and in order to get a clear insight into the subject, he considered the best thing to do was to write a paper about it.

Full of hope and happiness, he married Sarah Barnard, on June

12, 1821, and took his bride home to the Royal Institution, where he had been appointed superintendent.

Taking up original work in chemistry, Faraday made a number of discoveries, among them benzol, a basis for aniline dyes. Davy, recognizing his talents, made him director of the laboratory, where one of his first steps was to arrange for weekly meetings of members to discuss new discoveries and inventions. As time went on, Faraday became very much in demand as a lecturer, yet more and more he devoted time to research, and in 1831 he made the greatest of his discoveries—production of electricity from magnetism.

Gradually, Faraday's work in chemistry was eclipsed by his electrical discoveries, yet his three laws of electrolysis alone would have made him famous. Picking up where Ampère left off, Faraday proved that a conductor carrying a current also induced currents in neighboring conductors. On two wooden cores he wound insulated wire, and sent electricity through one, while the other was connected to a galvanometer which measured the current. He noticed that while the battery current flowed steadily through the coil, or helix, the needle of the galvanometer did not move, but when the current was started or stopped, the needle jerked back and forth. Thus he discovered that when a current starts in a conductor, it induces a current in a neighboring conductor, which continues for a moment and flows in the opposite direction to the existing current. In brief, Faraday discovered it is only during a *change* in the relations of the two conductors that induction manifests itself.

Concluding that since electricity produced magnetism, so magnetism might produce electricity, Faraday set out to test the idea; he wound a coil of insulated wire on each half of an iron ring. One coil was connected to a galvanometer, the other to a battery in order to magnetize the iron. When the current flowed in the magnetizing coil, the galvanometer needle whirled several times and stopped. He proved that the induced current was caused by magnetism and not by induction. This great discovery—that electricity could be produced by magnetism—was dated in Faraday's notebook as August 29,

1831. Faraday called it "magnetic-electricity." He reported his two discoveries of electrodynamic induction and magnetoelectric induction to the Royal Society on November 24, 1831.

Faraday refrained from applying these discoveries to practical use. He said he was more desirous of discovering new facts. His faith that the forces he had discovered would lead to epochal developments was justified by the induction coil, the electric generator, the magneto-telephone, and wherever the electric dynamo is used.

Faraday continued research and conducted a series of electrochemical experiments to learn more about the electric battery. He introduced the terms "electrode," "anode" and "cathode." His investigations caused him to wonder if some invisible force existed between the inducing body and the induced. He found that induction between one charged conductor and another was influenced by an intervening medium, or "dielectric"; also that electricity penetrated the dielectric and it seemed to be absorbed for a time and then restored. From this discovery the name "farad" was given to the unit of electrical capacity. For example, the capacity of a condenser may be rated at .002 farads, or 2000 microfarads.

To Faraday, *induction* was a powerful force linked with the future and progress. One day he remarked to an assistant, who was experimenting with a magnet, "How wonderful and mysterious is that power you have here. The more I think over it, the less I seem to know."

Faraday's use of a horseshoe magnet and a Nicol prism was a magnificent experiment which showed that magnetism was capable of affecting the luminiferous ether—the medium of light. It was the first proof of a relationship between light and electricity.

Faraday's three volumes, *Experimental Researches in Electricity*, covering his discoveries from 1831 to 1855, have been accepted as classics, and are described as "one of the richest treasuries of knowledge which has ever been presented to the world by a single intellect." Not only did he direct his thoughts to scientists, but his lectures to juveniles were extremely popular, as were his reports on the chemical history of the candle and other simple things of life.

No random experimenter, Faraday never trusted to chance. He planned his experiments. An associate said, "He moved quickly, yet calm and sure, like the process of his mind." He would never tolerate carelessness. He was extremely cautious and neat. It was said that forethought, skill and tidiness enabled Faraday to save both time and materials. Mingling with society had no appeal for him. His evenings were usually spent at home with his wife, for he had no children.

Faraday's honors would fill several pages of a book. Offered the presidency of the Royal Society, he declined it. Knighthood was offered him and he declined that also, saying, "I must remain plain Michael Faraday." He said that the sweetest reward of his work "is the sympathy and good-will which it has caused to flow in upon me from all quarters of the world."

When a student inquired of Faraday the secret of success, he replied, "Work, finish, publish." His fellow scientists regarded him as a born investigator with the gift of genius and a noble character. He boasted that he never made a mathematical calculation in his life, for he was not a mathematician.

A crowning satisfaction of Faraday's life was to see the electric light of Davy produced as the result of his own discovery of magneto-electricity, on June 6, 1862.

Of Faraday it is written "he discovered electromagnetic induction between two entirely separate circuits." He reasoned that if an electric current in a wire caused a magnetized needle to rotate, then a magnet should cause a wire carrying current to do likewise. He formulated the laws of magnetic induction, and by suspending a conductor so that it could rotate between magnetic poles, he demonstrated the basic principle of the electric motor, which led him to invent the first electric generator.

An invisible, mysterious force was at work. Electricity playing in one circuit caused something to happen in another coil or circuit not attached to it. Wireless?

What caused this mysterious transfer of energy? Was there an all-pervading medium? Faraday experimented in quest of proof. And as a result, he suggested a new theory—a revolutionary idea far removed from the old "elastic solid theory of light." Could the electrical action between two bodies be conveyed through a field of magnetic force? He thought that might explain it.

In 1845 he was on the outer frontier of wireless, as was realized years later when Sir William Thomson (Lord Kelvin) said:

> We all know how Faraday made himself a cage six feet in diameter, hung it up in mid-air in the theatre of the Royal Institution, went into it, and as he said, lived in it and made experiments. It was a cage with tinfoil hanging all around it; it was not a complete metallic enclosing shell. Faraday had a powerful machine working in the neighborhood, giving all varieties of gradual working-up and discharges by "impulsive rush"; and whether it was a sudden discharge of ordinary insulated conductors or of Leyden jars in the neighborhood outside the cage itself, he saw no effects on his most delicate gold-leaf electroscopes in the interior.
>
> His attention was not directed to look for Hertz sparks, or probably he might have found them in the interior. Edison seems to have noticed something of the kind in what he called "etheric force." His name "etheric" may, thirteen years ago, have seemed to many people absurd. But now we are beginning to call these inductive phenomena "etheric."[1]

While lecturing at the Royal Institution late in June, 1862, Faraday accidentally burned his notes. At the conclusion he bade a pathetic farewell to his audience saying that he had been before them too long. Those who had known him when "the heat of a volcano was beneath his intelligence" began to detect that his powers were failing.

Writing to his niece Faraday said, "My worldly faculties are slipping away day by day. Happy is it for all of us that the true good lies not in them. As they ebb, may they leave us as little children trusting in the Father of mercies and accepting His unspeak-

[1] Speech at a meeting of the Institution of Electrical Engineers, London, May 16, 1889.

able gift. I cannot think that death has to the Christian anything in it that should make it rare, or other than a constant thought; out of the view of death comes the view of life beyond the grave."

Paralysis crept upon him. Watching the sunset was one of his final pastimes, and one day as a rainbow spanned the sky he said, "He hath set His testimony in the heavens."

Faraday passed "almost imperceptibly away," as his end was described by friends about him, and he was buried in perfect silence in the Highgate Cemetery, London.

"Nature, not education," said Dr. A. M. Tyndall, "rendered Faraday strong and refined. . . . England contained no truer gentleman than he. Not half his greatness was incorporated in his science, for science could not reveal the bravery and delicacy of his heart."

Joseph Henry

AMERICA'S FARADAY

BORN: December 17, 1797
Albany, N. Y.

DIED: May 13, 1878
Washington, D. C.

JOSEPH HENRY, American physicist, conducted experiments in electromagnetism which formed the basis for development of the telegraph, telephone and wireless. In a letter dated 1831 he wrote: "I have lately succeeded in producing motion in a little machine by power, which, I believe, has never before been applied in mechanics —by magnetic attraction and repulsion." He called this machine "a philosophical toy." The same year Faraday, experimenting independently in England, built his first small dynamo; he observed the phenomenon of mutual inductance and by formally going on record won priority over Henry, who delayed in recording his discovery.

Henry began his career as a watchmaker's apprentice. But as a student at the Albany Academy he turned to chemistry, anatomy and physiology. He also became interested in engineering, and this led to another shift in his career in 1825, when he was appointed to survey a road across New York State from the Hudson River to Lake Erie.

Later he returned to the Albany Academy to teach mathematics, and it was there that electromagnetism won his interest. While experimenting with magnets, he made a number of discoveries and revolutionized the feeble electromagnet developed by William Sturgeon of England. Using such a magnet in an electric circuit containing a mile of wire, Henry in 1830 caused a small bell to ring at the end of the line. This is believed to have been the first electrical magnetization of iron at a remote point, which was fundamental to the telegraph.

Transferring to the College of New Jersey (later Princeton University) in 1832, Henry startled the students and other men of science in that vicinity by setting up a telegraph line between the laboratory and his house. He added the "relay" to his telegraph machine, and is believed to have been the first to use the earth return conductor. Adding to his magic and to his fame, he constructed an electromagnetic motor, recognized as a "forerunner of all electric motors."

Faraday and Henry paralleled in research, but were independent in the discovery of mutual induction and self-induction. According to their dates of publication, Faraday is credited with the discovery of mutual induction and Henry with self-induction. For this he was immortalized by the International Electrotechnical Commission which adopted the term "henry" for the unit of inductance.

Henry learned, from reports in two popular journals, of Faraday's discovery of the induced current. He made no claims to priority. In explaining his experiments, he said:

The secondary currents, as it is well known, were discovered in the introduction of magnetism and electricity by Dr. Faraday, in 1831. But he was at that time urged to the exploration of new and apparently richer veins of science, and left this branch to be traced by others.

Since then, however, attention has been almost exclusively directed to one part of the subject, namely, the induction from magnetism, and the perfection of the magneto-electrical machine; and I know of no attempts except my own, to review and explain the purely electrical part of Dr. Faraday's admirable discovery.

Accounting for Henry's failure to gain general recognition of his important work, friends said that it was no doubt his own fault, for he was always dilatory about publication. For example, he showed his magnets to the Albany Academy, but at the time published nothing about them. He delayed reporting his observations of the induced current, and was anticipated by Faraday. Henry seems to have underestimated the importance of his achievement, and did not realize that it was the forerunner of one of the most extensive applications of electricity.

After a trip to Europe in 1837, Henry began a comprehensive study of induced currents, in which he made his most important discoveries. He tested the apparent direction of the current in a circuit through which a Leyden jar was discharged. It led him to the important conclusion that the current in the spark gap was not a simple flow of electricity from one pole to another, but a succession of flows alternating in direction and rapidly diminishing in strength. It was while engaged in these experiments that he found the inductive action could be transmitted over considerable distances.

As early as 1840, Henry produced high-frequency currents with which he continued to experiment until his important announcement in a paper submitted to the American Philosophical Society on June 17, 1842:

The discharge (electric) whatever may be its nature, is not correctly represented by the single transfer from one side of the jar (Leyden jar condenser) to the other. The phenomena require us to admit the existence of a principal discharge in one direction, and then several reflex actions, backward and forward, each more feeble than the preceding, until equilibrium is obtained.

Further reports on his experiments contained ideas of a "wireless" nature:

. . . a single spark . . . thrown on the end of a circuit wire in an upper room, produced an induction sufficiently powerful to magnetize needles in a parallel circuit of wire placed in the cellar beneath, at a perpendicular distance of 30 feet with two floors and ceilings . . . intervening.

Henry's discovery was of vastly greater importance than anyone guessed at the time. Reiss, Wollaston and Helmholtz were quick to duplicate the Henry experiments, but it was not until 1853 that William Thomson (Lord Kelvin) presented the first mathematical conception of the nature of the condenser discharge. As in the case of numerous other discoveries, the full utility of the condenser appeared only after other discoveries were made, and relationships identified between the condenser discharge and phenomena previously thought of as something apart.

On October 21, 1842, in the hall of the American Philosophical Society in Philadelphia, Henry "communicated orally" by what he called "induction at a distance." He succeeded in magnetizing needles by the secondary current in a wire more than 220 feet distant from the wire through which the primary current was passing, excited by a single spark from an electrical machine.

In the later experiments, a wire for transmitting was stretched across the campus of Princeton University, in front of Nassau Hall, grounded at one end by a plate buried in the ground. A second wire for receiving was erected in the back campus. A high-frequency oscillatory current was produced in the transmitting wire when a battery of Leyden jars discharged. A small steel needle in the center of a spiral of wire formed a part of the receiving circuit. This needle was magnetized when the discharge took place in the transmitting circuit.

In reporting his experiments, Henry said:

. . . when it is considered that the magnetism of the needle is the result of the difference of two actions, it may be further inferred that the diffusion of motion in this case is almost comparable with that of a spark from a flint and steel in the case of light.

One of his students at Princeton made notes as follows:

. . . Hence, the conclusion that every spark of electricity in motion exerts these inductive effects at distances indefinitely great (effects apparent at distances of half a mile and more); and another ground for the supposition that electricity pervades all space. Each spark sent from the electrical machine in the College Hall sensibly affects the surrounding electricity through the whole village. A fact no more improbable than that light from a candle (probably merely another kind of wave vibration of the same medium) should produce a sensible effect on the eye at the same distance.

Henry's announcement in 1842 identifying the condenser's discharge as oscillatory helped to open the way for Maxwell's work in predicting "ether" wave phenomena twenty years later. Why not chop the sparks or "current flow" into dots and dashes and use them for signaling? Some day, someone would do just that—would use electromagnetic waves, not induction. But there would have to be a detector. The coherer, as the first detector, would come along later, and then there would be wireless!

Resigning the professorship of natural philosophy at Princeton in December, 1846, to become first secretary of the Smithsonian Institution, Henry is said to have remarked, "If I go, I shall probably exchange permanent fame for transient reputation."

Deeply interested in meteorology, while in Washington he also helped to organize the United States Weather Bureau. During the Civil War he directed mobilization of scientific effort.

The story is told that when Dom Pedro de Alcantara of Brazil made his historic discovery at the Philadelphia Centennial in 1876, that Bell's telephone actually talked, Bell invited Professor Henry to hold the receiver to his ear. Here was the man who had evolved the theory of the telephone a half-century before Bell's birth, now listening to it talk. Henry turned to Bell and said, "You are in possession of the germ of a great invention."

Bell replied with a confession that he lacked electrical knowledge. "Get it!" said Henry.

Many times after that, Bell related how those words were a lifetime inspiration to him.

It has been noted of Henry that he revealed "the greatness of his nature by being accurate in his descriptions of observed fact, but tentative, rather than cocksure, in his deductions." For instance, he wrote:

Man, with his finite faculties, cannot hope in this life to arrive at a knowledge of absolute truth; and were the true theory of the universe, or in other words, the precise mode in which Divine Wisdom operates in producing the phenomena of the material world, revealed to him, his mind would be unfitted for its reception; it would be too simple in its expression and too general in its application, to be understood and applied by intellects like ours.

Heinrich Daniel Ruhmkorff

IMPROVED THE INDUCTION COIL

BORN: *January 15, 1803*
Hannover, Germany

DIED: *December 20, 1877*
Paris, France

HEINRICH DANIEL RUHMKORFF, physicist, while specializing in precision instruments such as galvanometers in the early fifties, made important improvements in the induction coil by increasing the number of turns of wire on the secondary coil, and by winding it on a glass cylinder to improve its insulation from the primary coil. Perfected by Ruhmkorff, the induction coil became a "key" in experimental work in connection with the discharge of electricity through gases, with production of electrical oscillations, Hertzian waves, cathode rays and Roentgen rays.

Ruhmkorff was recognized as a skillful mechanician of Paris who made many mechanical improvements in construction of the induction coil. So many of these coils were constructed by Ruhmkorff that the coil was named after him. One of the largest coils, which he built in 1867, featured a secondary containing sixty-two miles of wire and it flashed a spark sixteen inches long.

In tracing the evolution of the induction coil we recall that Joseph Henry was the first to discover the electromotive force of self-induction, which he announced in 1832. He used a copper tape wound in spiral form, and upon passing a current through the spiral and suddenly interrupting it, he obtained a bright spark. In 1836, the Rev. N. J. Callan, of Maynooth College, built an electromagnet with two separate insulated wires, one thick and the other thin, wound on the same iron coil. The thick wire was copper, and through it the current passed. The thin wire was iron, and one end was connected to the copper winding. In 1837, Sturgeon, inventor of the electromagnet, constructed a coil on Callan's plan, but made use of an iron wire coil. A. Appes, in 1876, built a coil with a secondary consisting of 280 miles of wire in 341,850 turns; it produced a 42-inch spark.

Evolution of the alternating current transformer from the induction coil was a short step. The first intimation of it came in 1856, when S. A. Varley of London patented an induction coil in which the iron wire coil was extended and folded back on itself outside the coil, so that the ends overlapped and completed the magnetic circuit.

As an electrical instrument for producing high electromotive force, the induction or "spark" coil, consisting of two coils of wire wound one over the other, on a core formed of a bundle of thin iron wires or a number of thin iron sheets, pumped life into wireless. Many a pioneer experimenter, including Marconi, and hundreds of ships used the induction coil to crash the spark across the gap; hundreds of amateurs from 1900 to 1915 built wireless stations employing the spark coil, in many cases discarded from old automobiles, to stir the "ether" with dots and dashes.

While experimenting with the induction coil in 1853, Armand H. L. Fizeau,[1] French physicist, was the first to shunt a condenser across the terminals of the interrupter, increasing the length of the spark and the coil's efficiency. He also made valuable observations regarding the velocity of light and experimented to determine if any relative motion of the "ether" and matter could be detected.

[1] Born September 23, 1819, Paris, France; died September 18, 1896, Venteuil, France.

Hermann L. F. Von Helmholtz

HE GAVE HERTZ A PROBLEM

BORN: *August 31, 1821*
Potsdam, Germany

DIED: *September 8, 1894*
Charlottenburg, Germany

HERMANN L. F. VON HELMHOLTZ, German philosopher and physicist, is recorded as "one of the most distinguished men of science of the nineteenth century."

Helmholtz's father directed his thoughts toward the study of natural phenomena. His parents were poor, so he could not pursue a strictly scientific career, and that turned him to the study of medicine. He became assistant in the Berlin Anatomical Museum, and a professor of physiology at Königsberg, at Bonn and later (1858-71) at Heidelberg. Then, as professor of physics at the University of Berlin, he attracted considerable attention through experimental as well as mathematical physics.

In the classroom he inspired his students; in the biographical records of more than one noted man of radio science is proud testimony that "he studied under Helmholtz." His monograph *Sensations of Tone*, published in 1863, was considered the most important work on acoustics of the nineteenth century. An ardent student in various branches of science, especially acoustics and optics, he is regarded as one of the founders of the law of the conservation of energy.

Lecturing on "The Conservation of Force" before the Berlin Physical Society on July 23, 1847, von Helmholtz said, "We assume that the discharge of a jar [Leyden] is not a simple motion of the electricity in one direction, but a backward and forward motion between the coatings. . . ."

Von Helmholtz contributed to the development of the electromagnetic theory of light and indicated its general possibilities; he determined the velocity of the propagation of electromagnetic induction as

314,000 kilometers a second. It was this research into the phenomena of electrical oscillations and electromagnetic induction that fascinated his pupil, Heinrich Hertz, who demonstrated the existence of electromagnetic waves. Helmholtz encouraged him to study the problem, pursue the invisible impulses, prove that they existed and measure their length.

William Thomson (Lord Kelvin)

NATURAL PHILOSOPHER AND INVENTOR

BORN: *June 26, 1824*   DIED: *December 17, 1907*
Belfast, Ireland   *Largs, Scotland*

WILLIAM THOMSON (LORD KELVIN), through a rare combination of natural philosophy, brilliant mathematical reasoning, inventive ability, an insatiable curiosity and outstanding skill as an electrical experimenter, won world renown as a physicist. His father, James Thomson, was professor of mathematics at the University of Glasgow. Graduating in 1845 from St. Peter's College, Cambridge, William was appointed professor of natural philosophy at Glasgow, and continued in that position for fifty-three years—until 1899.

The study of electricity attracted him as early as his student days, and the articles he contributed to various scientific journals gained the interest and admiration of scientists. His discoveries in the mathematical theories of magnetism, electricity, elasticity and heat were outstanding. He invented the mirror galvanometer used for cable signaling, developed the siphon recorder and as an electrical engineer for the Atlantic cables, 1857-58 and 1865-66, made numerous contributions to the advance of communication over the cables, for which he was knighted in 1866, and raised to the peerage in 1892.

Lord Kelvin's inventive talents were by no means confined to the cables; he invented many electrical instruments, methods of measurement and deep-sea sounding apparatus, as well as a mariner's compass designed to be unaffected by the magnetic action of iron in a ship. His work on thermodynamics was of tremendous value. The past and future age of the earth, the electron theory, the wave theory of light, radium and wireless, the atom and the molecule, all entranced him.

Kelvin had a brilliantly original mind, and as Sir Ernest Rutherford remarked, "Kelvin hankers about information on every side."

While on a visit to Niagara Falls he tossed a bombshell into the controversy of scenic beauty versus electric power, at a time when it was being argued that to divert too much water from the river for power production would impair the scenic wonder. Said Kelvin: "I look forward to the time when the whole water from Lake Erie will find its way to the lower level of Lake Ontario through machinery doing more good for the world than that great benefit which we now possess in the anticipation of the splendid scene which we have presented before us at the present time by the waterfall of Niagara. I wish I could think it possible that I could live to see this grand development."[1]

This comment was printed far and wide, for the world respected Kelvin's opinions and bestowed many honors upon him. He was the first to receive the Order of Merit instituted by Edward VII in 1902; and the Grand Cross of the Victorian Order was awarded to him as were many honors from leading scientific societies and universities. Glasgow celebrated his jubilee as professor in 1896, and three years later he retired, but maintained his link with the University as a research student; in 1904 he was appointed chancellor of the University.

Kelvin, although a "cable man," displayed great interest and faith in wireless; he became a friend and admirer of Marconi. In fact, his enthusiasm for wireless was described as causing "a mild sensation" late in the nineties, and his recognition gained considerable prestige for Marconi.

[1] Interview by Orrin E. Dunlap, Sr., August 14, 1897, printed in the *Electrical Engineers*, August 26, 1897.

When in November, 1897, Marconi rigged up an aerial mast at Needles, on the Isle of Wight, Lord Kelvin had the distinction, on June 3, 1898, of sending the first paid Marconigrams to his friends, Sir George Stokes and Sir William Preece.

When Marconi was conducting his first tests of wireless in England, he became eligible for Italian military service that would cause him to abandon his experiments and return to Italy, but Kelvin urged Italian government officials to permit him to remain in England. As a result, he was appointed an assistant marine attaché of the Italian Embassy in London, in which capacity he continued his valuable work.

Indirectly, Kelvin approached wireless: He evolved the telegrapher's equation, which facilitated systematic studies and predictions to be made with long-distance cable telegraphy, and greatly stimulated thought in the field of blurring or distortion of electromagnetic waves traveling along conductors. Kelvin's work in this and allied directions improved cable telegraphy, produced improvements in telegraph circuits and even today is the ancestor of studies of television image degradation in normal circuits.

Rutherford, in presenting the Kelvin Gold Medal of the Institution of Civil Engineers to Marconi on May 3, 1932, remarked:

I am sure that if Lord Kelvin were here today, he would acclaim this award as to a kindred spirit, for Lord Kelvin combined to an extraordinary degree the quality of great theoretical insight with the power to realize his ideas in a practical form. It is interesting to recall on this occasion that Kelvin, in 1853, was the first to give the complete theoretical explanation of the oscillatory discharge of the Leyden jar, later verified experimentally by Fedderson, a theory which lies at the basis of all methods of generating waves.

Said Marconi in response, "Kelvin always believed in me."

Mahlon Loomis

PIONEER IN AERIAL TELEGRAPHY

BORN: July 21, 1826
Oppenheim, N. Y.

DIED: October 13, 1886
Terre Alta, W. Va.

MAHLON LOOMIS, an American dentist, became an experimenter and pioneer in "aerial telegraphy." His family moved to Virginia in the forties, and in 1848 went to Cleveland, Ohio, where Mahlon studied dentistry, later to set up his own practice at Earlville, New York. On May 2, 1854, he patented a mineral-plate (kaolin) process for making artificial teeth. About 1860, electricity began to interest him; he tried forcing plant growth by buried metal plates connected to batteries.

His interest shifted from earth to sky for a study of electrical charges which could be obtained from the upper atmosphere by kites carrying metal wires. He wondered if natural "static" might be used to replace batteries. From that experiment he observed that a kite wire sent aloft in one region would effect the flow of electricity to the ground in another kite wire some distance away. As a result, in 1868 he demonstrated this type of "wireless" to scientists and members of Congress.

Loomis visualized an "aura" around the globe and termed it "the static sea." He drew pictures to show that he knew what he was talking about; wireless to him was no idle dream. His United States Patent No. 129,971, dated July 30, 1872, was titled "Improvement in Telegraphing." He sent signals in 1886 from Cohocton Mountain, Virginia, to Beorse Deer Mountain, fourteen miles apart, and later between ships two miles apart on Chesapeake Bay. The patent covered "aerial telegraphy employing an 'aerial' used to radiate or to receive the pulsations caused by producing a disturbance in the electrical equilibrium of the atmosphere," and as such is recorded as "the first patent for wireless telegraphy issued in the United States."

Congress, on May 21, 1872, listened to a long speech relative to the "Loomis Aerial Telegraph Bill" requesting an appropriation of $50,000. The principle of operation of "aerial telegraphy" was described as follows:

. . . causing electrical vibrations or waves to pass around the world, as upon the surface of some quiet lake one wave circlet follows another from the point of the disturbance to the remotest shores, so that from any other mountain top upon the globe another conductor, which shall pierce this plane and receive the impressed vibration, may be connected to an indicator, which will mark the length and duration of each vibration; and indicate by any agreed system of notation, convertible into human language, the message of the operator at the point of the first disturbance.

The Washington *Chronicle* of Nov. 1, 1872, reported how Loomis conducted experiments with "kites covered with fine, light gauze of copper wire, held with a very fine string or tether of the same material, the lower end of which formed a good connection with the ground by laying the coil in a pool of water."

Loomis almost got the $50,000 from Congress to develop his invention, but the idea was called "absurd."

It was said of Loomis that there could be no question of his inventiveness, for his brain teemed with ideas, some altogether practical, others eminently impractical. It is to be noted that although he produced sparks when he touched the kite wire to the ground, and sent out electric waves, he had no means of detecting them. There was no Branly coherer at that time. Loomis was ahead of his time; he died, it is said, heartbroken.

PART II

PIONEERS OF THE RADIO AGE

David Edward Hughes

PIONEER OF THE MICROPHONE

BORN: *May 16, 1831*
London, England

DIED: *January 22, 1900*
London, England

DAVID EDWARD HUGHES, Anglo-American physicist, was born in London but spent the early part of his life in the United States. While professor of music at the College of Bardstown, Kentucky, in 1850, he was led to study sound, and that directed him toward science and the transmission as well as the amplification of sound. The professor turned inventor, and in 1855 he patented a type-printing telegraph instrument that went into extensive use in America and Europe.

As far as the records reveal, Sir Charles Wheatstone[1] in 1827 was the first to use the word "microphone" for an acoustic device he developed to amplify feeble sounds. Hughes, in 1878, revived the term in connection with his discovery that a loose contact in a circuit containing a battery and a telephone receiver (invented by Bell in 1876) would give rise to sounds in the receiver corresponding to the vibrations impinged upon the diaphragm of the "mouthpiece" or transmitter.

Hughes's microphone was built in the form of a carbon rod resting in grooves in two carbon blocks, the battery and telephone receiver being wired in series with the blocks. This "mike" was the forerunner of numerous carbon telephone transmitters. Hughes also is credited with discovering the principle upon which the wireless coherer depended.

The demands of the radiophone and broadcasting, also the talking pictures, brought about many refinements and improvements that led to a long line of microphones designed for realistic and high-

[1] Born February, 1802, in England; died October 19, 1875, in England.

63

quality sound, free of inherent noises. Development of the microphone has never ended.

Philip Reis of Germany designed a make-and-break platinum contact microphone in 1861, but it proved incapable of transmitting anything except the pitch of tones or the pitch of speech; it did not transmit their quality, only a musical buzz. It did not talk. Nevertheless, his epitaph reads *"Der Erfinder des Telephons."* He devised a vibrating membrane carrying a contact which made and broke an electric circuit to a small magnet wound with wire, when the membrane was vibrated by any sound wave in its vicinity.

Professor Amos E. Dolbear of Tufts College contended that he had improved Reis's telephone device, but a court decision rejected it for testimony is said to have revealed Dolbear's telephone "would squeak but not speak."

Emile Berliner in Washington observed in 1877 that the resistance of a loose contact varies with pressure and he applied the principle to microphone design for "sending the voice by electricity."

Edison in 1887 patented a telephone transmitter of a variable-resistance amplifying type in which the resistance element was a button of solid carbon.

The next year Francis Blake offered a telephone transmitter utilizing a block of hard carbon and a vibrating diaphragm. In 1884, Ader of France developed a multiple carbon pencil microphone for picking up music. Then Edison applied for a patent on a telephone transmitter filled with granules of hard coal.

Oddly enough music, which led Hughes to experiment with the microphone in 1850, has paced the research workers and inventors ever since, and with increased intensity since radio, the films and television took on music and speech. Evidence of the microphone's remarkable advance is found in the thousands of patents which have multiplied as the telephone and radio in conjunction with the electron tube opened not only new demands upon the microphone but new ways to improve it.

James Clerk Maxwell

DISCOVERER OF THE ETHER

BORN: *November 13, 1831*
Edinburgh, Scotland

DIED: *November 5, 1879*
Cambridge, England

JAMES CLERK MAXWELL, Scottish physicist, author, natural philosopher and eminent mathematician, discovered the ether. Modestly he referred to himself as an interpreter of Michael Faraday's ideas, but the world of science knew better, for his life was crowned by extraordinary electrical investigations.

Maxwell was well descended. His father had an aptitude for the mechanical arts, and his mother possessed artistic talents. It is recorded in his biography,[1] that Maxwell's memory went back to when he first remembered lying in the field, "looking at the sun and wondering."

The inquisitive lad was incessantly asking, "What's the go o' that?" He read every book he could get. Childhood marked by solitude in the country tended to make him shy. His mother died when he was nine, and in 1841 his father entered him in the Academy at Edinburgh. When, in 1844, he began the study of geometry, his talent became evident, and versatility marked his work for he also liked to draw and to versify. He left the Academy in 1847, with the first prize in English and mathematics, and enrolled at the University of Edinburgh where his professors soon saw evidence of a penetrating mind.

Electricity, magnetism, chemistry and optics led him into deep mathematical study, and the year 1850 found him at Cambridge steeped in science. His tutor is said to have described him as "a most extraordinary pupil, a man of genius with all its eccentricities, and a scientific luminary of the future." And he added, "It is not possible for that man to think incorrectly on physical subjects."

[1] *The Life of James Clerk Maxwell*, Lewis Campbell and William Garnet.

Said Maxwell: "He that would enjoy life and act with freedom, must have the work of the day continually before his eyes."

In 1856 he was appointed professor of natural philosophy in the Marischal College of Aberdeen. A year later he married Katherine Dewar, daughter of the principal, and in 1860 they moved to London, where Maxwell taught natural philosophy at King's College. In his attic "laboratory" at Kensington, he wrote scientific papers and conducted numerous experiments. For his researches on light Maxwell was awarded the Rumford Medal of the Royal Society in 1860, and a year later delivered his first lecture at the Royal Institution on the theory of the three primary colors.

Resigning from King's College in 1865, he retired to write, producing in 1870 his noted treatise on heat.

Fascinated by an idea gleaned from experiments that the attraction or repulsion produced by electricity and magnetism were caused by some "action at a distance"—by an unseen medium in space—Maxwell was determined to find the "missing link," mathematically at least.[2] As a result, he identified the ether—the medium of light and heat believed to permeate the universe. Light and heat, he concluded, were electromagnetic undulations in the ether. Maxwell was said to have discovered "an elemental ocean in which the truth may yet be found."

His masterful treatise *Electricity and Magnetism,* presented to the Royal Society in 1864, and in fully developed form in 1873, on the electrodynamic theory of light is remembered as "one of the most splendid monuments ever raised to the genius of a single individual." In that treatise he evolved the famous equation from which he predicted, solely from mathematical reasoning, the existence of ether

[2] Christiaan Huygens, physicist and astronomer (born April 14, 1629, at The Hague; died June 8, 1695), worked out a theory of undulation of light in an unseen conveying medium—an airy nothing filling the emptiness of space. He disclosed his theory at a time when scientists and philosophers were pondering the problem of a medium to account for the phenomenon of light. Otherwise how could light travel from the sun to the earth? Could interstellar space be filled with an invisible substance, a sort of liquid-filling matter? Huygens also won fame by applying the pendulum to clocks and through his researches in physical optics.

waves; he speculated on the possibility of the production of electromagnetic waves which would detach themselves from a source of origin.

Therefore, the history of wireless registers Maxwell as the discoverer, in 1867, of the ether, described as "an imponderable, electric medium supposed to pervade all space as well as the interior of solid bodies; the invisible, odorless, tasteless substance assumed to exist, through which light, heat and radio waves are transmitted."

Heinrich Hertz later produced the electromagnetic waves and proved Maxwell's theory to be correct.

By the time Marconi came along, Maxwell's theory made it possible for teachers to compare the ether with a pond, so that laymen might understand the mystery of wireless. The ether was pictured as a placid pool; toss in a stone and there is a series of ripples or waves, depending upon the force with which the stone strikes the water. That stone is the "transmitter." If tiny floating objects such as pieces of wood or cork float on the surface, they bob up and down in accordance with the waves; they are the "receivers."

It was all that simple!

Maxwell continued to contribute numerous papers to scientific societies; he wrote on atoms and molecules, on matter and motion. In 1874 the Cavendish Physical Laboratory, designed and built under his direction, was opened at Cambridge.

It was said that Maxwell contemplated the inner scene of Nature and envisaged an ethereal bond uniting the most diverse forms of matter. In 1877 his health failed; his brain refused new tasks.

Near the end he remarked, "I have been thinking, how very gently I have always been dealt with; I have never had a violent shove in all my life. The only desire which I can have is like David, to serve my own generation, by the will of God, and then fall asleep."

His doctor said, "No man ever met death more consciously or calmly," although he suffered great pain in his illness. After a memorial service in the Trinity College Chapel, the body of Maxwell, who had lived "a most perfect example of a Christian gentleman."

was removed to his old home Glenlair and buried in the churchyard of Parton.

A century later, the hundredth anniversary of Maxwell's birth was celebrated by the scientific world's "digging a grave for the theory of luminiferous ether," but at the same time honoring his mathematical genius. In 1931, his ether theory was called "that supreme paradox of Victorian science and yet a triumph of the scientific imagination," which as convenient fiction helped physicist and layman to bridge a mysterious gap, closed when the world realized that wireless waves are electromagnetic, not "ether."

In fact, it was remarked:

Maxwell could not believe in "action at a distance." To see a star the eye must touch it in a sense. To attract a needle a magnet must be "connected" with it. Maxwell invented an ether that satisfied the conditions. . . . Just as Newton's laws of gravitation unified the heavens so the ether unified energy and matter. . . . Maxwell's fate is much like Newton's. . . . Were he alive he would probably concede that his ether was no more real than the equator of the geographers—that it was necessary and convenient fiction without which science of his day was helpless.[3]

William Crookes

INVENTED THE CATHODE-RAY TUBE

BORN: June 17, 1832　　　　　　　　　　DIED: April 14, 1919
　　London, England　　　　　　　　　　　　London, England

SIR WILLIAM CROOKES, British chemist and physicist, invented one of the earliest forms of X-ray tubes, known as the Crookes tube. Although his career was devoted chiefly to chemical research, he conducted original investigations in wireless, and as a result, his prophetic writings were an inspiration and a chart for younger men of science, among them Marconi and De Forest, both fascinated by such words as these:

[3] The New York Times, October 5, 1931.

Here is unfolded to us a new and astonishing world, one which is hard to conceive should contain no possibilities of transmitting and receiving intelligence.

Rays of light will not pierce through a wall, nor, as we know only too well, through a London fog. But the electrical vibrations of a yard or more in wavelength . . . will easily pierce such mediums, which to them will be transparent. Here, then is revealed the bewildering possibility of telegraphy without wires, posts, cables or any of our present costly appliances.

Granted a few reasonable postulates, the whole thing comes well within the realms of possible fulfillment. At the present time experimentalists are able to generate electrical waves of any desired wavelength from a few feet upwards, and to keep up a succession of such waves radiating into space in all directions.

This is no mere dream of a visionary philosopher. All the requisites needed to bring it within grasp of daily life are well within the possibilities of discovery, and are so reasonable and so clearly in the path of researches which are now being actively prosecuted in every capital of Europe that we may any day expect to hear that they have emerged from the realms of speculation to those of sober fact. . . .

What remains to be discovered is . . . firstly, a simpler and more certain means of generating electrical waves of any desired wavelength. . . . Secondly, more delicate receivers which will respond to wavelengths between certain defined limits and be silent to all others. Thirdly, means of darting the sheaf of rays in any desired direction, whether by lenses or reflectors. . . .

Any two friends living within a radius of sensitivity of their receiving instruments, having first decided on their special wavelength and attuned their respective receiving instruments to mutual receptivity, could thus communicate as long and as often as they wished by timing the impulses to produce long and short intervals on the ordinary Morse code.[1]

Crookes had pictured radio; he suggested practical application of theories. His was a "road map" to broadcasting.

The Crookes tube was generally looked upon as a scientific plaything. In 1895, Roentgen changed that appraisal. He discovered that when a Crookes tube was enclosed in a darkened box, mysterious rays were emitted which rendered fluorescent materials outside luminous. For lack of a definite name, he used the algebraic symbol for the unknown quantity and called them X-rays.

[1] "Some Possibilities in Electricity," in the London *Fortnightly Review*, 1892.

Cathode rays, incidentally, are streams of negatively charged particles shot out from negatively charged electrodes, or cathodes. When streams of electrons in the form of cathode rays are directed against a target, the sudden loss of velocity causes radiation—the more sudden the stop the shorter the wavelength of the emergent X-rays.

Crookes' cathode-ray tube sprang from a study of creation of vacua within a sealed glass vessel by means of electricity. Through improvements in the air pump he made it possible to get an almost perfect vacuum, which swept many an obstacle from inventors' paths.

While experimenting with the cathode-ray tubes, Crookes recognized the existence of particles of matter smaller than the hydrogen atom. The luminous streams of cathode rays appeared to him as "a storm of projectiles"; he called them "a new or fourth state of matter." Although the precise nature of the particles was a mystery, he sensed the fact that they were different from ordinary molecules. It remained for J. J. Thomson to demonstrate that in general Crookes' hypothesis was correct, and to define the nature of the cathode ray—*electrons*. The cathode-ray tube became the "eye" of television.

The Crookes tube contained the germ of incandescent lighting and, of course, the X-rays. True, he missed identification of X-rays, but he revealed conclusions which upset the whole doctrine of chemistry. At the time of his death Crookes was called the greatest of British scientists in the realm of exact knowledge. Knighted in 1897, he also received the Order of Merit in 1910; the Royal Society elected him president from 1913-15.

Ubi Crookes ibi lux!

William Henry Preece

PIONEER IN "TELEGRAPHY BY INDUCTION"

BORN: February 15, 1834
Carnarvon, Wales

DIED: November 6, 1913
Carnarvon, Wales

SIR WILLIAM HENRY PREECE, British electrical and civil engineer, was educated at King's College, London. He began his career as a telegraph engineer. Electric signaling became his profession.

In 1854 he was assigned to investigate a system of "wireless" by means of conduction as developed by J. B. Lindsay. It was based on the theory that communication across a body of water could be accomplished by laying a wire on both sides of the water, each line being grounded at the ends. A battery and telegraph key were inserted in the sending wire, while a galvanometer placed in the receiving wire detected the signal impulses. It was this "wireless" that inspired Preece to use it for signaling between islands and the mainland. He introduced several improvements in the Lindsay system, chiefly a vibrator, or buzzer, at the sending end and a telephone receiver as the indicator at the receiver.

He later approached wireless by means of magnetic induction, using large loops of wire. For example, in 1877 he placed one such loop on the ground and one in a mine shaft and attempted communication.

Preece was commissioned in 1892 to experiment with communication between lighthouses and the shore without the use of a cable or connecting wire. When a cable broke between the mainland and the island of Mull in 1896, by laying lines of wire on the two shores, Preece telegraphed by induction over water and through the air, the distance being $4\frac{1}{2}$ miles. He sent 156 messages in the Morse code. He then experimented with a conductive system between Flatholm and Lavernock in the Bristol Channel. But the tests revealed the limitations, and furthermore, this system was not applicable to ships.

It was about this time that Marconi came to London to introduce his system of wireless, and Preece, who had been associated with the Post Office as electrician since 1877, and later as chief electrician, cooperated with the Italian, for the British were much interested. The resources of the Post Office, which had jurisdiction over communications, were placed at Marconi's disposal for experiment and trial. His wireless soon crossed the Bristol Channel so successfully that all thoughts of communication by conduction, induction or any other system quickly vanished.

Nevertheless, the British wondered why Marconi was declared the inventor, and not Preece or Admiral Henry B. Jackson,[1] but Preece explained:

He has not discovered any new rays. His recorder is based on the Branly coherer. Columbus did not invent the egg but he showed how to make it stand on its end, and Marconi has produced from known means a new electric eye, more delicate than any known instrument, and a new system of telegraphy that will reach places hitherto inaccessible. . . . Enough has been said to show that for shipping and lighthouse purposes it will be a great and valuable acquisition.

Preece was one of the first to recognize that Marconi "had something" of great value to Britain's far-flung empire. Because Britain gave the young Italian every assistance and encouragement when he arrived in London to demonstrate his invention, the early glory of wireless was reflected in the news throughout the world as coming from England, which became the center of wireless.

In June, 1897, Preece lectured at the Royal Institution on "Signaling Through Space Without Wires," and after referring to other and

[1] Admiral Jackson (Sir Henry Bradwardine), born in 1855 at Barnsley, entered. the Royal Navy in 1868. While commander of H.M.S. *Edinburgh* in 1893 he conceived the idea of using Hertzian waves for naval signaling. Under his direction the first wireless experiments in the British Navy began in 1896 on board H.M.S. *Defiance*. Using a Hertzian oscillator, energized by an induction coil, and with a coherer as detector, he established communication across $3\frac{1}{2}$ miles between the *Defiance* and the gunboat H.M.S. *Scourge*. In 1899, improved apparatus was installed on the *Europa*, *Juno* and *Alexandria* with Marconi in charge of the tests, collaborating with Jackson, then a captain.

older methods of "wireless," including his own, he exhibited Marconi's instruments. In reference to their capabilities he said:

In July last Mr. Marconi brought to England a new plan. Mr. Marconi utilizes electric or Hertzian waves of very high frequency. He has invented a new relay, which for sensitiveness and delicacy exceeds all known electrical apparatus. The peculiarity of Mr. Marconi's system is that, apart from the ordinary connecting wires of the apparatus, conductors of very moderate length only are needed and even these can be dispensed with if reflectors are used.

"It is impossible to predict what will happen in the twentieth century," said Preece in 1901. "Progress is slow; anticipations are wild. Mr. Marconi personally is to be congratulated on what he has already done, and everyone wishes him continued success."

Evidence of Preece's early pioneering along the frontiers of wireless is found in a statement by John Ambrose Fleming ten years before he filed his application for a patent on the valve detector: "This phenomenon (the Edison Effect) in carbon incandescent lamps was first observed by Mr. Edison in 1884, and further examined by Mr. W. H. Preece in 1885."

Preece was author and co-author of several books on telegraphy, electricity, incandescent lights and the telephone. In the annals of wireless he is remembered among the prominent electricians who were detoured by induction and conduction from reaching the goal of wireless electromagnetically, as did Marconi. But in his aid to the young man from Bologna, in London to seek support in developing his invention, Preece played a role similar to that of Queen Isabella. She aided Columbus. Preece helped Marconi find still another route to India—through space.

Amos Emerson Dolbear

INVENTED AN ELECTROSTATIC TELEPHONE

BORN: *November 10, 1837*
Norwich, Conn.

DIED: *February 23, 1910*
Medford, Mass.

Amos Emerson Dolbear, American physicist and teacher, after village schooling and boyhood spent on a farm in 1854 went to work in a pistol factory, and several years later in a locomotive works. There he began to show inventive talent through the design of a steam whistle that would "play any tune." Determined to have a college education, he studied to matriculate at Ohio Wesleyan, from which he was graduated in 1866. While at college he was particularly interested in physics, the telegraph, magnets and electricity.

In 1867 he was appointed professor of natural science at Bethany College, West Virginia, and later taught at Kentucky University. He went to Tufts College, Medford, Massachusetts, in 1874 as professor of physics, a position he held until his death. By 1876 he had done considerable experimenting and development work in telephony— chiefly the electrostatic telephone, which he patented in 1881. While working with this device a wire became disconnected, yet the instrument continued to "talk."

Studying the cause and effect led him to patent a system of communication in which the line was replaced by two conductors in the air, such as a tin roof or a wire suspended from a kite. The circuit was grounded at each end. Dolbear's patent on this was No. 350,299, dated October 5, 1886. He had first exhibited this "transfer of speech by communication without wires" on April 1, 1882, at a meeting of the Society of Telegraph Engineers and Electricians in London.

By means of his electrostatic telephone, Dolbear signaled across a quarter of a mile between Tufts College and a pond, using a 300-foot wire suspended from a kite as the aerial. Later he is said to have added the idea of a spark gap between the aerial and ground, thereby increasing the range from Medford to Boston, about 12 miles. Marconi, however, was in the field by this time. But promoters of wireless who gained control of Dolbear's interests claimed that his use of an elevated aerial pre-dated Marconi by ten years. In litigation the court held that Dolbear in his patent attempted to claim sole ownership of a basic principle, which, it was held, could not be done.

While electric radiation may have been present from his elevated aerial, no evidence was found that he recognized it or attempted to detect the signals as did Marconi. Dolbear's chief bid for fame was through the electrostatic telephone—but it was not wireless in the sense that Marconi developed it.

Reported to be sadly disappointed that Marconi, and not he, was first to succeed in spanning the Atlantic with a wireless signal, Dolbear nevertheless, when asked to comment upon the achievement, is said to have replied, "If Marconi says he has communicated across the sea, I know of no reason why I should not fully believe that he had solved the problem."

Dolbear at Tufts is remembered as the man who introduced the idea of wireless to the college, also as "a man in advance of his time."

In the announcement of his death, the Boston *Post* said:

Professor Dolbear was the inventor of several telegraph and telephone appliances, and always contended that the invention of the telephone should have been credited to him. He engaged in several costly suits over certain telephone patents, which he claimed were his, and the loss of these in the courts to Professor Bell of telephone fame preyed on his mind in his declining years. He always believed that he had been robbed of the fruits of his mechanical genius and carried this conviction to the grave.

Professor Dolbear, with all his accomplishments, was probably more an experimenter all his life than anything else. He strode along ahead even of inventors, left them ideas to apply to commercial and practical use and went on in new fields to discover fresh principles. In a book he wrote more than 40 years ago occurs this significant sentence: "Mechanism is all that stands between us and aerial navigation; all that is necessary to reproduce human speech in writing, and all that is necessary to realize completely the orator who shall at the same instant address an audience in every city in the world." The aeroplane and the phonograph remain as mementoes of his prophecies.

"His highest pleasure was in pioneer investigation," remarked a friend. "That was his life. His last writings on the science of the twentieth century were like the visions of a prophet."

Edouard Branly

INVENTOR OF THE COHERER

BORN: *October 23, 1844*   DIED: *March 24, 1940*
    Amiens, France   *Paris, France*

EDOUARD BRANLY, French physicist, invented the coherer, the first detector of wireless waves. At the Ecole Normal Supérieure in Paris, Desiré Edouard Branly was a brilliant student, also at the Lyceum de St. Quentin where his father was a professor. At the Sorbonne he worked in the physics laboratory and won his Doctor of Physics degree in three years. Later he was appointed professor at the Institut Catholique in Paris.

In his study of electrical conductivity, Branly observed that some materials, in powder form, were affected in their electrical conductivity by electromagnetic waves; he developed the coherer to study the properties of the waves, little realizing at the time that he had invented an essential element of wireless telegraphy which, in 1921, would win him the Nobel prize for Physics.

The idea of the coherer came to Branly rather accidentally about 1885 while he was studying medicine, testing different theories as to how nerves carry messages from the skin to the brain and back again. He learned that nerves are not continuous fibers, but are formed of neurons, massed closely but not necessarily in contact. The coherer resulted from the application of that observation and it became the first detector of wireless waves to be used by Marconi and other pioneers. Branly demonstrated it before the French Academy in 1891, thereby winning membership in that body.

Branly's coherer consisted of a glass tube filled with loose iron filings, a galvanometer and a battery in a closed circuit. Electromagnetic waves were produced twenty-five yards away and the effect caused the filings to cohere while the galvanometer revealed the deviation of the current.

He observed that the conductive effect on metallic filings in a small, thin glass tube, caused by an electric discharge in the vicinity, persisted after a comparatively long period. It was a fragile-looking device about like a thermometer in appearance, but as improved somewhat by later experimenters, it had two silver plugs so close together that a knife blade would scarcely pass between them. Fine nickel dust was sifted into the slit, and such particles enjoyed the strange property of being alternately conductors and nonconductors of Hertzian waves.

When the signals struck the metallic dust particles they cohered (thus the name coherer). A tapper arrangement was added; a tiny hammer like that of a doorbell struck against the tube and decohered the particles, stopping the current from a local battery. Each successive impulse reaching the antenna produced the same phenomena of coherence and decoherence, hence the recording of dots and dashes.

When Branly was ninety-three, Marconi died, and in tribute the Frenchman said, "He was the only man who could have carried on and developed my own finds [the coherer] to the greater glory of science."

On his ninety-fifth birthday Branly, irked by the use of radio for war propaganda purposes, was quoted from Paris as saying, in reference to broadcasting, "It bothers me to think that I had something to do with inventing it."

In his modest laboratory he caught the chill that brought his death in the spring of 1940, and it was recorded that M. Branly died a lonely, misunderstood, frustrated man, "about whom a whole sermon could be written." Through the simple, slender coherer he established his rendezvous with fame; France gave him a national funeral in Notre Dame Cathedral.

Study of the cohesion of metallic powders in a glass tube, caused by the action of a near-by electric spark, led to development of the coherer.

Guitard, 1850, noticed that when dusty air was electrified, the particles amalgamated into strings and flakes. This was rediscovered in 1866 by S. A. Varley, who made practical application of this principle of cohesion in a carbon-dust lightning protector for telegraph lines. Lord Rayleigh, in 1879, investigated similar effects in meteorological phenomena, such as the formation of snowflakes under the influence of atmospheric electricity.

The principle of coherence also was studied by an Italian professor, Calzecchi Onesti. He discovered that copper filings between two brass plates were ordinarily nonconductors of electricity, but that they became conductive when subjected to the high-voltage discharge of an induction coil. Then the resistance dropped from millions to hundreds of ohms. He published his discoveries in *Il Nuovo Cimento* in 1884, but his work attracted little attention until after the publication, six years later, of Branly's researches. Then the earlier discoveries of Varley and Onesti were recalled.

Branly investigated the variations of conductivity of a large number of conductors under different electric influences. His results were disclosed by him in *La Lumière Electrique*, May-June, 1891. He reported that a coat, or varnish, of fine copper dust was a bad conductor under ordinary conditions, but fell sharply in resistance when a spark occurred in the vicinity. The substances most suitable for demonstrating this effect were filings of iron, aluminum, copper, brass, antimony, cadmium, zinc and bismuth. He also found that the conductivity could be made to disappear rapidly by a shock, as by tapping the tube in which the filings were contained.

Several of Branly's patents of 1890 and 1891 related to the electrical conductivity of radio-conductors and to the operation of a local relay circuit from a distance. Branly made the extremely important observation that an electric spark *at a distance* had the power of suddenly changing the conductivity of loose masses of powdered conductors.

Sir Oliver Lodge, who had done some work in the same direction, was attracted by Branly's experiments. He immediately tried Branly's tube of filings and found it far superior in manageability to the apparatus he had been using. He used it in demonstrations and lectures at London and at Oxford in 1894. Lecturing in June, 1894, at the Royal Institution, he described the Branly tube and, in referring to it as the *coherer*, is believed to have been the one to name it.

Marconi improved the Branly tube by modifying its relative dimensions. He used tightly fitting silver end plugs, slightly amalgamated at the ends, and introduced a mixture of nickel and silver filings, the proportion being that giving best results. He also exhausted the air from the tube and sealed it. This Marconi coherer was far more dependable in its action than any detector previously designed.

Thomas Alva Edison

AMERICA'S GREATEST INVENTOR

BORN: *February 11, 1847*   DIED: *October 18, 1931*
       Milan, O.   *West Orange, N. J.*

THOMAS ALVA EDISON, greatest and most prolific of American inventors, first saw the light of day in Milan, Ohio, and moved northward with his parents to Port Huron, Michigan, when he was seven years old. The Edisons were of Dutch ancestry. Thomas's forebears arrived in America before the Revolutionary War. In Ohio his father operated a shingle factory; in Michigan he was a dealer in grain and feed.

Young Tom was a restless youth, more anxious to work than to go to school. He obtained the newspaper concession on the Grand Trunk

Railway between Port Huron and Detroit, not only to sell papers on the trains but to establish newsstands at the stations. That enterprise combined with truck gardening on a vacant lot near his home started him on a business career.

He became a popular hero of Port Huron when he saved the station agent's little boy from an onrushing train. In appreciation, the station agent taught him the Morse code, for Edison had long had his eye on the telegraph. To make good use of the news items that came over the wire from Detroit, he installed a printing press in the mail car and printed the *Weekly Herald* en route, selling it to passengers and at stations along the way. He also used the mail car as a mobile vegetable stand from which he sold produce from his garden. To make even greater use of the car he built a laboratory in one corner, but a chemical experiment started a fire. That ended the mail car as a printing shop, vegetable stand and laboratory. He decided to become a professional telegraph operator and for several years moved from town to town.

While he was working as a newsboy, a railroad conductor lifted him by the ears when he was trying to climb into a freight car with both arms full of papers. Edison said he felt something snap inside his head, and after that his hearing declined. But he never looked upon his deafness as a serious handicap. At times he considered it a blessing because it enabled him to think without disturbance from noise and chatter.

Edison in his teens was described as "a typical story-telling, tobacco-chewing, fun-loving, hard-working telegraph operator, slovenly in dress, awkward in manner, and always a great practical joker"—the latter often stemming from an imaginative mind. The most prolific period of his inventive career was in the 1880's while he was in his thirties. Asked what he considered the most wonderful thing in life, Edison is quoted as saying, "A blade of grass."

Electrical gadgets of all sorts fascinated him, but it was the electric telegraph that put his ever-active mind on the inventive track. He first displayed a flair for invention in 1864 at Indianapolis by building an automatic telegraph repeater, the forerunner of his many inventions. In all, he was granted more than 1,200 patents. It was in Boston that he invented a stock ticker, for which, to his great amazement, he was paid $40,000; he had expected about $3,000. This enabled him to establish a laboratory at Menlo Park and at West Orange, New Jersey. With his application for a patent, in 1877, on a "phonograph, or speaking machine," there was plenty of evidence that inventing was becoming a profession for Edison, who, later in life, defined genius as "2 per cent inspiration and 98 per cent perspiration."

Probably no inventor touched upon wireless more indirectly yet with greater effect than Edison. As a "road builder" he paved and pointed the way; he left the direct approach to others for he was "too busy with other things." Nevertheless, as the wizard of Menlo Park, he had a profound influence on development of radio through his electric lights, batteries, dynamos, motors, motion pictures, microphones, "etheric force," mimeograph, the talking machine, recordings and "the Edison Effect."

In 1875 he was on the track of wireless when he observed "new manifestations of electricity through mysterious sparks of an oscillatory nature." Curiosity caused him to investigate this "true unknown force" he had been witnessing during various experiments, so he built what became known as Edison's famous black box. Inside, two carbon points formed a micrometer gap across which tiny sparks could be seen through a window. Here was a strange force that had a tendency to diffuse or spread in all directions; he could even draw the sparks from a gas pipe in the laboratory. He called it "etheric force"; it remained for Hertz to prove the existence of wireless waves.

Dr. George M. Beard, physicist, in commenting on Edison's "find" remarked, "The honor of a scientific discovery belongs, not to him who first sees a thing, but to him who first sees it with expert eyes; not to him who drops an original suggestion, but to him who first makes that suggestion fruitful of results." In wireless, Marconi did that.

Edison took out only one patent on "telegraphy without wires," but it involved the principle of induction, not exactly wireless as Marconi developed it. The application was filed May 23, 1885; the patent, No. 465,971, was issued December 29, 1891. In the specifications Edison stated: "I have discovered that if sufficient elevation be obtained to overcome the curvature of the earth's surface and to reduce to the minimum the earth's absorption, electric telegraphing or signaling between distant points can be carried on by induction without the use of wires connecting such distant points." He called the receiving machine an "electromotograph," and the system in general "grasshopper telegraphy." Edison sold this patent to the Marconi Company in 1903 for what he termed "a song."

As a pioneer in witnessing curious electrical phenomena, while developing the incandescent lamp, Edison caught sight of a mystery taking place inside the glass bulb. During his tests of carbon filament lamps, molecular bombardment inside the bulbs caused a black deposit to form on the glass. William J. Hammer, one of Edison's laboratory assistants, noticed that in several instances there was a narrow line of "no deposit" on the glass. This he termed "the phantom shadow" or "ghost." He showed it to Edison in 1880, who tried in several ways to eliminate the black deposit. He placed a coating of tinfoil outside the bulb, with a "counter charge" applied to it. In experimenting with this, he found that if he connected a galvanometer in series with the tinfoil and the positive terminal of the filament, a direct current flowed through the galvanometer. When he reversed the process by connecting to the negative terminal, no current was observed. This phenomenon, observed in 1883, was called "the Edison Effect."

Pursuing the tinfoil experiment, Edison placed a metal plate inside the bulb, connected to the outside by a wire sealed through the glass. Again applying the galvanometer, he obtained the same results. At the Philadelphia Exposition he placed a telegraph sounder in the galvanometer circuit, and found that sufficient current flowed to operate the instrument.

In another series of experiments Edison installed two filaments—the second as a spare—so that when one burned out the other could be put into the circuit, thereby doubling the life of the lamp. By means of a galvanometer he observed that there seemed to be a current in the idle or spare filament. Induction was suspected. He assigned William Kennedy Laurie Dickson, a laboratory assistant, to the job of exploring the mystery. Again "the Edison Effect" was at work.

The "effect" became the signpost that led Fleming to the invention of the valve, or first electronic tube detector, and also De Forest to the audion. In 1883 Edison applied for a patent on an electrical indicator employing an Edison Effect lamp bulb, for he had found that the current varied sharply with the voltage. This was, in effect, an electronic voltmeter, but it was not found to be commercially practical.

While Edison apparently did not recognize that in this instance he had at his fingertips a great and wonderful clue—in fact, a master key to radio and its unlimited future—he nevertheless recognized the possibilities of wireless signaling.

At the turn of the century, Edison told a friend that he thought some time there might be daily signals across the Atlantic without wires, but that he did not know when, and being preoccupied he did not think he would have time to do it himself. When Marconi did the trick in 1901, Edison said, "I would like to meet that young man who had the monumental audacity to attempt and succeed in jumping an electric wave across the Atlantic."

Recounting the story of the historic transatlantic signal, Marconi said, "I shall never forget Mr. Edison's laconic comment, 'If Marconi says it's true, it's true.' Nothing ever pleased me as these words."

How the Edison dynamos and batteries have pumped the life into radio, how the phonograph has whirled music through the air and recorded sounds of voices and melody for posterity, are stories well known, for Edison's "talking machine" now has talked around the world on the wings of "etheric force." Wherever there is a phonograph, radio or motion picture on the screen or on television, Edison, "the lamplighter," lives on. As was remarked at the time of his passing, after long years of almost superhuman labor, "He reigns still in his viewless empery."

Commemorating the ninety-seventh birthday of Edison, Charles Seymour, President of Yale University, saluted him as "one of the greatest of Americans and the supreme inventive genius of the industrial age," and added:

The staggering list of his inventions compels us to realize the extent of his contribution to the United States and to the world, not merely in our own days, but for all time to come. Already he has, through the disciplined activity of his ideas, produced billions of dollars of new wealth.

Much more important than the new material wealth which his inventions have brought forth are the new paths in the pursuit of human happiness indicated by them. He sought the secrets of nature and devised the means to exploit these secrets in order that they might be applied for the betterment of man. What seemed even more important than genius was his extraordinary capacity for unflagging hard work, which led him to "scorn delights and live laborious days." He refused to accept at any time the idea of defeat and regarded the failure of an experiment as merely an incitement to further effort.[1]

Alexander Graham Bell

INVENTOR OF THE TELEPHONE

BORN: *April 3, 1847*   DIED: *August 2, 1922*
      Edinburgh, Scotland   *Baddeck, Nova Scotia*

ALEXANDER GRAHAM BELL invented the telephone. He electrified the human voice and by putting the spoken word on wires left no doubt in the minds of wireless pioneers that some day radio also would talk. Bell's invention contributed much to the development and to the service of radio; from the telephone, radio inherited numerous

[1] Excerpt from broadcast, February 11, 1944.

devices and techniques. The magnetic telephone receiver was adopted by radio as its universal earphone for reception. The microphone also had its inception in telephony. And radio called upon the wire lines to form its broadcasting networks to supplement its ethereal activity. Wires became the runways of radio on its flight into space. As radio progressed it reciprocated by supplying new devices and supplemented the service of the telephone. The radio-electron tube became a master key in the advance of telephone engineering and in extension of its service.

Bell was a Scotsman. Educated at the University of Edinburgh and the University of London, he moved across the ocean with his father in 1870 and Brantford, Ont., became his new home. Much interested in his father's system of "visible speech" instruction, used successfully in teaching deaf-mutes to speak, Bell in 1872 became professor of vocal physiology at Boston University. His specialty was referred to as "the mechanics of speech" and led him into what might well be called "the electrics of speech."

He began experiments to develop apparatus for electrical transmission of the spoken word. An attic in Boston was his laboratory. There under the rafters history was made; a vast communication system and one of man's great utilities was born. Bell and his assistant, Thomas A. Watson, built a number of machines which turned words into strange noises—none articulate. One day, however, while they were experimenting Bell called, "Mr. Watson, come here, I want you." Watson standing near the contraption heard it produce Bell's voice, and he ran into the next room exclaiming, "I can hear you. I can hear the words!"

That was the birth of the telephone—March 10, 1876.[1]

Bell put the instrument on exhibit at the Philadelphia Centennial Exposition that year, but without attracting much attention until

[1] Twenty-five days passed after Bell applied for a United States patent on February 14, 1876, before he first made the telephone transmit speech. Patent No. 174,465 was granted to him on March 7, 1876, and three days later, while tinkering with the contraption, he made it talk. Extensive litigation with other inventors followed over the question of priority. The United States Supreme Court sustained Bell.

Dom Pedro de Alcantara, emperor of Brazil, on a tour of the exposition stopped to watch a demonstration of the device. In amazement he exclaimed, "My word—it talks!"

That discovery by Dom Pedro gave the telephone royal recognition in the news and focused new attention on its performance and possibilities. Continued experiments led to its improvement and a company was organized for its development. Five years later, in 1881, the first telephone line between Boston and Providence was opened; Boston to New York in 1885; New York to Chicago in 1892; New York to Denver in 1911; New York to San Francisco in 1915.

Bell lived to hear the radiophone talk and sing. The year he died there were 14,347,000 telephones in the United States,[2] and the first ship-to-shore two-way conversations were conducted between Deal Beach, New Jersey, and the S.S. *America*, 400 miles at sea. The S.S. *Gloucester* off the New Jersey coast also talked to Deal Beach, which relayed the voice from the air over telephone lines to Long Beach, California, then by radiophone to the Catalina Islands. By this time broadcasting stations were springing up everywhere, and the year after Bell's death, New York and Boston stations were hooked up by telephone wire for the first "chain broadcast"; and the first multiple station network was formed with stations in New York, Schenectady, Pittsburgh and Chicago linked in a copper web of telephone wires.

Recognizing the telephone's important relationships to radio, Marconi saluted Bell as one of the great contributors to the art:

"I have built very largely on the works of others, and before concluding I would like to mention a few names, Clerk Maxwell, Lord Kelvin, Professor Henry and Professor Hertz. I do not know if you are aware that the message received at St. Johns was received through a telephone receiver, and in connection with the telephone the name of Bell is inseparable."[3]

---

[2] 26,381,000 on January 1, 1944.

[3] Speech at a dinner of the American Institute of Electrical Engineers, January 13, 1902, in celebration of the first transatlantic wireless signal.

Adolph K. H. Slaby

FUNKENTELEGRAPHIE OCCUPIED HIS MIND

BORN: April 18, 1849
Berlin, Germany

DIED: April 6, 1913
Charlottenburg, Germany

ADOLPH KARL HEINRICH SLABY, physicist, was known as "the German Marconi," because of his experiments in the field of wireless. He began his academic professional career in 1876 at the Berlin Trade Academy, having been a student at the Royal Trade School in Potsdam. In 1882 he was appointed professor of electrotechnics, and in 1884 director of the electrotechnical laboratory of the Technical High School at Charlottenburg; in 1892, he attained distinction as honorary professor on the Philosophical Faculty of the University of Berlin. His scientific investigations in the early nineties were related to thermodynamics, motors and gas engines.

Hertz's electromagnetic wave experiments naturally attracted a man of Slaby's aptitude for science into "spark communication." Try as he might he could not make the electric waves go beyond the limits of the Charlottenburg high school. When he read that Marconi had been able to exceed his maximum range of 100 meters, he hurried to England to discover how the Italian had solved the problem that baffled him. He arrived in time to witness Marconi's demonstrations on May 14, 1897, between Lavernock Point and Breen Down, a distance of eight miles.

Enthusiastic about what he had heard and seen Slaby returned to Berlin with hopes of duplicating Marconi's performance and of improving upon it if possible. Interest in wireless was running high in Germany, and on August 27, Slaby reported on his trip to England as part of a lecture on wireless telegraphy which he delivered at the Sailors' Home at Potsdam, with Kaiser Wilhelm and the king of Spain in the audience. To reveal the practical development of wireless, in

October he sent wireless messages between a church and the marine station at Potsdam, and shortly after between Peacock Island and Potsdam. Using captive balloons to hold the aerial aloft more than 800 feet he increased the range of his apparatus and communicated across 21 kilometers. He used the Branly coherer as the detector. Making a direct contribution to the art, he introduced resonant coils, known as "Slaby rods," for measuring wavelengths, and they were of use in the early days before the more accurate wavemeter was developed.

Professor Slaby as author of an article, "The New Telegraphy," in the *Century Magazine*, April, 1898, said:

In January, 1897, when the news of Marconi's first successes ran through the newspapers, I myself was earnestly occupied with similar problems. I had not been able to telegraph more than 100 meters through the air. It was at once clear to me that Marconi must have added something else—something new to what was already known, whereby he had been able to attain wavelengths measured by kilometers. I traveled to England, and in truth what I saw there was something quite new.

Marconi had made a discovery. He was working with means the entire meaning of which no one before him had recognized. Only in that way can we explain the secret of his success. In the English professional journals an attempt has been made to deny novelty to the method of Marconi. It was urged that the production of Hertz rays, their radiation through space, the construction of his electrical eye—all this was known before. True; all this had been known to me also, and yet I was never able to exceed one hundred meters.

In the first place, Marconi has worked out a clever arrangement for the apparatus which by the use of the simplest means produces a sure technical result. Then he has shown that such telegraphy (writing from afar) was to be made possible only through, on the one hand, earth connection between the apparatus and on the other, the use of long extended upright wires. By this simple yet extraordinarily effective method he raised the power of radiation in the electric forces a hundredfold.

Considerable rivalry developed between Marconi and Slaby, the latter taking out German patents to cover the invention of wireless, although Marconi had been granted German patents a year earlier. Slaby, however, claimed to have modified Marconi's antenna system. In collaboration with Graf George von Arco,[1] his assistant at Charlottenburg, he developed the Slaby-Arco system, which in 1903 was amalgamated with the Braun and the Siemens-Halske systems, thus forming the German national system known as Telefunken.

In the history of wireless, Slaby's activity may be summed up about as follows:

Funkentelegraphie owes no great discovery to him, yet he rendered pioneer service well worthwhile, in that he brought to the public view this new means of communication, by his lectures and his experiments, in such a way that he popularized it. He helped to put Germany on the wireless map.

He was one of the first to give a technically correct explanation of the creation of oscillations in the sending and receiving antenna, and was one of the first to measure wavelengths. As a result, he was able to aid in solving the problem of tuned oscillatory circuits. . . . Not only Count Arco but all German engineers of the early days of spark telegraphy were students at his school, and as a result of the stimulation which he gave to the art the Algemeine Electricäts Gesellschaft, the first Continental factory for wireless apparatus was organized.

As a teacher and investigator of wireless, Slaby was a pioneer, but the irresistible speed at which the art progressed quickly outmoded all of his developments.

[1] George Wilhelm Alexander Hans von Arco was born August 30, 1869, in Grossgorschuetz, near Ratibor; died May 7, 1940, in Berlin. In 1903, he was appointed manager of Gesellschaft für Drahtlose Telegraphie. In 1906, he telephoned by wireless over 21 miles, and in 1912 his high-frequency apparatus was exhibited at the International Radiotelegraphic Conference, London. Von Arco's inventions in the field of wireless involved Siemens and Halske and the German General Electric Company in long litigation until the dispute was settled by intervention of Kaiser Wilhelm. That led to formation of the Telefunken Gesellschaft, which merged various German wireless companies; von Arco was appointed chief engineer.

John Ambrose Fleming

A DETECTOR WON HIM KNIGHTHOOD

BORN: November 29, 1849
Lancaster, England

SIR JOHN AMBROSE FLEMING, English physicist and electrical pioneer, invented the thermionic valve, or tube, the first electronic detector of wireless waves.

John Ambrose, the son of the Rev. James Fleming, completed his schooling at University College School, London, to which city his parents moved from Lancaster. He matriculated at the age of sixteen in the University of London. Graduating with a Bachelor of Science degree in 1870, he was for a brief period science master at Rossall School, returning to London to the Royal College of Chemistry to work under the eminent chemist, Sir Edward Frankland. In 1874 he was appointed a science master at Cheltenham College, and the first paper to be read before the newly formed Physical Society of London was one on the theory of the galvanic cell by J. A. Fleming.

Three years later he went to Cambridge to work under Professor James Clerk Maxwell. For a short time he was first professor of mathematics and physics at University College, Nottingham. In 1881, when electric lighting began to attract public attention, Fleming was appointed electrician to the Edison Electric Light Company of London, a position which he occupied for the ensuing ten years. His great practical knowledge qualified him to practice as a consulting electrical engineer, and he became adviser to many city corporations on their electric lighting plans and problems.

In 1885 Fleming was appointed the first professor of electrical engineering at University College, London, a position which he held for more than forty years. His abilities as a lecturer and teacher brought him many invitations to speak before audiences of the Royal

Institution and the Royal Society of Arts. His treatise on electric-wave telegraphy was for many years a standard book on the subject.

It was natural that his work in connection with the introduction of the telephone and electric light in England should have led him into the field of wireless. For more than twenty-five years he served as scientific adviser of the Marconi Wireless Telegraph Company, and he was partly responsible for the design of the first transatlantic station at Poldhu. Since there had been much controversy regarding the wavelength used by Poldhu to flash the first transatlantic signal, Fleming was asked by the author in 1935 what wave was used. He replied:

The wavelength of the electric waves sent out from Poldhu Marconi station in 1901 was not measured because I did not invent my cymometer or wavemeter until October, 1904. The height of the original aerial (1901) was 200 feet, but then there was a coil of a transformer or "jigger" as we called it in series with it. My estimate was that the original wavelength must have been not less than about 3,000 feet, but it was considerably lengthened later on.

I knew at that time that the diffraction or bending of the rays around the earth would be increased by increasing the wavelength and after the first success I was continually urging Marconi to lengthen the wavelength, and that was done when commercial transmission began. I remember I designed special cymometers to measure up to 20,000 feet or so.

It was not Poldhu, however, that made Fleming a name to be remembered. Poldhu's triumph belonged to Marconi. It was a small electric bulb—an offspring of the electric incandescent lamp—that gave Fleming his claim to fame.

Telling the story of how he came to invent the valve detector, Fleming said:

In 1882, as electrical adviser of the Edison Electric Light Company of London, I was brought into close touch with the many problems of incandescent lamps and I began to study the physical phenomena with all the scientific means at my disposal. Like everyone else, I noticed that the filaments broke easily at the slightest shock, and when the lamps burned out the glass bulbs became discolored. This discoloration of the glass was generally accepted as a matter of course. It seemed too trifling to notice. But in science it is the trifles that count. The little things of today may develop ino the great things of tomorrow.

Wondering why the glass bulb grew dark, I started to investigate the matter, and discovered that in many burned-out lamps there was a line of glass that was not discolored. It was as though someone took a smoked glass, drew a finger down it, and left a perfectly clean line behind. I found that the lamps with these strange, sharply-defined clean spaces were covered elsewhere with a deposit of carbon or metal, and that the clean line was immediately in the plane of the hairpin-shaped carbon filament and on the side of the loop opposite to the burned-out point of the filament.

It was obvious to me that the unbroken part of the filament acted as a screen to that particular line of clear glass, and that the discharge from the overheated point on the filament bombarded the remainder of the bulb with molecules of carbon or vaporized metal shot out in straight lines. My experiments at the end of 1882 and early in 1883 proved that I was right.

Edison in 1883 noticed the phenomenon called "the Edison Effect"; but he could not explain it, nor did he use it in any way.

In October, 1884, Sir William Preece turned his attention to investigation of "the Edison Effeot." He decided it was associated with the projection of carbon molecules from the filament in straight lines, thus confirming my original discovery. There Sir William Preece let the matter rest, just as Edison had done. He did not satisfactorily explain the phenomenon nor did he seek to apply it. "The Edison Effect" remained just a peculiar property, a mystery of the incandescent lamp.[1]

At this point other work sidetracked Fleming's attention, but in 1888 he obtained several special carbon-filament lamps made by Edison and also by Sir Joseph Swan in England and resumed his experiments. The filaments, as Fleming described them, were "bent like a horseshoe," and within the bulbs or in the side of the tubes metal plates were attached. He enclosed the negative leg of the carbon filament in a glass bulb, and noticed that the bombardment of electrified particles was stopped. By altering the position of the metal plates he could vary the intensity of the bombardment. When he placed a metal cylinder around the negative leg of the filament without touching it, the galvanometer registered the strongest current. It was

[1] *Popular Radio*, March, 1923.

obvious to Fleming that the metal cylinder was catching the electrified particles that streamed from the incandescent filament. By study of the fundamental causes of "the effect," he found that the plate-filament combination could be used as a rectifier of alternating currents, not only those of commercial frequency but also those of the high frequencies used in wireless.

Fleming's appointment in 1899 as electrical adviser to the Marconi Wireless Telegraph Company thoroughly acquainted him with the capricious coherer as a detector of wireless waves. To find a better detector he tried to develop chemical rectifiers, until one day the thought occurred to him: "Why not try the lamps?"

First he constructed an oscillatory circuit, with two Leyden jars, a wired wooden frame and an induction coil. He then made another circuit, in which one of the lamps and a galvanometer were inserted. Both circuits were tuned to the same frequency.

It was about 5 o'clock in the evening when the apparatus was completed [said Fleming, recalling the experiment]. I was, of course, most anxious to test it without further loss of time. We set the two circuits some distance apart in the laboratory, and I started the oscillations in the primary circuit.

To my delight I saw that the needle of the galvanometer indicated a steady direct current passing through, and found that we had in this peculiar kind of electric lamp a solution of the problem of rectifying high-frequency wireless currents. The missing link in wireless was found—and it was an electric lamp!

I saw at once that the metal plate should be replaced by a metal cylinder enclosing the whole filament, so as to collect all the electrons projected from it. I accordingly had many carbon filament lamps made with metal cylinders and used them for rectifying the high-frequency currents of wireless telegraphy.

This instrument I named an oscillation valve. It was at once found to be of value in wireless telegraphy, the mirror galvanometer that I used being replaced by an ordinary telephone, a replacement that could be made with advantage in those days when the spark system of wireless telegraphy was employed. In this form my valve was somewhat extensively used by Marconi's Telegraph Company as a detector of wireless waves. I applied for a patent in Great Britain on November 16, 1904.

For that invention the Royal Society of Arts, London, in 1921 awarded Fleming its highest distinction—the Gold Albert Medal. His honors were many, including the Kelvin Medal, the Faraday Medal of the Institution of Electrical Engineers and the Franklin Medal of Franklin Institute, Philadelphia. In March, 1929, he received the honor of knighthood for his "valuable service in science and industry."

Augusto Righi

EMINENT SCIENTIST AND TEACHER

BORN: *August 27, 1850*
Bologna, Italy

DIED: *June 8, 1920*
Bologna, Italy

AUGUSTO RIGHI, Italian physicist, educated at Bologna University, became professor of physics from 1873 to 1880 at the Bologna Technical Institute; 1880 to 1885 at the Palermo University; 1885 to 1889 at Padua University and then at the University of Bologna. From 1872 to 1918, Righi published more than 200 scientific papers on such subjects as "electro-atomic phenomena," "the action of magnetism;" "electrified particles in gases;" "electric waves;" "electric oscillations;" "Hertzian waves" and "telegraphy without wires." After Hertz announced his discovery of electromagnetic waves, Righi investigated them, especially their optical properties, and published the results in a treatise, *Optice Elettrica,* in 1897. He noticed that the smaller the spheres on the "exciters," the shorter the waves, approaching those of light.

It was remarked by a veteran Marconi engineer that "before describing methods Marconi devised by which he realized his ambition, it is advisable to refer to the work of those pioneers who influenced Marconi in his early experiments, and of whose work he had knowledge: Maxwell, Hertz, Righi and Branly."

Bologna was Marconi's home. It was there that Righi, professor of Physics at the University, propagated electric waves as short as 2.5 centimeters, whereas Hertz had produced them 30 centimeters in length. Righi improved the Hertz oscillator that generated the waves; he placed the spark gap in vaseline oil and made the waves more consistent and steady. He contributed a new "detector" by cutting thin lines on the back of a mirror, dividing the metallic surface with a diamond point into narrow discontinuous strips. This provided a spark-distance much finer than could be attained by a micrometer gap, hence affording greater "sensitivity." But it is said that Righi's work in generation and detection of electric waves was not in itself as important as the fact that it was partly through him that Marconi found encouragement. Although Marconi was never enrolled as a student at the University of Bologna, he did hear Righi lecture.

In Marconi's first test of wireless he used the induction coil as the electric-wave emitter, and the ball discharger or spark gap described by Professor Righi in his scientific papers. It consisted of four brass balls separated by small gaps and immersed in vaseline oil. To control the electric discharge across the gap a telegraph key was connected in the primary circuit of the induction coil. This, of course, permitted the formation of dots and dashes.

After Marconi's success in opening transatlantic wireless service in January, 1903, with an exchange of greetings between President Theodore Roosevelt and King Edward VII, he returned to Bologna; the entire town turned out to greet him, and in the throng was Professor Righi, who at the reception said:

"Perhaps no one can appreciate better than I his exceptional inventive power and his unusual intellectual gifts. It is to the credit of Marconi that he has proved how much those are in error who regard with disdainful or indifferent eyes the work carried on in the silence of the laboratory by modest students of science."

Oliver Heaviside

FOUND THE RADIO "ROOF"

BORN: May 13, 1850
London, England

DIED: February 4, 1925
Torquay, England

SIR OLIVER HEAVISIDE, English telephone engineer and mathematician, while in the service of the Great Northern Telegraph Company devoted considerable study to the possibilities of quadruplex telegraph. It is believed that he may have been influenced to enter this field since he was a nephew of Sir Charles Wheatstone, noted telegraph engineer. Increasing deafness at the age of twenty-four caused Heaviside to leave the telegraph company, and he took up mathematical research. As an ardent student of Maxwell he delved into the electromagnetic theory and wave propagation.

Independent and shy, especially in later life, he lived as a recluse, even cooking and looking after his home alone. Shielded by solitude, here was a profound thinker who looked afar, as evidenced in his last book, *Electromagnetic Theory* in which he described the universe "as boundless one way toward the great, so it is equally boundless the other way, towards the small. . . . We do not know where life begins, if it has a beginning. There may be and probably is no ultimate distinction between the living and the dead."

Heaviside's voluminous scientific writings were said to be difficult even for the advanced mathematician. His fame is pinnacled upon the laws governing propagation of energy in electrical circuits, which led him to investigate the effects of land, water and the upper atmosphere on the propagation of wireless waves.

Said Heaviside in 1902:

Sea water though transparent to light, has quite enough conductivity to make it behave as a conductor for Hertzian waves, and the same is true in a more imperfect manner of the earth. Hence the waves accommodate themselves to the surface of the sea in the same way as waves follow wires. The irregularities make confusion, no doubt, but the main waves are pulled round by the curvature of the earth, and do not jump off.

There is another consideration. There may possibly be a sufficiently conducting layer in the upper air. If so, the waves will, so to speak, catch on to it more or less. Then the guidance will be by the sea on one side and the upper layer on the other. But obstructions, on land especially, may not be conducting enough to make waves go round them fairly. The waves will go partly through them.[1]

So in the science of radio it has become recognized that high in the sky, at an altitude of sixty miles and higher, billowing up and down like the big top of a circus, is "the Heaviside layer." It is the "ceiling" or "mirror" that reflects radio waves back to the earth. For that discovery Sir Oliver is linked with world-wide radio, since his theory accounts for the ease with which short waves hop, skip and jump around the globe.

Karl Ferdinand Braun

DEVELOPED THE CATHODE-RAY TUBE

BORN: June 6, 1850
Fulda, Germany

DIED: April 14, 1918
Brooklyn, N. Y.

KARL FERDINAND BRAUN, physicist, was "the Fleming" of the cathode-ray tube. As Fleming developed the valve detector, to which De Forest added the grid to create the three-element audion, so Braun developed the cathode-ray tube to the point where it remained chiefly to add the electron gun control to bring the Kinescope, or television picture tube, into being.

Educated at Marburg and Berlin, Braun became professor of physics in 1895 at Marburg and afterwards at Karlsruhe; later, director of the Physical Institute at Strasbourg. Electrical phenomena of cathode rays, oscillographs and the riddles of wireless were his

[1] *Oliver Heaviside*, by F. Gill, Bell Telephone Laboratories, 1925.

specialties in research. Noted for development of the Braun cathode-ray tube, he shared the Nobel prize for physics with Marconi in 1909.

Cathode rays were not originated with Braun for they had been used by Crookes and Roentgen, but up to the time of Braun the cathode-ray streams had been like a rushing torrent, uncontrolled. It remained for Braun to apply older knowledge systematically in order to deflect the cathode rays. He produced a narrow, guided stream of electrons; he deflected that stream electrostatically and thus made it trace patterns on a fluorescent screen. This was a great step forward in two fields: First, in oscillography, it enabled study of fluctuating voltages and currents even if their frequencies were extremely high. In fact, the modern cathode-ray oscillograph, except for refinements and details, was born in Braun's laboratory as a most useful tool in electrical, electronic and radio research.

In television, the Braun tube found its second major field of usefulness. It lacked only one element to enable it to reproduce luminous pictures in motion. Braun used an electron stream of constant intensity. Later, von Rosing modulated the electron stream in the Braun tube to follow the lights and shadows of an image—and electronic television was on its way, so near did Braun come to the Kinescope. He had the electron gun, the deflecting plates and the fluorescent screen; the gun control was his only missing link.

Braun was not without contacts and influence on the early development of wireless telegraphy. In 1903, five wireless systems were being tested in the United States—the Marconi system; the Slaby-Arco, by the Navy; the Braun, by the Army; the Fessenden, by the Weather Bureau; and the De Forest, by the Navy. Also the Germans and French had the Braun system, while the Russians in the Russo-Japanese War used a variation of it. Sir Oliver Lodge and Braun in 1898 were apparently working in the same direction as Marconi; they described inductively coupled methods and also recognized the necessity for adjusting the transmitter and receiver to the same wavelength.

Braun was described by an American radio engineer who knew

him well as a steady, thoughtful, typical German professor, guarded in his speech, careful in his statements, modest, good-natured and friendly. As a very skilled radio engineer, he utilized the rudimentary technique of his time but added to it and improved it; his circuits were well designed, and his cathode-ray tube was a beacon that helped to light the future.

Emile Berliner

MAKER OF THE MICROPHONE

BORN: *May 20, 1851*
    Hannover, Germany

DIED: *August 3, 1929*
    Washington, D.C.

EMILE BERLINER lived, as his biographer put it, as "a restlessly active spirit in the endless Kingdom of the unexplored." His story is the story of the microphone and of the "lateral cut" phonograph disk record, both of which contributed to the art of broadcasting.

Emile's father was Samuel Berliner, a merchant in Hannover, Germany; his mother was Sarah Fridman. Of their family of eleven children, Emile was the fourth. His hobby as a boy was "a craze for music." He was graduated at the age of fourteen from the Samsonschule in Wolfenbüttel, about two hours by rail from Hannover. That ended his schooling. His parents, hard put to care adequately for their extensive brood, urged Emile to seek work, first as a printer's devil and then as a clerk in a dry-goods store. At sixteen he began to display a flair for invention by developing a weaving machine.

Stories of "free America" turned his thoughts westward, and in 1870, young Berliner was a passenger when the *Hammonia* sailed from Hamburg. Nathan Gotthelf, old friend of the family, gave him a job in his store in Washington, D.C. Next he tried his luck in New York, then Milwaukee, and then back to New York.

At the Philadelphia Centennial in 1876 Berliner scented the dawn of the Industrial Age; he saw Bell's telephone on exhibit there. He sensed that the telephone was "the coming thing." From then on, his room in a lodging house in Washington looked like an electrical laboratory. He rigged up telephones between his window and the barn and experimented no end to improve the telephonic voice.

It is strange what a little thing will serve as a clue when you are groping for a new idea [said Berliner]. One of the men I used to visit occasionally in those days was Alvan S. Richards, chief operator at the Washington fire-alarm telegraph office. I told him one day that I was learning to transmit messages.

"Let me hear what you can do," he said, pointing to a sending instrument. I placed my finger on the key and started. "Hold on," he exclaimed, "that isn't right, you must press down on the key, not simply touch it. There must be a firm contact or your message may not be understood at the other end." He explained that in long-distance transmission, where the resistance is high, more current passes through the contacts when more pressure is used on the key.

With that explanation I knew I had what I had been seeking. I went home, rigged up a diaphragm and made a contact with a steel button. I began to adjust it until the galvanometer showed that current was flowing. Then I pressed gently and I found that each time I pressed, the galvanometer deflected through a larger angle.

Thus Berliner caught sight of the microphonic principle; he had found the solution to overcome the shortcomings of the telephone transmitter, or mouthpiece. The new microphone rendered faint sound vibrations audible, and varying the contact pressure registered the sound's intensity. His caveat describing the microphone was filed in the United States Patent Office April 14, 1877; the patent was granted on November 17, 1891.

Discovering that the carrying power of the microphone was enhanced by using it in a circuit with an induction coil, Berliner introduced the continuous current transformer.

From the microphone, Berliner turned his attention to the "talking machine." He developed the lateral cut method of etching the human voice on a gramophone disk, or "phonoautogram."

By devising a disk gramophone record and working out a means of cutting it laterally at an even depth, I could get accuracy and purity of tone impossible with the cylinder records with their up-and-down cuts of uneven depth [explained Berliner]. More than that, however, I solved the problem of making unlimited copies of one original record.

The tremendous commercial success of the talking machine is, of course, due in some measure to the genius of Eldridge R. Johnson, president of the Victor Talking Machine Company, who covered both technical and business fields. My part in it you may gather from the statement issued by the Victor Company several years ago as a warning to infringers.[1]

The statement read:

The manufacture and sale of the gramophone was first conducted by the United States Gramophone Company, followed by the Berliner Gramophone Company, and then by the Victor Talking Machine Company, which latter company acquired its rights from the former companies.

We now control the original Berliner basic patents, and we have the gramophone developed to its present condition. Through our efforts and improvements, the gramophone has become an important factor in the market, in spite of the general opinion among talking-machine manufacturers, at the time of its advent, that it was destined to remain nothing more than a toy.

In May, 1913, on the twenty-fifth anniversary of his first exhibition of the gramophone before the Franklin Institute, Berliner was awarded the Elliott Cresson Medal "in recognition of important contributions to telephony and to the science and art of sound production"—which became the heritage of radio broadcasting.

When beyond three score and ten, Berliner was asked at what age an inventor was most productive.

"The young man is the most prolific inventor every time," he replied unhesitatingly. "Most of the great inventions have been made by men between the ages of 22 and 27. More original ideas are evolved in youth than at any other time, but, of course, a man who is a born inventor keeps producing all his life."

Emile Berliner at seventy-five was still discovering and inventing; his was a spirit powerless to curb. He had three qualities indis-

[1] *Scientific American*, July, 1927.

pensable in scientific exploration: driving force, unconquerable optimism and utter contempt for failure.

The heart beats 40,000,000 times in a year [said Berliner], and the lungs inhale 700,000 gallons of air in the same period. All this and a great many other functions of the human body, one more elaborate than the other, continue without undue friction or disturbance—unless it be our own trespasses —for 70 years. All that is required of us to do is to eat and drink good things of earth; for the rest of the organs of the body take care of themselves. Thus, and through countless other wonders, by teaching humility to its disciples, Science assumes the role of the most potent religion.

Oliver Lodge

GREAT PHYSICIST AND THINKER

BORN: June 12, 1851   DIED: August 22, 1940
     Penkhull, England   Amesbury, Wiltshire, England

SIR OLIVER LODGE, English physicist, was educated at Newport Grammar School where he made his first acquaintance with science. Later, on a visit to London, he heard a series of Tyndall's lectures and began the study of chemistry by attending afternoon classes at Wedgwood Institute. And in 1872 he enrolled for a course at the South Kensington Chemical Laboratory.

By work and study at odd hours he matriculated at the University of London where he became much interested in mathematics. He received his Bachelor of Science degree in 1875, and was selected to fill the post of demonstrator of physics at University College. He published several papers on the flow of electricity, which attracted considerable attention in the scientific world. The next year he exhibited before the British Association a model derived from Maxwell's theories for the purpose of illustrating mechanically the passage of electricity through metals, electrolytes and dielectrics.

Lodge was appointed professor of physics and mathematics in

the University College, Liverpool, in 1881, where he remained until 1900. He was awarded the Doctor of Science degree in 1887. Also, while lecturer at Bedford College, London, Lodge continued his research work. In 1889 he wrote a little book titled *Modern Views of Electricity*, with the exposition based entirely on models. He compared the ether, of which he was one of the most persuasive and lucid interpreters, to an elastic jelly filling all space; he compared magnetism to whirlpools in that jelly, or more crudely to interlocking wheels. To him the universe was a gigantic machine.

Lodge, writing in the *London Electrician* in 1894, discussed the discoveries of Hertz, described his own experiments with electromagnetic waves and commented upon the phenomenon of resonance or tuning. He pointed out that some circuits were by their nature persistent vibrators—that is, they were able to sustain for a long period oscillations set up in them—while other circuits were so constructed that their oscillations were rapidly damped. He said that a receiver of the rapidly damped type would respond to waves of almost any frequency, while one that was a persistent vibrator would respond only to waves of its own natural period, or wavelength. Lodge found that the Hertz transmitter "radiates very powerfully" but that "in consequence of its radiation of energy, its vibrations are rapidly damped," therefore it could excite sparks in conductors barely in tune with it.

On February 1, 1898, Lodge applied for a patent which was allowed on August 16, 1898, as No. 609,154. It disclosed an adjustable induction coil in the open or antenna circuit of a wireless transmitter or receiver, or in both, to make it possible to put the transmitter and receiver in tune with each other. He used a Branly coherer as the detector. He broadly claimed that making the antenna coil or inductance variable made tuning of the antenna circuits in a system of wireless communication possible.

This "syntonic" or tuning patent won him a high place in the history of wireless, for it established him as a pioneer in experiments that recognized the necessity of tuning in order to select a desired station. This patent, incidentally, was acquired by the Marconi Company on March 19, 1912.

Lodge's tuning patent was appraised by the United States District Court (Eastern District of New York) in 1914, as "the realization of the advantages to be derived in the matter of sharpness of tuning." But it was proved that Marconi's original patent was more specific; he had specified that his elevated capacity plates (antenna) were preferably electrically tuned with each other.

Said the Court in regard to Lodge:

> He increased the persistence of vibrations of his radiating circuit at the expense of its radiating qualities, and increased the cumulative power of his receiving circuit at the expense of its absorbing qualities.
>
> Effecting this compromise by means of the introduction of an inductance coil in an open circuit, he obtained a train of waves of approximately equal amplitude, and this rendered effective syntony (tuning). But the syntony thus obtained was utilized for selectivity alone. It was attained at the expense of the radiating and absorbing qualities of the circuit; and Lodge still supposed that for distant signaling the single pulse, or whip crack, was best.

Where Lodge compromised, as the Court pointed out, Marconi reconciled, so to the Italian went the crown!

Of Sir Oliver, Marconi said,

> He is one of our greatest physicists and thinkers, but it is particularly in regard to his pioneering in wireless, which should never be forgotten. In the very early days, after the experimental confirmation of Maxwell's theory as to the existence of electric waves and their propagation through space, it was given to only a very few persons to possess clear insight in regard to what was considered to be one of the most hidden mysteries of nature. Sir Oliver Lodge possessed that insight in a far greater degree than perhaps any of his contemporaries.

As the British asked with regard to Preece, so they inquired why Lodge was not the rightful inventor of wireless? Sir Oliver explained it this way: "I was too busy with teaching work to take up telegraphic or any other development nor had I the insight to perceive what has turned out to be its extraordinary importance to the navy, the merchant service, and indeed, land and war services too."

The first transoceanic wireless, "an epoch in human history," as Lodge referred to it, inspired him to remark, "Marconi's creation like that of the poet who gathers words of other men in a perfect lyric was none the less brilliant and original. . . . One feels like a boy who has been strumming on a silent keyboard of a deserted organ, into the chest of which an unseen power begins to blow a vivifying breath."

In recognition of his scientific contributions, Lodge received the Rumford Medal of the Royal Society in 1898 and was knighted by King Edward VII in 1902. As one of the pioneers in wireless telegraphy, he was presented with the Albert Medal of the Royal Society of Arts in 1919. From 1900 to 1919, Sir Oliver was principal of Birmingham University. After 1910 he became increasingly prominent as a spiritualist leader and a strong believer in the possibilities of communicating with the dead; he interested himself in a serious endeavor to reconcile science and religion. He expressed a belief in telepathy and the opinion that the easiest way to communicate with the planet Mars would be by means of gigantic geometrical figures drawn on the Sahara Desert.

As the years passed, Sir Oliver became more and more a believer in speech with the dead, manifestations from the mysterious unknown, even in nebulous forms that were produced from ectoplasm at séances. At the age of eighty, he announced that he would try to communicate with the world after his death. He placed a sealed document in the custody of the English Society of Psychical Research, saying that his message from the beyond would correspond with what he had recorded in the document.

Lodge had the power of crystallizing into clear statement an entire collection of thoughts or arguments. Once during a discussion about the forces that bind atom to atom he picked up a stick that lay on the lecture table, and he seemed merely to be toying with it, when suddenly he said, "The whole problem of physics lies in this: why, when I pick up one end of the stick, does not the other end come up too?

The forces that hold the stick in one are those also which bind the universe together."

"I think of him," said Sir William Bragg, "as a really magnificent figure, tall and impressive, a marvelous teacher, an enterprising thinker and a great worker, who had a remarkable influence on his contemporaries and students. He was a very distinguished man of science."

Elihu Thomson

FOREMOST AMONG SCIENTISTS OF HIS AGE

BORN: March 29, 1853   DIED: March 13, 1937
    Manchester, England   Swampscott, Mass.

ELIHU THOMSON, American inventor, was recognized in the nineteenth century as "one of the foremost among great men of science of this age."

Asked to trace the beginning of his long and useful career, Thomson said:

I must go back to the year 1853, when I was born in Manchester, England, coming to America with my parents at the age of five and settling in Philadelphia. The year of my graduation from the Central High School in that city was 1870. I was then seventeen, and before the end of that year I was made a member of the faculty as assistant professor of chemistry. In 1876, when I was twenty-three, I was appointed to the full professorship of chemistry and mechanics.

Throughout my youth I was interested in physics, mechanics, and electricity. I began making electrical experiments when I was eleven years of age, constructing my first frictional machine at that time. From then until about 1880 I was frequently engaged, during my spare moments, in producing experimental electrical devices; then, about 1877-78, I built a complete dynamo-electric machine and thereafter gave some demonstrations of electric lighting circuits, including the demonstration of 1879 in which induction coils connected in parallel were employed, foreshadowing the transformer practice of the present time. Some of these early patents were taken out jointly with Edwin J. Houston, Professor of Natural Philosophy at the Philadelphia High School.

Thomson and Professor Houston made their first experiments with the Ruhmkorff coil in 1871. They noticed while electricity was flowing between the points of the coil that long sparks could be drawn from any metallic object within eight or ten feet and from a small steam engine which was thirty feet away from the coil. Edison, about the same time, reported on similar experiments and referred to such sparks as "etheric forces." Thomson is said to have believed the "force" was in reality transmission of electrical impulses through the air—wireless!

In 1875, as a twenty-two-year-old high school teacher in Philadelphia, Thomson noticed that sparks caused by a Ruhmkorff coil in the physics room jumped from the brass doorknobs to a pencil point. While at the time he was unaware of the full implications, he said:

I realized that if we had been able to go down the street probably a quarter of a mile away, the same tests might have been productive of positive results and I further realized that we had the germ of a new system of electric signaling.

In 1879 I began designing an electric arc-light system for the commercial market, having the financial support of George S. Garrett, of Garrettsford, Penn. My first dynamo would supply four arc lights, but its capacity was soon increased, by re-arranging the windings, to furnish current for eight lights. The inherent design of the dynamo made it adaptable also as a three-phase alternator—I believe it was the first three-phase winding ever brought out.

In 1892—the year in which the Thomson-Houston Electric Company was combined with Edison's company to form the General Electric Company—Thomson wrote an article for the *New England Magazine* which was accompanied by a drawing of a lighthouse flashing electric waves along with the light to penetrate a fog.

"Electricians are not without some hope," he said, "that signaling or telegraphing over moderate distances without wires or even through a dense fog may be an accomplished fact soon."

For sixty-six years Thomson was an outstanding pioneer in electrical engineering, in physics, chemistry and astronomy. He was so retiring, so modest and so busy in his research laboratory that the public scarcely knew he was alive. Yet leading technical societies in America and abroad honored him. In a broadcast over WGY, his biographer said:

Thomson's word on scientific subjects was law. As a teacher, and giver of common, sound advice, he was a legendary figure. His kindness and understanding, his genius for taking others into his confidence and inspiring them, have not been equaled by any scientist since Faraday.

Thomson was born six years after Edison. Edison was spectacular. His mind worked like a steel trap biting to the heart of a problem by some God-given instinct for mechanical things. Elihu Thomson's mind was as wide and deep as the sea. He had a tremendous knowledge and instinct for the fundamental laws of nature. His inventions and discoveries were not made by brilliant intuition but by steady reasoning and logic. . . . In 1878 he invented the most compact and foolproof dynamo machine so far made, and founded an industry. At that time he devised the alternating current system of electric distribution. . . . Professor Thomson was giving a public demonstration in Philadelphia one night in 1877 when by accident he produced an electric weld. Nine years later he patented the process and founded a company to market it. . . . The amount of electric current the world uses is measured by millions of recording wattmeters which are the direct descendants of the Thomson meter invented in 1889. It was Thomson who discovered the repulsion induction motor, whose descendants now run vacuum cleaners and electric fans. He invented the centrifugal separator; the magnetic blow-out principle in lightning arresters and electric switches; the oil-cooled type of transformer; electric resistance welding; electric air drill; the constant-current transformer; and the process of commercially treating fused quartz.

Thomson was more than an inventor; he was a scientist, a philosopher and a great human being as well. He built a large telescope and became an authority on the planets and stars. His lifetime hobby was astronomy. He was one of the first scientists to believe that sun spots caused the aurora and the earth's magnetic storms.

Thomson was a Lincoln of the scientific world. When he died he became a permanent American tradition. We cannot live through a single day without relying upon the inventions and the discoveries of truth that he made. At the time of his death he held more than 700 patents.[1]

Thomson was recognized as "always more the scientist than the contriver." It was said of him that in the field of electrical science there was scarcely any aspect in which he had not been active at some time or other. While affiliated with the General Electric Company as director of research at Lynn, Massachusetts, Thomson remarked, "When I see need for a thing I settle down to discover what is the best thing to do to fill that need."

Of him it was said in 1933, by President Compton of Massachusetts Institute of Technology, "More than any other man now living or, in fact, more than any man in history, Professor Thomson has combined in a most remarkable way the constructive powers of the inventor, the thoroughness and soundness of the man of science, and the kindly balance of an ideal philosopher, teacher and friend."

To which tribute was later added at the time of his death, "He had a many-sided mind: astronomy, chemistry, mechanics and electricity —he enriched them all."

Joseph John Thomson

DISCOVERER OF THE ELECTRON

BORN: *December 18, 1856*
Manchester, England

DIED: *August 30, 1940*
Cambridge, England

SIR JOSEPH JOHN THOMSON, English physicist, "found" the electron —the key to a new age in electrophysics. As a student of electricity and magnetism, he concentrated on conduction of electricity through gases, and upon his classical investigations into the behavior and properties of electrons, the modern theory of thermionic emission was founded.

[1] David O. Woodbury, March 29, 1943.

Educated at Owens College and Trinity College, Cambridge, Thomson was appointed Cavendish Professor of Experimental Physics in 1896. The same year, at Princeton University, he delivered a series of lectures published in 1897 under the title, "Discharge of Electricity through Gases." In 1903 he returned to the United States and received honorary degrees from Princeton, Columbia and Johns Hopkins. He was professor of physics at the Royal Institution, London, in 1905. The Nobel prize for physics was awarded to him in 1906. Knighted in 1908, he was honored throughout the world of science for his development of the modern ionic theory of electricity, the theoretical and experimental discussion of radioactivity and the electrical theory of inertia of matter.

When wireless pioneers, including Marconi, were puzzled over why the signals traveled greater distances at night than in the daytime, Professor Thomson showed that the illuminated and ionized air absorbed considerable energy of the electric waves.

Physicists had recognized that matter was composed of molecules and that molecules were combinations of atoms. What were the atoms made of? Thomson found the answer—electrons. In 1897 he demonstrated the true character of the electron as the smallest particle of the electrical structure of the atom. This epochal discovery of the electron did not mean that he isolated or saw it; he simply verified that something much smaller than an atom existed, and that these entities had the same mass and electric charge regardless of the kind of metal from which they were produced.

Scientists were intrigued and at loss to discover an immediate value—but not for long. They soon learned that electrons were infinitesimal particles carrying negative charges of electricity, and recognized them as the basic material of atomic architecture—the corpuscles of radio science. Despite its tiny character, scientists have continued to learn more about the electron. They report that it is 1,840 times lighter than the hydrogen atom—the lightest of all atoms. In the atom, the electrons are found to travel in orbits about the central nucleus (the proton) in much the same way as the planets move around the sun. Thirty billion billion billion electrons, it is estimated, might weigh an ounce. And the electron stream travels at one-tenth the speed of light—at a velocity of 20,000 miles in a second. Since electricity is believed to consist of millions of free electrons in motion—flowing through a conductor—the electron stream may well be called the lifeblood of modern radio communications.

Electrons pervade all matter. Fortunately, they can be liberated from the atoms of matter to which they ordinarily are bound. They may be distilled into a vacuum by heating the filament in a radio tube; they may escape under the influence of light as in the photoelectric tube; or they may be freed from the atoms of some substances by methods of bombardment.

The electron became the nucleus of a new branch of science—electronics, born of the incandescent electric lamp, and with the radio tube as its heart. Such wonders as X-rays, world-wide broadcasting, the electron microscope, television "eyes" and no end of new developments attest the ever-growing importance and power of the electron tube.

Electronics deals with the liberated electrons. When the metal filament, or cathode of a radio-electron tube is heated, the tube comes to life and the action begins. Electrons are set free. The radio tube generates electrons, liberates them, harnesses them and puts them to work. It gives man a new grip on electricity; it greatly widens the concepts and scope of electrical engineering. Electricity is no longer wire-bound. Electrons are no longer imprisoned, but are free to move through a vacuum or gases, and when brought under control they perform a myriad of tasks.

Scientists generally agree that electrons are basic building blocks from which the ninety-two stable chemical elements are formed. It is explained that the chemical differences between these elements—from hydrogen, the lightest, to uranium, the heaviest—depend chiefly on the number and arrangement of the outermost electrons in each of the ninety-two kinds of atoms. Thus it is recognized that all material substances are composed of electrons. As Faraday called upon the world to become electrically minded, Thomson directed it to be electronically minded.

Acclaimed as the foremost physicist of his generation, Thomson was known among his associates as "JJ." At the time of his death, the New York *Times* observed that he had bridged the enormous gap between the old physics and the new—the old physics that conceived the atom as the smallest unit of matter, and the new based upon the far smaller electron.

"JJ's" whole professional life was spent probing the deep and hidden nature of matter and electricity. Before him there were two different entities; after him, one and the same. Through his mathematical skill of the highest order he even foreshadowed the solar-system type of atom and furnished relativity with one of its important props by showing the relation between the mass and the charge of the electron.

It may be recalled that when Sir Humphry Davy was asked to name his greatest discovery he waved his hand toward Michael Faraday. Thomson, with ability, kindliness and understanding of young men, could point to Rutherford and fifty others who became noted physicists because he had "discovered" them and helped them along the way.

Unlike some of the most eminent Victorians, Thomson could throw a useless theory overboard and develop a new one which, it was said, left even his associates gasping at its boldness. Recalling a statement by Thomas Huxley, "God give me strength to face a fact though it slay me," the *Times* remarked that "JJ" had that strength, and for that reason even in his old age he was as young in mind as any later-day chaser of neutrons.

"He, more than any other man," said Sir William Bragg, "was responsible for the fundamental change in the outlook which distinguishes the physics of this century from that of the last, namely, the electrical conception of the constitution of matter."

Thomson is remembered as a mathematical physicist, not as a

manipulator of apparatus. In his experiments he had assistants expert in handling instruments. He was "all fingers," awkward with his hands. He figured how things ought to go and pointed the way; he stimulated and encouraged thought and work among others. He is said to have considered a slide rule a waste of time. His way of measuring the diameter of a rod was to wrap a thread around it and measure the length of the thread.

Thomson's intellect coupled with great perseverance made a powerful combination; his fellow workers described him as "a sticker"—a man utterly unpretentious, whose great mind was inseparable from simplicity of character.

Heinrich Rudolph Hertz

DISCOVERER OF ELECTRIC WAVES

BORN: February 22, 1857
Hamburg, Germany

DIED: January 1, 1894
Bonn, Germany

HEINRICH RUDOLPH HERTZ, German physicist, was the first to create, detect and measure electromagnetic waves, and thereby to confirm Maxwell's theory of "ether" waves. He found a close relationship between "wireless" and light by observing that the velocity of the electric impulses was the same as that of light, and that the law of this electrical radiation was the same as the corresponding law of optics. He demonstrated that the invisible waves could be reflected, refracted and polarized like the waves of light, and he expressed belief that if the rate of oscillation could be increased a millionfold, the electromagnetic waves actually would "wash" upon the frontiers of light.

Hertz's father was a lawyer, and his mother, the daughter of a physician, was descended from a long line of Lutheran ministers, all of cultural tastes and attainments. At the age of twenty he went to school in Munich to pursue an engineering career, but at the last moment changed his plans and took up the study of natural science, specializing in mathematics and magnetics. In 1878 he went to Berlin, and having enrolled as a student under Helmholtz and Kirchhoff, he wrote to his parents, "I am now thoroughly happy and could not wish things better."

In 1879 the Berlin Academy of Science offered a prize for research on the problem of establishing experimentally any relation between electromagnetic forces and the dielectric polarization of insulators. Helmholtz drew Hertz's attention to the problem and promised him the assistance of the Physical Institute if he decided to take up the work and aim for the prize. Do electric and magnetic forces, like light, require time for their propagation? Are there waves?

The riddle was complicated by the fact that oscillations of sufficiently high frequency were not then available.

Recalling the challenge, Hertz said:

I reflected on the problem, but abandoned it for the time. In 1886 I took it up again, and by using apparatus that was available I produced electric waves, and found that by the use of parallel conductors I could determine the presence or absence of these waves, in the form of nodes or loops, by means of tiny sparks across various positions on these parallel rods.

In this same year Sir Oliver Lodge found the same effects while investigating the operation of the lightning conductor. This work of mine was in 1886-7, and was described in a paper "On Very Rapid Electric Oscillations."

Hertz became professor of experimental physics at the Technical High School at Karlsruhe in 1885. A year later he married Elizabeth Doll, daughter of a professor. In 1888 he received his doctorate and was appointed assistant to Helmholtz; he also lectured on theoretical physics at the University of Kiel. Called to succeed the noted Clausius at the University of Bonn in 1889, at the age of thirty-two, he had what was recognized as a position in the academic world not ordinarily attained until much later in life.

As a preliminary experiment directed toward proving the existence of electromagnetic waves, Hertz connected a spiral coil in series with a condenser and spark gap, and found that every charge of the condenser produced an oscillatory discharge. This was the key to solving the big problem for now he could produce high-frequency oscillations.

Later he replaced this combination with an oscillator, or "exciter," as he called it, and spread the field of force. In fact, real radiation occurred. By means of his search coil, or resonator, he detected the presence of the elusive waves some distance from their source.

The resonator, or detector circuit, comprised a short length of wire in the form of a circular loop, containing a micrometer gap across which sparks could be seen when the room was darkened. The effect was more pronounced when the resonator was in electrical resonance, or tune, with the exciter.

Hertz was not content to stop there. He demonstrated that the electric waves could be reflected from plane or curved metal surfaces in accordance with the same laws as those of light waves. Also he showed that the electromagnetic impulses were refracted when passing through prisms of pitch, paraffin and other insulating materials. From actual measurements of the wavelengths and computations of the frequency of the impulses he calculated the velocity and found it to be the same as light—186,000 miles a second.

The oscillator was nothing more than a short metal rod with a spark gap in the middle and capacity plates at the outer ends of the rod. The sparking terminals consisted of small knobs or spheres which were connected to the terminals of a Ruhmkorff induction coil; the small inductance and capacitance of this simple linear conductor, together with the proper functioning of the spark gap, accounted for its success.[1] By such means Hertz obtained wavelengths from a few meters to 30 centimeters—ultra-short waves.

Said Hertz with characteristic constraint, "Such researches as I have made upon this subject form but a link in a long chain. Lack of time compels me, against my will, to pass by the researches made by many other investigators; so that I am not able to show you in how

[1] "Hertz," by Julian Blanchard, in *Proceedings* of the Institute of Radio Engineers, May, 1938.

many ways the path was prepared for my experiment, and how near several investigators came to performing these experiments themselves."

In an electrical journal he described how he radiated electromagnetic waves. A young man in his 'teens happened to read the story while vacationing in the Alps; for him it contained the germ of a big idea. Why not use the sparks for signaling? Guglielmo Marconi cut short his vacation and rushed back to his home in Italy to try what seemed to be fantastic.

In the summer of 1892, Hertz suffered an illness which developed into chronic blood poisoning. He died at the age of thirty-seven. Few scientists ever accomplished so much in so short a span of life as did Hertz, who passed the torch of wireless to Marconi.

Hertz's epochal experiments were described in a paper entitled "Electromagnetic Waves in Air and Their Reflection," published in May, 1888.[2] As summarized by Hertz, "the hope of these experiments was to test the fundamental hypotheses of the Faraday-Maxwell theory and the result of the experiments is to confirm the fundamental hypotheses of the theory."

In was admitted in 1890 that Hertz's discovery "is working a revolution in our ideas about electricity."

The English mathematical physicist, Sir Oliver Heaviside, observed in 1891: "Three years ago electromagnetic waves were nowhere. Shortly afterward they were everywhere."

Sir Oliver Lodge remarked:

Hertz stepped in before the English physicists and brilliantly carried off the prize. He was naturally and unexpectedly pleased with the reception of his discovery in England, and his speech on the occasion of the bestowal of the Rumford Medal by the Royal Society will long be remembered by those who heard it for its simple-hearted enthusiasm and good feeling. His letters are full of the same sentiment. There is not a student of physical science on the planet who will not realize and lament the sad loss conveyed by the message, "Hertz is dead."

     [2] Hertz's collected papers edited by Dr. Philipp Lenard and translated into English by Professor D. E. Jones comprise three volumes.

In a memorial address, Professor Herman Ebert, before the Physical Society of Erlangen on March 7, 1894, expressed this tribute to Hertz:

In him there passed away not only a man of great learning, but also a noble man, who had the singular good fortune to find many admirers, but none to hate or envy him; those who came into personal contact with him were struck by his modesty and charmed by his amiability. He was a true friend to his friends, a respected teacher to his students, who had begun to gather around him in somewhat large numbers, some of them coming from great distances; and to his family he was a loving husband and father.

As the founder of a new epoch in experimental physics, modestly Hertz had once remarked, "The theory of electricity is so foreign to me."

Of her son, the mother said, "He was really not ambitious, only very eager."

Hertzian waves carry his name into posterity, for "on the unerring accuracy of this brilliant physicist rests the foundation of wireless."

Nikola Tesla

GENIUS WAS APPLICABLE TO HIM

BORN: July 10, 1857
Smiljan, Serbia

DIED: January 7, 1943
New York, N.Y.

NIKOLA TESLA, through his wide range of electrical experiments and discoveries, became one of the world's foremost electricians. His invention of the induction motor and the Tesla coil and his discovery of the rotary magnetic field principle won him widespread recognition as "the electrical wizard" of the nineties.

His father was a Greek clergyman and orator; his mother, Georgina Mandic, was an inventor. Mathematics was Tesla's forte; theories and high-frequency currents his delights. Young Nikola's education began with one year in elementary school, four years of the lower Realschule at Gospic, Lika, and then a higher school at Carlstadt, Croatia, from which he was graduated in 1873. He studied for four years at the Polytechnic School at Gratz, devoting most of his time to mathematics, physics and mechanics, and subsequently had two years at the University of Prague, where he studied philosophy. At Gratz, he had seen Z. T. Gramme's electrical dynamo armature. Struck with the objections to the use of commutators and brushes on dynamo-electric machines, he determined to remedy that "defect" and to simplify the machine.

While employed by the Austrian government in its telegraph engineering division, Tesla made his first practical invention—a telephone repeater. Later he engaged in electrical engineering in Budapest. In 1881 he went to Paris, where he worked as an electrical engineer, and the following year he moved to Strasbourg.

Attracted to America by the remarkable progress of the electrical industry, the twenty-seven-year-old Tesla, with four cents in his pocket, stepped off the boat at the Battery in 1884. America as a land of opportunity was soon apparent, for as he walked up Broadway he met a group of workmen trying to repair an electric motor. They paid him $20 to fix it.

Tesla, like many a foreign enthusiast in electricity who came to these shores, arrived with high hopes of finding work with Edison. His luck continued; Edison gave him a job in the laboratory at Orange, New Jersey, designing motors and generators.

Before long a proposal was made that Tesla start his own company. Early in 1887 the Tesla Electric Company was formed, but it was not a financial success. It was in 1888, however, that Tesla produced his epoch-making motors for alternating current. His system of electrical conversion and distribution by oscillatory discharges was developed the following year, and in 1891 the famous Tesla coil, or transformer, was introduced; also he demonstrated the principle of tuning at Columbia University.

He devised a system of wireless transmission in 1893 and began to talk about transmitting power through the air. He developed the

principle of the rotary magnetic field embodied in early power transmission at Niagara Falls, and invented an arc-lighting system as well
as innumerable dynamos, transformers, coils, condensers and other
electrical apparatus. In 1895, at Niagara, his new method for
generating electricity (alternating current) for transmission over
long distances produced 100,000 hp—an output of electrical energy
equaling that of all other generating stations operating at the time
in the United States. The press observed that "the electric revolution
has started."

Tesla was no tinkerer. He was recognized as a first-class mathematician and physicist "whose blueprints were plausible, even though
they were far ahead of the technical resources of his day." He belonged, as a friend remarked, "to the passing age of heroic invention
of which Edison was the most distinguished exemplar—the age of
technical poets who expressed themselves in generators, inductance
coils and high voltages rather than in drama or verse and who were
the real architects of culture."

Tesla was called "the lone scientist"—a wizard to some, a fanatical
prophet to others; always his vivid images were of the future.

When Hertz demonstrated that electromagnetic waves could be
reflected by means of reflectors, he was far ahead of his time in the
science of radio-location. But it remained for Tesla to recognize
and to point out the practical application of the radio "echo," so
vital in the Second World War. Describing his 1889 method and
transmission of wireless energy in *Century* (June, 1900), he said:

That communication without wires to any point of the globe is practical
with such apparatus would need no demonstration, but through a discovery
which I made I obtained absolute certitude. Popularly explained, it is
exactly this: When we raise the voice and hear an echo in reply, we know
that the sound of the voice must have reached a distant wall or boundary,
and must have been reflected from the same. Exactly as the sound, so an
electrical wave is reflected, and the same evidence which is afforded by an
echo is offered by an electrical phenomenon known as a "stationary" wave
—that is, a wave with fixed nodal and ventral regions. Instead of sending
sound-vibrations toward a distant wall, I have sent electrical vibrations

toward the remote boundaries of the earth, and instead of the wall the earth has replied. In place of an echo I have obtained a stationary electrical wave —a wave reflected from afar.

Stationary waves . . . mean something more than telegraphy without wires to any distance. . . . For instance, by their use we may produce at will, *from a sending station*, an electrical effect in any particular region of the globe; *we may determine the relative position or course of a moving object, such as a vessel at sea, the distance traversed by the same, or its speed.*

That was Tesla the prophet at his best, revealing one of his vivid images of the future.

Light cannot be anything else but a longitudinal disturbance in the ether, involving ultimate compressions and rarefactions. In other words, light can be nothing else than a sound wave in the ether. As a matter of fact radio transmitters emit nothing else but sound waves in the ether. The shorter the waves the more penetrative they become.

When Tesla patents were brought forward in the court (1914) as prior to Marconi's "four circuit" tuner, the court stated the impossibility of obtaining wireless communication with apparatus such as Tesla described. By calculation it was shown that the local oscillatory circuits of the Tesla transmitter were vibrating at a wavelength of 1,200 meters, while the elevated wire (antenna) which he suggested would be somewhere in the vicinity of six or seven miles in height, and would have a natural wavelength of 28,000 to 56,000 meters. Therefore, it could not be tuned by the apparatus with which Tesla proposed to pick up the signals. As winner of the Edison Medal in 1916, he was said to be "power-minded rather than communication-minded." Transmission of power by wireless was his big dream. He felt that "anyone could communicate by wireless—it was a task already understood."

As he advanced in years, Tesla's ideas bordered increasingly on the fantastic. On his seventy-eighth birthday he announced that he had invented a "death beam" powerful enough to destroy 10,000 airplanes at a distance of 250 miles and annihilate an army of 1,000,000 soldiers instantaneously.

In his late seventies Tesla said that he expected to live beyond 140. At the age of 86, with more than 700 patents to his credit, he died as he had spent the last years of his life—alone in the New York hotel room which he had made his home.

Death had brought to an end an engineering career of unique and unconventional nature, and the Institute of Radio Engineers in final tribute observed: "He consistently lived in a land of brilliant concepts, idealized dreams and aspirations so lofty as to be foredoomed. . . . Tesla was a catalyst in the realm of technology, a daring originator, and a dreamer on a grand scale. His passing seems in a sense the end of an epoch."

Editorially, the New York *Times* said:

. . . His practical achievements were limited to the short period that began in 1886 and ended in 1903. And what achievements they were! Polyphase currents and alternating current engineering, applied against the opposition of Lord Kelvin and Edison in the first hydroelectric plant of Niagara Falls, the induction motor, the use of oil in transformers, remarkable work in wireless at a time when Marconi had yet to make his mark, electric arcs fed by direct current in a magnetic field, later applied by Poulsen in the first radio telephone, gas-discharge lamps which were in some respects the forerunners of the neon lights that now shine on every Main Street, the medical application of high-frequency currents in what he called "electrical massage"—those crucial seven years of his youth were crowded with triumphs out of which came the whole modern apparatus of high-voltage electrical engineering.

Yet all this he affected to regard as of minor importance. It was the Jules Verne future that engrossed him, for which reason the last half of his life was spent in the isolation of a recluse. For forty years he lived and worked in a world of fantasy crackling with electric sparks, packed with strange towers to receive and emit energy and dreamy contrivances to give utopian man complete control of nature. It was a lonely life. . . . If that abused word "genius" ever was applicable to any man it was to him.[1]

Shy of manner and ascetic in his tastes, Tesla always preferred his workshop to society. He never married. He ate sparingly and drank neither coffee nor tea. On the other hand, he regarded alcohol in

[1] January 9, 1943.

moderation as virtually an elixir of life. It was his habit to stay up until daylight and then to sleep only for a few hours before resuming his work.

In one of his last interviews with this author, Tesla in his eighties still dreamed of power transmission by radio. The tall, lean inventor in a cutaway coat entered the room, laid his black derby on the table and then, looking out across the skyline of New York, spoke in almost a whisper:

There is something frightening about the universe when we consider that only our senses of sound and sight make it beautiful. Just think, the universe is darker than the darkest ink; colder than the coldest ice and more silent than a silent tomb with all bodies rushing through space at terrific speeds. What an awe-inspiring picture, isn't it? Yet it is our brain that gives merely a physical impression. Sight and sound are the only avenues through which we can perceive it all. Often I have wondered if there is a third sense which we have failed to discover. I'm afraid not [he said after some hesitation and thought]. If there were, we might learn more about the universe.

Tesla commented on the vast change that had come over the art of invention in the streamlined era of speed. Man, he observed, had little chance to think. The egg of science, he said, is laid in the nest of solitude.

It is providential that the youth or man of inventive mind is not "blessed" with a million dollars [he continued]. The mind is sharper and keener in seclusion and uninterrupted solitude. Originality thrives in seclusion free of outside influences beating upon us to cripple the creative mind. Be alone, that is the secret of invention; be alone, that is when ideas are born. That is why many of the earthly miracles have had their genesis in humble surroundings. The young man need not deplore that he has no million dollars to develop an idea. It does not cost a million dollars to think; and by the thinking process the idea is created.

Tesla, who hurled man-made thunderbolts in the nineties, when man marveled at such tremendous power, believed that every person, to be content, must have an ideal. And if not! He shook his head in despair at such a thought.

Religion is simply an ideal [he remarked]. It is an ideal force that tends to free the human being from material bonds. I do not believe that matter and energy are interchangeable, any more than are the body and soul. There is just so much matter in the universe and it cannot be destroyed. As I see life on this planet, there is no individuality. It may sound ridiculous to say so, but I believe each person is but a wave passing through space, ever-changing from minute to minute as it travels along, finally, some day, just becoming dissolved.

Michael Idvorsky Pupin

IMMIGRANT, INVENTOR, TEACHER

BORN: October 4, 1858   *DIED: March 12, 1935*
     Ivor, Hungary   *New York, N.Y.*

MICHAEL IDVORSKY PUPIN, electrophysicist, inventor and educator, of Serb ancestry, came to the United States in 1874. He was graduated from Columbia University in 1883, and after further study at Cambridge, England, and at the University of Berlin under Helmholtz, he returned to New York to be appointed professor of mathematical physics at Columbia University in 1891. His researches covered the wide field of telegraph, telephone and wireless. He discovered secondary X-ray radiation in 1896.

Pupin's crowning triumph was the invention of the telephone repeater or Pupin coil, which greatly extended the long-distance telephone through a system in which localized inductance coils placed at predetermined intervals in the line are used to maintain tone distinctions. The Bell Telephone Company acquired the patent in 1901.

Pupin's contributions to wireless included research on the electrolytic detector, tuning, and development of the loading coil. His patents on "electrical selectivity" (tuning) were licensed to the Marconi Company in 1903.

When the skeptical world scoffed at the idea of wireless, at the time Marconi announced reception of the first transatlantic signal in

1901, Pupin was not among the doubting Thomases. He knew wireless was possible. He said, "The faintness of the signals had nothing to do with it. Distance was overcome! . . . Marconi deserves great credit for pushing the work so persistently and intelligently."

Always the admirer of Marconi, Pupin added at the time of the *Titanic* disaster, "Marconi did an immortal job. . . . When he grounded the transmitter and then the receiver, and let the spark go, then the world had wireless, and no one had ever done that before."

Pupin's road to fame was long and steep. Once a shepherd boy, he left home with his parents' blessing at the age of fifteen, with a small bundle of food and clothing, eventually to reach America in the autumn of 1874, as he described it "with five cents in my pocket and a piece of apple pie in my hand." He did chores on farms, worked at all sorts of odd jobs, went to night school, learned English, saved his pennies and entered Columbia University in 1879. It was remarked that he "read messages in every star and flower, in every vibrating atom and ethereal wave." But there was none of the tinkerer or whittler in him; he was a trained physicist, not a blind performer who goes through endless experiments to find success. His was powerful mathematical equipment; he was no empiricist. He had the imagination of a great artist. In 1917 he was President of the Institute of Radio Engineers. The Edison Medal was his in 1920.

"Pupin was a man of complete intellectual honesty; if he made an error in an equation on the blackboard he would quickly admit the mistake, rub out the blunder and begin again," said one of his students, who became a noted radio engineer. "There was no pretense about Pupin. And he was a man of two moods—the earthly realist, and the highly abstract inventor and dreamer. He had an impish humor."

Aside from invention, Pupin scored as a teacher at Columbia who not only taught electrical principles but inspired his students, fired their imaginations and pointed out to them the paths of invention. Defeat was not in his vocabulary. *From Immigrant to Inventor,* his inspiring autobiography, is the story of a great life, a fascinating career and of America as a land of opportunity.

Jagadis Chunder Bose

PIONEER IN "WAVE-TELEGRAPHING"

BORN: *November 30, 1858*
    Rarikhal, East Bengal, India

DIED: *November 23, 1937*
    Giridih, Bengal, India

SIR JAGADIS CHUNDER BOSE, Hindu physicist and botanist, was once referred to as Marconi's "immediate predecessor." His father was a noted 'scholar and mathematician. After graduating from St. Xavier's College, Calcutta, young Bose entered Christ's College, Cambridge, England. He was graduated with high honors in 1884, and then went back to India as professor of physics at Presidency College, Calcutta. Fascinated by Hertzian waves, Bose delved into the subject of "wave-telegraphing."

During a lecture in Calcutta he demonstrated the ability of electric waves to penetrate walls of wood and brick. His radiator was a small platinum ball between two small platinum beads, connected to a two-volt battery. When a key was pressed the ball sparked and, as he explained, started a wave through the ether in all directions like a wave produced by dropping a stone into a pond.

The Bose receiver was about seventy-five feet distant from the radiator with three thick walls between them, yet the electric wave was made to fire a pistol and ring a bell. The energy was concentrated as rays of light are concentrated by a lens placed close to the radiator; Bose used "lenses" of various materials—sulphur, ebonite and pitch.

What is the law describing the intensity or power of the wave at any given distance? Bose was asked.[1]

"Exactly the same as the law of light," he replied. "Generally speaking, these electric waves act like rays of light."

Do you mean to say that you could telegraph in this way through houses as far as you could send a beam of light with a searchlight?

[1] Interviewed for *McClure's Magazine*, March, 1897.

"I would not like to say it in these terms, but generally speaking, such is the fact."

How far could this ether dispatch be sent?

"Indefinitely; that depends upon the exciting energy," said Bose.

And what other unknown forces also lie in the upper regions?

"That remains for the future," replied Bose. "It is impossible to forecast what new facts the study of the ether is destined to give us. It is a tremendous field, from which we may expect new facts, new forces—new forms of energy—results now unthought of and unthinkable."

Though named as a discoverer of "the new telegraphy," it was said that Bose had no interest in it, for he had done little more than was announced by Hertz in 1888. Nevertheless, he had done great work, understood and appreciated by other investigators.

He explained that his study had pertained to electric radiation, more particularly electric waves, varying between about one-quarter and about one-half inch in length. His results were represented in the apparatus which he described before the British Association at Liverpool in 1896—apparatus for the verification of the laws of reflection, refraction, selective absorption, interference and polarization of these waves. He used a coherer as the detector. Dr. Bose came on the scene in London at the time Marconi was said to have "opened new doors in the electric wing of the temple of truth."

As professor emeritus of Presidency College, in 1915, he founded the Bose Research Institute in Calcutta for the study of plant and insect life. The botanical world had lured him away from wireless; more important to him was hearing the "heart beat" of plants. To study the "nervous reaction" of plants he invented the crescograph, a recorder said to be capable of magnifying a small movement as much as ten million times. It was observed that if he had not deliberately turned his back on commercialism, he might have anticipated Marconi.

Alexander Stepanovitch Popoff

RUSSIA'S MARCONI

BORN: *March 16, 1859*
Perm, Russia

DIED: *January, 1906*
St. Petersburg, Russia

ALEXANDER STEPANOVITCH POPOFF was the Russian pioneer in wireless, yet his compatriots have noted that "by the irony of fate his discoveries have been given very little credit in Europe or America." Popoff entered the wireless field through his attempt to develop a device to detect thunderstorms in advance. He conceived the idea of using the Branly coherer to pick up the static or atmospheric electricity—the clue to the electric storm's approach.

In May, 1895, at a meeting of the Russian Physicist Society of St. Petersburg, using Hertz apparatus and a coherer, Popoff is reported to have sent and received a wireless signal across 600 yards. In March, 1897, he established a station at Kronstadt, and equipped the cruiser *Africa* with his apparatus. As the story of Popoff's record goes, in 1899 wireless communication was established between the battleship *Admiral Aprasin* and the coast, a distance of forty-five miles. In 1900, a wireless dispatch from St. Petersburg, using Popoff apparatus, was flashed to the icebreaker *Ermak* in the Baltic, instructing the crew to rescue a group of fishermen stranded on floating ice in the Gulf of Finland. A year later the Russian Army used Popoff's equipment, and in 1903 the Ministry of Postal-Telegraph opened its first commercial wireless service.

Popoff is said to have refused to take out a patent on his wireless system, contending that the discovery should benefit the scientific world at large. In 1908 a special commission led by Professor O. D. Hvolson of St. Petersburg is reported to have established Popoff's findings and the application of them. He had disclosed the successful use of the coherer in the *Journal* of the Physico Chemical Society,

St. Petersburg, in 1896. Popoff expressed the hope that wireless telegraphy could be accomplished by means of Hertzian waves, but as the courts later pointed out, neither he nor anyone else "described and demonstrated a system of wireless adapted for the transmission and reception of definite intelligible signals by such means," until Marconi came on the scene. Such was the "irony of fate" that befell Popoff.

Paul Nipkow

INVENTOR OF THE TELEVISION DISK

BORN: *August 23, 1860*   DIED: *August 24, 1940*
      Lauenburg, Pomerania   *Berlin, Germany*

PAUL NIPKOW, television pioneer, was educated in the local school at Lauenburg and at Neustadt, where his interest in telescopes, optics and the telephone caused him to ponder about sending pictures over wires. Astounded with the simplicity of the telephone, Nipkow constructed a microphone out of nails and succeeded in transmitting noises from one attic to another. To learn about wireless he attended lectures by Helmholtz and Slaby in Berlin and Charlottenburg.

On Christmas Eve, 1883, the solution of the general idea for television came to him. It was the perforated spiral distributing disk or scanner, for which a *"Patentschrift"* was granted to him on January 6, 1884. The Nipkow disk was the basic scanner used in all of the early television systems—in fact, right up to the late twenties when electronic scanning was adopted. The scanning disk is remembered as the device that whirled television into being; it proved that pictures in motion could be flashed over wire and radio.

Nipkow, however, was ahead of his time; he lacked the light-sensitive cells, neon lamps, cathode-ray tubes, photoelectric cells and radio-electron tubes that later experimenters had available for use in the circuit with his disk.

There was no wireless in 1884, for as Nipkow said, "It was television over the telephone wires that appeared before me. Hertz had not yet taught; Marconi had not yet telegraphed. How then could such far-flung ideas as pictures through the air have come to a modest student of philosophy?"[1]

While the wireless was being unfolded by Marconi and others, Nipkow turned his attention to the development of a practical system for making railroad traffic safe. And then, as he described it, he chased another phantom, the use of a set of paddle wheels on an airplane. Instead of the paddles being lined up parallel, he arranged them to swing around on the main crosscurrents, enabling the flying machine to be steered in any desired direction, vertically straight, obliquely up, forward or backward, without shifting the rotation of the motor.

In 1933 he wrote: "They are building an airplane of this type in Berlin right now. Compare it with the wing movements of insects which enable them to stay in one place in a room."

Nipkow lived to see the cathode-ray tube used as the television scanner, and he confessed that it had "the most prospect for realization."

The occupation of Paul Nipkow in the Berlin directory of the 'thirties read, "head engineer, retired."

Arthur Edwin Kennelly

PUT A CEILING ON RADIO

BORN: December 17, 1861
Bombay, India

DIED: June 18, 1939
Boston, Mass.

ARTHUR EDWIN KENNELLY, mathematical physicist of British parentage, was educated in England, Scotland, France and Belgium. His first position was that of assistant secretary of the Telegraph Society of London, and in 1876 he joined the Eastern Telegraph

[1] Letter to the author dated Berlin, February 27, 1933.

Company, concentrating on submarine cables and mathematical treatment of the phenomena of transmission lines. In 1887 he came to America as an electrical assistant to Thomas A. Edison and held that position until 1894. Appointed professor of electrical engineering at Harvard in 1902, he occupied that chair until his retirement as professor emeritus in 1930; from 1913 to 1924 he also was professor of electrical engineering at Massachusetts Institute of Technology; and in 1916 president of the Institute of Radio Engineers.

Kennelly probed the vagaries of the ether, and he is best remembered in the realm of radio for his explanation of the mechanism of transmission of electric waves. In the beginning of wireless it was supposed that long-distance communication was hopeless, because of the curvature of the earth. It was reasoned that with the field strength varying inversely as the square of the distance, the energy would be attenuated rapidly. Marconi's first transatlantic signal put this idea to a test, and proved it was not so. Some unknown factor intervened.

Could it be that high in the earth's atmosphere a conducting layer of ionized air reflected radio waves back to the earth, so that the curvature was overcome and the energy spread restricted to two dimensions? If so the attenuation of signals would vary with the first power of the distance instead of the square. Kennelly proved this and went further.

He did not assume the existence of a purely speculative conducting stratum but showed (in 1902) that an electrically conducting stratum must exist because of rarefaction of the atmosphere, at a height of about fifty miles, with conductivity several times as great as that of sea water. Thus Kennelly and Sir Oliver Heaviside, working independently, one in America and the other in England, were recognized as co-discoverers of the "radio mirror" or "roof," and the engineering world hyphenized their names to call it the Kennelly-Heaviside surface, or layer.

For "meritorious achievement in electrical science, electrical engineering and electrical arts" Professor Kennelly was awarded the

Edison Gold Medal of the American Institute of Electrical Engineers in 1933.

Said Kennelly in 1926: "Through radio I look forward to a United States of the World. Radio is standardizing the peoples of the earth. English will become the universal language because it is predominantly the language of the ether. The most important aspect of radio is its sociological influence."

George Owen Squier

CHAMPION OF WIRED WIRELESS

BORN: March 21, 1865
Dryden, Mich.

DIED: March 24, 1934
Washington, D.C.

MAJOR GENERAL GEORGE OWEN SQUIER, "Army scientist," was wartime chief signal officer and chief of the American Air Service from 1916 to 1918; in February, 1917, he was appointed the chief signal officer of the Army.

Squier was graduated from West Point in 1887, with high honors, having specialized in physics. In London, at the time Marconi first demonstrated wireless there, Squier witnessed the tests in the laboratory of Sir William Preece at the Post Office, where British officials including Army and Navy officers were invited to hear the sparks and the resultant signals. Squier's training and his interest in electricity as it applied to communications qualified him as chief signal officer of the Third Army Corps during the Spanish-American War, and in 1900 he was sent to the Philippines to lay the cable telegraph system.

Upon return from the Far East, Squier studied at Johns Hopkins, and received his Ph.D. in 1903. He was interested also in aeronautics, but while in the laboratory of the Signal Corps at Washington, he developed "wired wireless," which he patented and dedicated to the public. It was described as a "method of using wireless currents for telephony along the line of a wire"; guidance by the wire, it was explained, would insure greater accuracy, secrecy and dependability than would be gained from broadcasting.

Wired wireless brought Squier to the front pages of the press and he had considerable publicity, as also happened in 1919, when he attracted attention by using trees as radio antennas. He drove a spike into the trunk of a tree on the outskirts of Washington and picked up signals from Germany. He called such messages "flora-grams," and the tree-telegraph was described as a "floragraph"; the receiver a "floraphone."

Squier retired from the Army and from the radio field in 1924 with many medals and honors as evidence of his work in wireless, especially as applied to military operations. His awards included the Elliott Cresson Gold Medal, in 1912, for his researches in multi-plex telephony, and in 1919, the Franklin Medal and the Distinguished Service Medal, U. S. Army.

Charles Proteus Steinmetz

ELECTRICAL WIZARD

BORN: *April 9, 1865*   DIED: *October 26, 1923*
    Breslau, Germany   *Schenectady, N.Y.*

CHARLES PROTEUS STEINMETZ arrived in the United States in 1889 as a penniless immigrant and became one of America's outstanding electrical engineers. Described standing on the steamer's deck as "a seeming pygmy, a dwarf in stature, not conscious of his destiny and with no intimation that he was to solve some of the riddles of the electrical era," he had no thought of an electrical career as he stepped down the gangplank in New York to set foot on American soil.

In fact, he was almost "sent back home." Immigration officers were determined to deport him, but the friendship and financial support of a fellow student, Oscar Asmussen, who accompanied him in steerage and took full responsibility for Steinmetz's future, gained him entry to America. He soon found a job as an electrical drafts-man at $12 a week in the office of Eickemeyer & Osterheld at Yonkers, New York.

Three years later, in 1892, this same young man spoke before the American Institute of Electrical Engineers and revealed new mathematical laws to leaders of the American electrical engineering profession. He was acclaimed for throwing light into dark corners of electrical engineering. In 1893 the General Electric Company bought Eickemeyer's plant and patents, but the odd young fellow with the hunched shoulders, jet-black hair, keen eyes and brilliant mind was appraised as Eickemeyer's "most pronounced asset." He had distinguished himself by making known the mathematics of the law of hysteresis. Steinmetz left Yonkers to become a General Electric engineer at the Lynn plant. In 1902 he was appointed professor of electrical engineering at Union College.

Steinmetz, as seen shortly after his arrival on these shores by E. W. Rice, Jr.,[1] was described as "a small frail body, surmounted by a large head with long hair hanging to the shoulders, clothed in an old cardigan jacket, cigar in mouth, sitting cross-legged on a laboratory work table. I instantly felt the strange power of his piercing but kindly eyes; his enthusiasm, his earnestness, his clear conception and marvelous grasp of engineering problems convinced me that we had indeed made a great find."

It was said that no workshop in America, perhaps in all the world, had as much Bohemian environment, bizarre atmosphere, as did Steinmetz's laboratory during those years when the new century was coming in, and with it the gleaming, blue-white lamps. He never tired of laboratory work, and his associates observed that he had the creed of a searcher—he lost himself for long hours in his laboratory. He never thought of sleep and yielded to slumber only with regret.

Eating was a necessary evil to him, but he took the burden upon himself and cooked on a little gas stove, not as a chef but as a chemist. He was partial to yellow, so eggs were a favorite diet.

[1] President of the General Electric Company, 1913-22.

An inveterate cigar smoker, he bought cigars in lots of 500 and when the General Electric Company erected signs in the plant "No Smoking," he used a piece of chalk to make the placard near his laboratory read: "No Smoking—No Steinmetz." Those who worked alongside him described him as "mathematician, inventor and a marvelous human being." As inventor he assigned more than 201 patents to the General Electric Company, among them his aluminum cell lightning arrester and the magnetite arc lamp which went into use all over the country.

"Steinmetz was particularly good in instructing people how to tackle a new job—just the way to go at it, the trouble to be expected, and the way to get around it,"[2] said J. T. H. Dempster, one of Steinmetz's oldest associates in research.

A Frenchman, Henri Amiel, differentiated between talent and genius: "You are talented if you can *do easily* what is hard for *others* to do. But to be a *genius*, you must do things that are impossible for others—impossible for even talented persons to do."

"Steinmetz was both talented and a genius," said Dempster, recalling these definitions of Amiel. "And he tried to show others the way by asking: 'Who can say what is impossible?' and by advising young and old to 'Do what no one else does.' So, he was more than a mathematician, even more than an inventor—he was also an inspired genius."

Although he had several hundred patents, the outstanding contribution of Steinmetz to electrical science is listed as "investigations on magnetism resulting in his discovery of the law of hysteresis, which enabled losses of electric power due to magnetism to be calculated before starting the construction of transformers, motors, generators and other electrical devices utilizing iron."

His intricate equations simplified one aspect of the art of designing efficient electric power-consuming apparatus. He applied mathematics to the phenomenon of alterations, cycles and phases—and did it so simply, compared to the hitherto slow, complicated methods,

[2] The *Monogram*, October, 1943.

that formidable difficulties of alternating current were mastered, although the Steinmetz formula was not easy to comprehend.

Devoting considerable time to investigations of lightning phenomena at "the House of Magic" in Schenectady, Steinmetz, through his study of magnetism and electricity, became identified with wireless.

Steinmetz, like Dr. Albert Einstein, pointed out that the conception of the ether was one of those hypotheses made in an attempt to explain some scientific difficulty. He declared that the more study was applied to the ether theory the more unreasonable and untenable it became. He held that it was merely conservatism or lack of courage which had kept science from abandoning the ethereal hypothesis. Steinmetz called attention to the fact that belief in an ether is in contradiction to the relativity theory of Einstein, since this theory holds that there is no absolute position or motion, but that all positions and motions are relative and equivalent. Thus, if science agreed that the theory of relativity is correct the ether theory must be abandoned.

Scientists in general, therefore, discarded the ether theory. They derided the radio ethereal medium as fiction, calling it a makeshift fabricated to explain something for which scientists have not had the correct explanation.

In the pre-Marconi era the only real things were bodies, space and time. Those were the constructive elements from the physical viewpoint. Faraday introduced the idea of an electric or magnetic field, such as surrounds an ordinary magnet. Scientists, therefore, introduced a new body called the ether to represent a physical state. This, theoretically, allowed the electromagnetic phenomena to occur in space.

Steinmetz asserted shortly before his death that "there are no ether waves." He said that radio and light waves are merely properties of an alternating electromagnetic field of force which extends through space. Scientists, he contended, need no idea of ether. They can think better in terms of electromagnetic waves. Consequently, Steinmetz heralded the Einstein theory of relativity as "the greatest contribution to science of the last fifteen years."

If there are no ether waves, what are radio listeners and television spectators to think of as the mechanism of the broadcast wave?

Steinmetz explained that the space surrounding a magnet is a magnetic field. To produce a field of force requires energy, and the energy stored in space is called the field. This is supposed to be an accumulation of the forces of all the electrons in existence. In broadcasting, the radio transmitter disturbs the energy stored in the vast reservoir of space which listeners tap to hear music and voices, or to see pictures. The earth is also surrounded by a gravitational field. When a ball is thrown skyward it falls back because it does not have sufficient force behind it to overcome the power of the gravity which acts upon it.

If a coil of insulated wire surrounds a piece of soft iron and a direct current is sent through the coil we have what is called an electromagnet. The space around the coil is the magnetic field. When the current is decreased the breadth of the field is reduced. If the current is reversed the field is reversed. When an alternating current is sent through the coil the magnetic field alternates. The field becomes a periodic phenomenon or wave, described by Steinmetz as "an alternating magnetic field-wave."

"The space surrounding a wire that carries an electric current is an electromagnetic field," said Steinmetz, "that is, a combination of a magnetic field and an electrostatic field. If the current and voltage alternate, the electromagnetic field alternates; it is a periodic field or an electromagnetic wave."

Thus, the broadcast listener, or television observer, who wants to forget the ether can think of the aerial at the transmitter, setting up electromagnetic waves in a field of electric force which fills all space (and therefore every receiving wire is within the field). This electromagnetic field, however, is supposed to be in a state of rest until the radio transmitter causes it to vibrate. The action of the transmitter is like tapping a mold of Jello. Waves pass through it. The receiving set detects the vibrations.

Old associates tell how all conversation stopped when Steinmetz entered the laboratory. All heads turned in his direction; all eyes focused on the impressive figure, diminutive in stature, yet suggestive of a power beyond physical strength.

For nearly thirty years he opened the day at office or laboratory with the same greeting, "Good morning! Good morning!" and added, "What's new?"

Reginald Aubrey Fessenden

AMERICAN PIONEER IN WIRELESS

BORN: October 6, 1866
East Bolton, Quebec

DIED: July 23, 1932
Bermuda

REGINALD AUBREY FESSENDEN, physicist, radio pioneer and inventor, won fame through his early wireless experiments at Brant Rock, Massachusetts, after which Elihu Thomson called him "the greatest wireless inventor of the age—greater than Marconi."

Fessenden was born in the rectory of a small parish at East Bolton, on Lake Memphremagog, Lower Canada. When he was nine years old the family moved to Niagara Falls, and the boy entered DeVeaux Military College, alongside the Whirlpool Rapids. In 1877 he went to Trinity College School at Port Hope, Ontario, after which he attended Bishop's College at Lennoxville, Quebec. He next served for two years as principal of the Whitney Institute in Bermuda. His talent in mathematics steered him into electricity, which fast became the center of his interest, and so strong was the urge to work in this field that he decided to give up teaching and go to New York with the hope of fitting himself for a job under Edison. In Fessenden's mind only one inventor in all history ranked with Edison, and that was Archimedes.

Finally obtaining a job as tester with the Edison Machine Works engaged in putting down telephone conduits in New York, Fessenden worked his way to becoming one of Edison's assistants at the

Llewellyn Park Laboratory. Edison encouraged him to specialize in chemistry because there were so many electrical problems that required chemistry for solution.

Interviewed in a New York newspaper in 1887, Edison was quoted: "I can take a Yankee boy and a china mug and get more results than all the German chemists put together." He is believed to have referred to Fessenden because several days later he said, "Fezzy, you will take charge of the chemical laboratory in the future." Thus Fessenden acquired the title of chief chemist of the Edison Laboratory.

The pendulum of his career swung back to teaching, for he left Edison in 1889, and after several positions, he went to Purdue University in 1892 as professor of electrical engineering. From there he moved to the University of Pittsburgh—then Western University of Pennsylvania, at Allegheny City. At both of these institutions he lectured on Hertzian waves and conducted numerous experiments to indicate their possibilities.

Speaking before the American Institute of Electrical Engineers in November, 1899, Fessenden said, "Having been forced some years ago into X-ray work with much loss of time and very little results to show for it, I considered myself proof against the seduction of liquid air and wireless telegraphy."

But wireless lured him and he soon was recognized as a leader in the field, first serving for a time as wireless expert of the United States Weather Bureau. At Cobb Island, Maryland, he began to conduct his own wireless experiments—to develop the Fessenden System. He believed the wireless art had started on the wrong track, and he aimed to set it right—on sound, scientific principles. At Roanoke Island, North Carolina, he conducted further tests of "prolonged oscillations," or continuous waves, also some of the earliest radiophone experiments.

In 1902 the National Electric Signaling Company was formed with Fessenden wireless patents as its backbone. In 1905 Fessenden's wireless activity shifted to a new station at Brant Rock, Massachusetts, where he developed the high-frequency alternator, radio telephony, the electrolytic detector and a heterodyne, or "beat" receiver. Brant Rock in 1906 attracted much attention as one of the pioneer transatlantic stations, having established communication with Machrihanish, Scotland. On Christmas Eve, in 1906, phonograph music and speech were broadcast; ships reported reception as far down the coast as Virginia, and later the voices were reported received in New York, Washington and New Orleans.

As the result of his Brant Rock experiments, Fessenden foresaw much that was needed to advance the art of wireless, and he encouraged Alexanderson to develop the alternator that won renown in World War I.

Fessenden also invented the rotary spark gap,[1] and pioneered in the development of the wireless direction finder. He was one of the first to realize the importance and possibilities of short waves. On September 28, 1901, he applied for a United States patent covering "improvements in apparatus for wireless transmission of electromagnetic waves, said improvements relating more especially to transmissions and reproduction of words or audible sounds."

Charles J. Pannill, a pioneer in wireless, who later became President of the Radiomarine Corporation of America, said:

I worked with Fessenden from 1902 to 1910. He was a great character, of splendid physique, but what a temper! Many of us were fired on more than one occasion, and usually on some slight provocation. When he cooled off, he was sorry and hired us back, always at higher pay. He had a marvelous vision; he told me in 1903 of things that would happen in wireless 20 years later, and they have all come true.

[1] The rotary gap consisted of a wheel or disc with projecting knobs or points which whirled past a stationary electrode on each side of the wheel. The pitch of the signal was varied by the speed of the wheel; the fanning effect of the wheel was self-cooling.

The quenched spark gap, designed to produce a violin tone in comparison with the rotary gap's whistle note, was introduced by Max Wien, physicist, born in 1866 at Königsberg. A student of Helmholtz, he specialized in electromagnetic waves and assisted Roentgen, 1891-93. The quenched gap comprised a number of flat copper or silver discs, three or four inches in diameter at the sparking surfaces, with their faces separated by a space about the thickness of heavy paper. A fan or blower cooled the gaps when high power was used; the gaps also had fins to help radiate the heat. The quenched gap aided in production of a so-called pure wave, one sharply tuned, and it had the further advantage of noiseless operation.

Fessenden could think best when flat on his back smoking Pittsburgh stogies; that's when he got his real ideas. At Old Point Comfort, Va., he had a radio shack built on the sands away from the main shop at Old Point, so he could go off by himself and think.

Late in 1903, Fessenden set up stations at Washington, Collingswood, N.J. and Jersey City, N.J.—that was the first overland wireless. In 1904, we made tests of the Fessenden apparatus for the Navy on board the U.S.S. *Topeka*. The Navy installed a station at Navesink Highlands, N.J. (Sandy Hook), and we had a Fessenden "interference preventer" receiver at the Brooklyn Navy Yard. We were able to communicate with the *Topeka* at sea from Sandy Hook! Later we tried to establish communication between Lynn, Mass., and Schenectady, N.Y., but even with a 5-kilowatt spark we couldn't make it, apparently because of ore deposits in the intervening Berkshires, but Schenectady heard the Brant Rock signals without any trouble.

Fessenden, whose experimental stations were usually located on the seashore, "ran his office in a bathing suit." Reminiscing one day, Roy Weagant, one of his early assistants, said:

He could be very nice at times, but only at times. His voice boomed like a bull. . . . He had no regard for cost; he once sent for a 100-horsepower boiler and had it shipped by express. The more anything cost the better he liked it. He was sometimes unsound technically, but he more than made up for this by his brilliant imagination. He was the greatest inventive genius of all time in the realm of wireless.

If he had confined himself to being a discoverer and a creator, and had let the commercial designing end of the business alone, his company would have dominated the world. But he wanted to boss the design of everything, to every last detail, including the binding posts. He demanded high speed from his alternators and from his men. Results, plenty of results, and results quickly, were what he wanted. He had an utter disregard of money.

More than 500 inventions were attributed to Fessenden in the varied fields of electric waves, sound and light. His electrolytic, or chemical detector, introduced in 1902, increased the range and effectiveness of wireless. It used a solution of 20 per cent sulphuric or nitric acid into which dipped a silver-coated platinum wire about the thickness of a horse hair. As a detector, it was a step between the coherer and the crystal to the electron tube. It was said of Fes-

THALES OF MILETUS

WILLIAM GILBERT

OTTO VON GUERICKE

BENJAMIN FRANKLIN

LUIGI GALVANI

ALESSANDRO VOLTA

ANDRE MARIE AMPERE

HANS CHRISTIAN OERSTED

GEORG SIMON OHM

SAMUEL F. B. MORSE

MICHAEL FARADAY

JOSEPH HENRY

HERMAN VON HELMHOLTZ

LORD KELVIN

MAHLON LOOMIS

DAVID EDWARD HUGHES

JAMES CLERK MAXWELL

WILLIAM CROOKES

SIR WILLIAM PREECE

AMOS DOLBEAR

EDOUARD BRANLY

THOMAS A. EDISON

ALEXANDER GRAHAM BELL

ADOLPH K. H. SLABY

SIR AMBROSE FLEMING

AUGUSTO RIGHI

OLIVER HEAVISIDE

KARL FERDINAND BRAUN

EMILE BERLINER

SIR OLIVER LODGE

ELIHU THOMSON   SIR JOSEPH THOMSON

HEINRICH HERTZ   NIKOLA TESLA

MICHAEL IDVORSKY PUPIN   SIR JAGADIS CHUNDER BOSE

ALEXANDER S. POPOFF

PAUL NIPKOW

ARTHUR EDWIN KENNELLY

MAJ. GENERAL GEORGE OWEN SQUIER

CHARLES P. STEINMETZ

REGINALD AUBREY FESSENDEN

CHARLES FRANCIS JENKINS

LOUIS WINSLOW AUSTIN

WILLIS R. WHITNEY

VALDEMAR POULSEN

JOHN STONE STONE

SIR ERNEST RUTHERFORD

ARTHUR KORN

GEORGE WASHINGTON PIERCE

LEE DE FOREST

WILLIAM D. COOLIDGE

GUGLIELMO MARCONI

FRANK CONRAD

WILLIAM H. ECCLES

GREENLEAF W. PICKARD

ERNST F. W. ALEXANDERSON

A. HOYT TAYLOR

CHARLES SAMUEL FRANKLIN

ALBERT W. HULL

IRVING LANGMUIR

ROY A. WEAGANT

ILIA E. MOUROMTSEFF

HERBERT E. IVES

FREDERICK A. KOLSTER

HAROLD DE FOREST ARNOLD

EMORY LEON CHAFFEE

JOHN H. DELLINGER

LOUIS A. HAZELTINE

HENDRIK J. VAN DER BIJL

ALFRED N. GOLDSMITH

JOHN HAYS HAMMOND, JR.

WILLIAM DUBILIER

RAYMOND A. HEISING

JOHN LOGIE BAIRD

LLOYD ESPENSCHIED

RICHARD RANGER

J. V. L. HOGAN

VLADIMIR K. ZWORYKIN

GEORGE C. SOUTHWORTH

MAJOR EDWIN H. ARMSTRONG

RALPH BOWN

SIR ROBERT WATSON-WATT

HAROLD BEVERAGE

IRVING WOLFF

NILS ERIK LINDENBLAD

STUART BALLANTINE

C. W. HANSELL

RUSSELL VARIAN

CHARLES J. YOUNG

HARRY F. OLSON

B. J. THOMPSON

ALLEN B. DUMONT

PHILO T. FARNSWORTH

JOSEPH LYMAN

GEORGE H. BROWN

senden that he discovered vital principles that paved the way for broadcasting, and a friend remarked, "When he took hold of an idea his mind glimpsed it as if looking through 1,000 windows."

Said Dr. E. F. W. Alexanderson: "Fessenden had a dynamic, inspiring imagination."

"The first actual transmission of speech by wireless was accomplished in December, 1900," said Fessenden when interviewed in 1915. "It was gradually improved until 1904, when it was working for 25 miles, and was tendered to the United States Navy. . . . On December 11, 1906, an exhibition of wireless telephony was given at Brant Rock, attended by Dr. Kennelly of Harvard and Professor Elihu Thomson."

During the First World War, Fessenden turned his attention to submarine signaling and developed what he called "the fathometer" for depth finding. He also is credited as originator of the turboelectric drive for battleships.

Fessenden, an indefatigable worker, tired by the strain of invention, the hectic pace of wireless and court battles in defense of his contributions to the art, passed away on the island of Bermuda far from the madding crowd, and it is there that he rests.

"His great spirit had passed," said his devoted wife, "merged, so it seems to me it must be, in the vast controlling force of the Universe."[2]

Charles Francis Jenkins

PUT PICTURES ON THE AIR

BORN: *August 22, 1867*
  near Dayton, O.

DIED: *June 5, 1934*
  Washington, D.C.

CHARLES FRANCIS JENKINS, American television pioneer, spent his boyhood on a farm near Richmond, Indiana. He attended country

[2] *Fessenden, Builder of Tomorrow*, Helen M. Fessenden, 1940.

school, high school and Earlham College; then in 1890, he went to Washington as secretary in the United States Life Saving Service, but resigned in 1895 at the age of twenty-three "to take up inventing as a profession."

Photography as a hobby fired Jenkins's interest in motion pictures, and in 1892 he projected a "moving picture" before an astonished group of friends, using a silk handkerchief as the "screen." A year later he added an arc light, and this machine was a forerunner of the motion-picture projector. He sold his invention for a few dollars, but lived to see the movies grow into a billion-dollar industry.

The films led Jenkins into radio facsimile and television. As early as 1894, he outlined a scheme for the electrical transmission of pictures. Other high spots in his career include his proposal on September 27, 1913, of "wireless moving-picture news"; and in 1923 he transmitted pictures of President Harding by radio from Washington to Philadelphia, 130 miles. In December, 1924, clear images of the signature of Herbert Hoover, then Secretary of Commerce, were sent from Washington to Boston, 450 miles.

From pen-and-ink photoradio Jenkins turned to television, and on June 13, 1925, in Washington, he demonstrated a mechanical scanning system using a revolving disk, the rim being lined with tiny lenses. Collaborating with the Navy, in 1926, he flashed weather maps from Arlington, Virginia, to ships at sea, using a "mysterious radio pen."

In March, 1932, he described a new principle far advanced from the early "shadowgraph" stage. Now the images, estimated to be 3,600 times brighter, appeared on a sensitized emulsion on "an animated lantern slide." Incoming signals quickly changed the surface from opaque to clear, equivalent to the lights and shadows, thereby "painting" an ever changing pattern corresponding to the scene transmitted. Several of the Jenkins motor-driven mechanical scanners were demonstrated in New York; the receivers had a large glass bull's eye-like screen. Through this instrument many people witnessed television for the first time during the early thirties.

Jenkins died on the threshold of television.

It's easy [he had remarked in explaining television]. Don't you remember when we were little tykes, mother entertained us by putting a penny under a piece of paper, and by drawing straight lines across the paper, she made a picture of the Indian appear? Well, that's the very way we do it. The incoming radio signals turn the light up and down as it moves swiftly over the screen and you see the distant scene. Easy, isn't it? You can go out in the woodshed and build yourself one now. Of course, if you have only a fine laboratory and no woodshed, where you can get off by yourself and think clearly, you are out of luck. If your woodshed is on a farm, the probability of clear thinking is greatly enhanced.

Louis Winslow Austin

CORRELATED RADIO WITH NATURE

BORN: October 30, 1867   *DIED: June 27, 1932*
Orwell, Vermont   *Washington, D.C.*

LOUIS WINSLOW AUSTIN, physicist, was educated at Middlebury College, graduating in 1889; Ph.D., University of Strasbourg, 1893; instructor and assistant professor, University of Wisconsin, 1893-1901; research work at University of Berlin, 1901-02; in 1904 he became associated with the Bureau of Standards. Appointed chief of the Bureau's laboratory for special radio transmission research in 1923, he concentrated on the study of static, the influence of temperature, humidity, magnetic storms and sunspots on radio.

Dr. Austin headed the United States Naval Research Laboratory, 1908-23, and was chief of the Radio Physics Laboratory, 1923-32. As a result, in 1927, he was awarded the Medal of Honor of the Institute of Radio Engineers for "his pioneer work in the quantitative measurement and correlation of factors involved in radio transmission." He was president of the Institute in 1914.

Under the direction of Austin, as head of the Naval Radio Telegraphic Laboratory at the Bureau of Standards, the Navy Department, in 1909 and 1910, conducted long-distance wireless tests between the scout cruisers *Birmingham* and *Salem* and the Fessenden station at Brant Rock, Massachusetts. While the cruisers voyaged to Liberia and back, Austin measured the received impulses from the ships on the 3,750 and 1,000-meter wavelengths, in order to determine whether absorption varied with frequency. The signals were plotted from day to day, and Austin, assisted by Dr. Louis Cohen, research engineer for the National Electric Signaling Company, aimed to determine as nearly as possible the law which governs long-distance transmission of electric waves—to establish the relations which connect the principal factors such as distance, wavelength, height of antenna, with the relative strength of the current at the sending and receiving stations. It had been known for some time that over comparatively short distances the received current falls off approximately in inverse ratio with the distance. The Austin-Cohen formula resulted. Thus, for a given signal current on a given wavelength, it was possible to derive by formula the received current which would result at a distant point.[1]

Austin also attacked the popular belief that lightning is the sole source of static; what he described as "upside-down" lightning he believed to be the major cause, since it consisted of the steady discharge of electrical energy into a conducting layer estimated to exist at a height of from sixty to eighty kilometers above the earth. He added that he believed the Heaviside layer produces refraction of waves rather than reflection.

"Our knowledge concerning the atmospheric disturbances is still

[1] Duddell and Taylor in 1905 had determined that the received energy vanished over water nearly in proportion to the distance. Their observations were confined to short distances over the English Channel. Austin found that their theory held true from 100 to 200 miles, beyond which the values of the received current disappeared more rapidly. This was caused by absorption. Austin assumed that absorption was proportional to the distance. Cohen, however, discovered the law connecting absorption and frequency. This took Austin's work out of the realm of the empirical, for he had dealt chiefly with two wavelengths, and gave the formula a general nature. Thus it was appropriate that the formula became universally known as the Austin-Cohen formula.

very meager," said Austin.[2] He catalogued the observed facts as follows:

In general, atmospherics are stronger on the longer wavelengths. Except for the effects of local storms, they are nearly always stronger in the afternoon and night, while for the higher frequencies this increase in strength is confined usually to the night alone. Static is stronger in summer than in winter, in the south than in the north and on the land than on the ocean. A large proportion of the atmospherics appear to be directive—that is, to come from definite regions, or centers, as mountain ranges, rain areas or thunderstorms. It is also reasonably certain, Austin found, that at least most of the long-wave disturbances travel along the earth with a practically vertical wave front like the signals—that a considerable portion of static is oscillatory in character.

Austin observed that in Europe about 30 per cent of static disturbances originated in thunderstorms, while 75 per cent were associated with rain areas. In the United States, near the Atlantic coast, disturbances in general came from the southwest, while on the California coast they came from permanent centers in the neighboring mountains. In the Middle West the direction was found to be variable depending upon thunderstorms and rain areas.

"It is believed," said Austin, "that even in thunderstorms some of the heaviest disturbances do not come from the lightning itself, but the nature of these non-luminous sources of such great power is still a matter of conjecture."

Called "the government's radio patriarch," Austin trailed atmospheric disturbances from Goat Island, California, to Bar Harbor, Maine, observed the pranks of static in Florida and the Panama Canal Zone and out of it all concluded, "Static probably never will be eliminated entirely."

[2] At a meeting of the Section of Terrestrial Magnetism and Electricity of the American Geographical Union, Washington, D. C., April 30, 1925.

Willis Rodney Whitney

INSPIRING LEADER IN RESEARCH

BORN: *August 22, 1868*
  Jamestown, N. Y.

WILLIS RODNEY WHITNEY, American Doctor of Science, of Philosophy and of Laws, a teacher, inventor and executive, conducted research and inspired others in the conquest of the unforeseen.

A microscope, which his parents gave him, opened new worlds to the boy and started him on his career. He enrolled at Massachusetts Institute of Technology in 1886, very much interested in nature, biology, chemistry and electrical engineering. He majored in chemistry, but never neglected the closely related fields of biology, physics and electricity. He went to the University of Leipzig to study under Wilhelm Ostwald, and there received the degree of Doctor of Philosophy. He studied for a short time at the Sorbonne, then returned to M.I.T. to teach and to do research.

In 1900, E. W. Rice, vice president of the General Electric Company, thought of forming a research organization as a gateway into the future. He reasoned that the electrical industry was based on discoveries of such scientists as Faraday, Henry and Maxwell, that more discoveries were sure to follow and that the growing industry should have the benefit of them. Research creates wealth and jobs; it improves products, provides new services and lowers prices.

Other industries maintained laboratories. They tested materials to be sure that they came up to specifications. They were used to investigate unexpected difficulties but they did not investigate the unknown as such. Mr. Rice wanted a laboratory to conduct research in pure science. He invited Whitney to organize such a laboratory—later to be termed "the House of Magic." It was there that Whitney, as director of research, won distinction for his leadership in industrial scientific research.

His first valuable find in the borderland between chemistry and physics, which proved a fruitful field for exploration, was the metallized carbon filament for incandescent lamps. It resulted from an experiment by Whitney to see if he could prevent the blackening of lamp bulbs, which limited the useful life of the lamps. The new filament gave 25 per cent more light from the same wattage. That was in 1902. Ductile tungsten filaments were next, a discovery by Dr. W. D. Coolidge. From there it was a natural move into the realm of radio-electron tubes. Whitney directed his corps of experts to aim at improving the tube's sensitivity and stability, to develop its amplification properties, give it longer life, make it more economical to operate and design it to produce great power for transmitting purposes. It was Whitney who hired Langmuir, and in 1909 put him on a track which led him to make important improvements in electron tubes.

Always an inspiration to his fellow workers, Whitney once said: "We should let our imaginations work, and forget the critics of ideas. . . . Someone digressed with his pure imagination to establish new and useful things, like Franklin's lightning rod, Faraday's electromagnetic generator and Marconi's wireless."

Under Whitney's supervision radio therapy was opened up and machines were built to create "radio" or artificial fever. The Edison Medal was presented to him in 1934 "for his contributions to electrical science, his pioneer inventions, and his inspiring leadership in research."

He also received the honorary degrees of Doctor of Science from Union College (1919), Syracuse University (1925), University of Michigan (1927), University of Rochester (1932); Doctor of Chemistry, University of Pittsburgh (1919); and Doctor of Laws, Lehigh University (1929). The Willard Gibbs Medal was bestowed upon Whitney in 1916, the Chandler Medal in 1920, the Perkin Medal in 1921, the gold medal of the National Institute of Social Sciences in 1928, and the Franklin Medal in 1931. He was awarded the distinguished service gold key of the American College of Physical Therapy in 1935, and the Marcellus Hartley Award of the National Academy of Science in 1938.

The John Fritz Medal awarded since 1902 for "notable scientific or industrial achievement, without restriction on account of nationality or sex," put Whitney on a roster of noted scientists, for past recipients include Bell, Edison, Marconi and Wright. The 1943 presentation to Whitney carried this citation: "For distinguished research, both as an individual investigator and as an outstanding and inspiring administrator of pioneering enterprise, coordinating pure science with the service of society through industry."

Modestly, in accounting for the achievements which brought him high honors, Whitney explained that he allowed himself "to be led by Nature along lines seemingly desirable." He turned to the "Testament of Beauty" of Robert Bridges, formerly poet laureate of England, to let the poet express a truth better than he thought the scientists might: "Conduct lies in the masterful administration of the unforeseen."

At no time in history was there such a great mass of the "unforeseen" available to us [said Whitney]. This applies to every bud and tip of countless branches in the forests of trees of knowledge. These can never die and they await appreciation. I have thought of this in connection particularly with modern chemistry and the new electricity, but it applies as well to all our mental activities. We still fail to realize our possibilities.

The experience of organic chemistry was repeated in electrical science. The new field seems infinite again. There is room enough here for a world of scientists.

I have lived to see that bothersome Edison Effect of vacuum lamps develop into the boundless areas of electronics. Hard, round, indivisible atoms of centuries' endurance began to emit some of their components. Nothing could have been more unforeseen than that. And now photographs of some of those organic chemical molecules are actually made without light, by electrons which give us a magnification scores of times higher than was ever optically possible. The wildest imagination never foresaw what has actually come from this truly "unforeseen."

In summarizing advances in practical electronics, I like to compare the electron with Archimedes' lever. Electrons do their work by using imaginary dimensions and almost nothing for the levers. The length, the fulcrum, and the material have disappeared. Disembodied electrical power itself is guided by unhuman electrical senses. Resembling our human senses, they are much more exact and tireless. The power of screws, the use of wheels, hydraulic rams and presses, pulley blocks, belts and trunnions, and races of ball bearings came directly from the principle of the lever. Certainly one could lift the world if a fulcrum were ready. Perhaps the same should be said of the electron. Employed first for speaking, hearing, seeing, smelling, tasting, and feeling, it can record its findings and it can also present its records at any time in any part of the world. It can use a subconscious integrating entity for directing and controlling any amount of power while performing any kind of work at any desired rate.

The strange thing about it is that this is all done, not by "mirrors", but by next to nothing in a vacuum. Electronics seems to me as extensive and promising a new science as the whole of electricity seemed but a few years ago.[1]

John Stone Stone

SHARPENED THE WIRELESS TUNERS

BORN: *September 24, 1869*
Dover, Va.

DIED: *May 20, 1943*
San Diego, Calif.

JOHN STONE STONE, physicist, began his career as a telephone engineer and found it a natural step into the field of wireless, which at the opening of the century was attracting electrical engineers as California did prospectors in '49.

General Charles Pomeroy Stone was in the Union Army during the Civil War, and it was while campaigning in the Mississippi Valley that he met Miss Jeannie Stone, a southern girl. The duplication of names explains why their son John Stone Stone was so baptized.

In later years General Stone was chief of staff for the khedive of Egypt, having been officially designated by the United States

[1] January 27, 1943, upon presentation of the John Fritz Medal by AIEE.

government. During his son's boyhood, he traveled through many countries bordering on the Mediterranean, which accounts for the fact that John was as fluent in French and Arabic as he was in English.

John's education in America was obtained at the Columbia Grammar School, New York City, at the Columbia School of Mines (two years) and at Johns Hopkins University (two years) from which he was graduated in 1890. For the next nine years he was with the Research and Development Laboratory of the American Bell Telephone Company at Boston, Massachusetts, where his exceptional ability in mathematical analysis came into full play. Among his early inventive achievements were the Stone common battery system for telephony, the use of uniformly spaced inductance coils for loading telephone wires and a carrier current system of transmission over wires.

Stone's special study of electrical oscillations and radiation at Johns Hopkins, and his further study of the work of Professor Elihu Thomson, Nikola Tesla and others along the line of electromagnetic waves, led H. V. Hayes, chief engineer of the Telephone Company, to ask him to investigate the possibility of transmitting speech telephonically by Hertzian waves without the use of wire conductors. Stone made a masterly report of this work. He also filed patents covering his work on carrier current, or "wired wireless," as it was termed later.

Stone did not have wireless particularly in mind when in 1899 he set himself up as consultant, but ensuing events forced his hand. His first client was Herman W. Ladd, who had developed a method of radio direction finding based on a cylindrical metal screen around a vertical receiving antenna. The screen had an up-and-down slit through which electric waves were supposed to strike the antenna as the screen rotated. Stone had two stations set up to test the contraption, and while working on it became so interested in wireless telegraphy that before long he had taken it up as his major effort.

It became more and more evident to him that the wireless needed sharper tuning. This, and his practical work with Ladd's apparatus, finally brought him into the wireless telegraph fold, and in the summer of 1899 he conceived a system of selective wireless communication.

Stone applied for a patent on tuning on February 8, 1900, and it was allowed February 2, 1902 (No. 714,756). This was a year and a half before the grant of Marconi's American patent No. 763,772 on tuning. Stone's arrangement featured a four-circuit wireless telegraph apparatus substantially like that later specified and patented in America by Marconi, who had previously been granted an equivalent British patent, the famous No. 7,777. Stone's patent described adjustable tuning, by means of a variable inductance, of the closed circuits of both transmitter and receiver. It also recommended that the two antenna circuits be so constructed as to be resonant to the same frequencies as the closed circuits. Stone made it clear that he had found it was possible not only to originate high-frequency oscillations in a circuit, and to determine their frequency by proper choice of capacity and self-inductance in the circuit, but also to transfer those oscillations to another circuit and retain their original frequency.

In those days, spark transmitters were closely coupled, and hence were broadly tuned so that overlapping of waves caused interference. At the transmitter, Stone took advantage of loose coupling, bringing about the emission of a single, sharply defined wave. The use of loading coils as "swamping inductances" was also a feature of his system. His receivers likewise embodied loose coupling, and included an intermediate "weeding-out circuit," which greatly enhanced selectivity.

To make these ideas and developments available as apparatus, Stone formed the Stone Wireless Telegraph Syndicate in 1901, which was followed soon after by the Stone Telegraph and Telephone Company.

Stone's methods revolutionized spark telegraphy in the United States, particularly at government stations. Soon his ideas as to the emission of a single wave, and his requirements as to selectivity, were made a part of specifications for government-purchased wireless equipment. Almost all of the older sets in service, particularly in the United States Navy, were changed over to loose-coupled types. In 1905 the Navy contracted for the Stone system to be installed at the navy yards at Boston, Massachusetts, and Portsmouth, New Hampshire, and for the first time these stations were so sharply tuned that a relay station between the two Navy yards was no longer necessary.

Another early investigation of the Stone Company was in the field of marine radio direction finding, but tests revealed that while the bearings were accurate, the method was not practical. It remained for F. A. Kolster, who assisted in the tests, to develop a workable system of direction finding for the Navy about nine years later.

In the story of radio, there is registered a historic day in the autumn of 1912, when De Forest, with the assistance of his old friend John Stone Stone, demonstrated the audion as an audio amplifier to engineers of the American Telephone and Telegraph Company. They proved that although weak and imperfect, and incapable of carrying any considerable voice load without a blue haze forming inside the bulb, nevertheless, the audion *was* capable of amplifying speech.

Stone, one of the leaders in the formation of the Institute of Radio Engineers, was a director of the Institute in 1912, vice president in 1913-14, and president in 1914-15. He was awarded the Edward Longstreth Medal of the Franklin Institute in 1913 for a paper on the practical aspects of the propagation of high-frequency waves along wires, and the Medal of Honor of the Institute of Radio Engineers "for distinguished service in radio communication" in 1923. He had obtained about 120 patents on telephonic and radio subjects in the United States, as well as a similar number in foreign countries.

Stone was a gentleman of the old school, a deep thinker, and one of the most practical mathematicians in the field of radio. "His calculations and analysis went so deep into mathematics that we could never follow him," said an associate, "but Nature always agreed and confirmed his findings."

Said the Institute of Radio Engineers in tribute:

Very much of an individualist, possessed of an interesting personality, of an artistic temperament, a gracious sense of humor, and a very high sense of honor, Stone lived a good life. Well trained technically and given to the classical scientific method of analysis as it were, Stone was one of the last of the pioneers who witnessed the very inception of radio and gave his whole life to it and lived to see it flower into a great industry.[1]

Valdemar Poulsen

HARNESSED THE ARC TO WIRELESS

BORN: November 23, 1869
Copenhagen, Denmark

DIED: August 6, 1942
Denmark

VALDEMAR POULSEN, Danish scientist, the son of a judge in the highest court of Denmark, harnessed the electric arc to wireless to extend its range. After studying for a degree in natural sciences at the University of Copenhagen, 1889-93, he entered the technical department of the Copenhagen Telephone Company. *Telegrafonen* became his specialty. It was an ingenious apparatus for recording telephone conversations electromagnetically on a steel wire, for repetition at will.

After inventing the telegraphone, Poulsen left the telephone company in order to be free to conduct a series of experiments and to follow a new line of investigation that had suggested itself to him. In 1900 his telephone research gained for him the Grand Prix of Paris. Three years later he initiated a new method of generating continuous electric waves by means of the arc. In 1904 he was transmitting the voice over appreciable distances.

In 1907 Poulsen received the Gold Medal of the Royal Danish

[1] *Proceedings* of the Institute of Radio Engineers, September, 1943.

Society for Science, and in 1909 the University of Leipzig conferred upon him the honorary degree, Doctor of Philosophy. He received from the Danish government the Medal of Merit, an honor he shared at that time with Nansen, Georg Brandes, Sven Hedin and Amundsen. At his death Dr. Poulsen was a fellow of the Danish Academy of Sciences, the Danish Academy of Technical Science and the Swedish Institute for Engineering Research.

Poulsen's arc as a generator of continuous waves differed from the usual arc since it burned in an atmosphere containing hydrogen in a strong transverse magnetic field. The Federal Telegraph Company, specializing in arc transmitters, brought Poulsen's arc to America. When NAA, the United States naval spark station at Arlington, Virginia, went into commission in 1912, an arc also was installed; thus two rivals—Fessenden with the spark, Poulsen with the arc— met on a common proving ground.[1]

Arc transmitters up to 500 kilowatts were tested by the Navy. One main disadvantage was found in that the arc emitted harmonics and "arc mush"; the heat was so terrific that a water-cooling system was required. Nevertheless, during the First World War a number of battleships carried arc transmitters and later the U.S.S. *George Washington*, which took President Wilson to the Peace Conference, was equipped with an arc in hopes that communication might be maintained all the way across the sea. It was a triumph for radio when the *Washington* entering the harbor at Brest flashed signals from its arc which were picked up at Otter Cliffs, Bar Harbor, Maine, and a 600-word message was received without the loss of a word.

Then came the Alexanderson alternator, a more efficient generator of radio waves, and the arc transmitter, along with the spark, became

---

[1] William DuBois Duddell, British electrical engineer, born 1872; died November 4, 1917, was educated at Cannes. In 1900 he discovered that an electric arc could be made to generate high-frequency energy, in fact, to "sing." Poulsen took up the idea and harnessed "the singing arc" to a wireless transmitter, thereby producing an early wireless telephone. Duddell's arc produced continuous oscillations at a frequency of about 10,000 a second; Poulsen raised it to 100,000 by employing a cooled metal electrode and an atmosphere of hydrocarbon gas.

a wonder of the past; the powerful electron tube was destined to do the same for the stentorian but costly and massive alternator.

Arthur Korn

PIONEER IN PICTURE TRANSMISSION

BORN: May 20, 1870
Breslau, Germany

ARTHUR KORN, pioneer in electrical transmission of pictures by wire and wireless, studied at Leipzig and Paris, majoring in physics and mathematics. Appointed professor of physics at the University of Munich in 1903, he retired from the position in 1908 and from 1914 to 1936 served as professor of electrophysics at the Berlin Institute of Technology. It was in 1904 that he developed a system of "seeing by wire."[1]

A photo-film was put on a revolving glass drum inside a cylinder, lighted only by a small aperture. The light was permitted to traverse both film and glass. The light ray regulated by the lights and shadows of the picture was caught by a prism and thrown on a selenium cell, connected with a battery. With this system in 1904 Korn sent telephone wire-photos from Munich to Nuremberg, over 600 miles, also the first wire-photos from the Continent to England, heralded as a sensation in 1907.

It was announced in 1922 that he had a new method of signaling by radio: The apparatus associated with the ordinary receiver was merely a typewriter or other mechanical printer so modified that it wrote dots of various sizes instead of letters. Pictures radioed by this method were described as "half-tone groups of dots." On May 6, 1922, Korn wired a picture from Centecello, near Rome, to Berlin,

[1] Experiments directed toward sending pictures over wires are almost as old as the art of telegraphy, for in 1842 Alexander Bain, an English physicist, first produced a device to transmit pictures from one place to another over electric wires.

from which point it was radioed across the sea to the Navy radio station at Otter Cliffs, Maine, in about forty minutes. Korn's transatlantic ĥadiophoto of Pope Pius XI, which appeared in the New York *World* on June 11, 1922, was reported in the press as "a miracle of modern science."

Asked what he did next Korn said, "From 1922 I worked out a transmitter with alkali-cells and amplification by electronic tubes. This wireless system has been used by the German police stations since 1928."

Another Korn development was a 40-pound radio outfit to enable aircraft to pick up weather maps and military sketches in a minute and a half and aerial pictures in about five minutes. His radio or wire printer was called a "phototelegraph"; the method, "phototelegraphy." It was used by both sides during the Spanish Civil War and was taken up by military authorities in Russia, Poland, Italy and Germany.

The year 1939 found Professor Korn an émigré with his wife and son from Germany, teaching in the department of electrical engineering at Stevens Institute of Technology, Hoboken, New Jersey.

Ernest Rutherford

THE NEWTON OF ATOMIC PHYSICS

BORN: *August 30, 1871*
Spring Grove, New Zealand

DIED: *October 19, 1937*
London, England

SIR ERNEST RUTHERFORD, British physicist, invented the radio magnetic detector and "in 1911 introduced the greatest change in our idea of matter since the time of Democritus." Such was the tribute of Sir Arthur S. Eddington.

Rutherford was born at Spring Grove, later named Brightwater, thirteen miles from the town of Nelson, New Zealand. He was a student at Nelson College, Canterbury College at Christchurch and

New Zealand University, after which he entered Trinity College, Cambridge, England. Following several years of research at Cavendish Laboratory, Cambridge, in 1898 he was appointed MacDonald Professor of Physics at McGill University, Montreal; 1919, Cavendish Professor of Experimental Physics at the University of Cambridge; and in addition, in 1920, professor of physics at the Royal Institution, London.

As Rutherford remarked, he lived in the "heroic age of physics." Recognized by fellow scientists as a man of colossal energy and tireless enthusiasm, he opened a new road which led no one knew where; he discovered and named the alpha and beta rays from uranium—he played not only with atoms but with the nuclei of the atom. Radioactivity was systematized, the nucleus discovered and transmutation achieved.

Rutherford's early researches concerned electromagnetic waves. Like many a youth with an aptitude for science, he was impressed with Hertz's discovery of the waves. In fact, like many a wireless amateur experimenter he set up a Hertz oscillator in "a miserable, cold, draughty, concrete-floored cellar." There he generated high-frequency alternating current and found it quite possible to magnetize or demagnetize iron and steel by rapidly alternating currents.

These experiments led him to develop the magnetic detector described by him in 1895 as "far and away the best metrical detector of electrical waves." It was a new hope for long-distance wireless communication, since it was far more sensitive than the coherer. In his experiments he had noticed that a small magnetized needle, when suspended at the end of an electromagnet, was deflected by the rise and fall of the curre..i in the coils of the magnet. A pair of horseshoe permanent magnets slowly revolved over an electromagnet, the coils of which were connected to the earphones. Fluctuations in the current, caused by the incoming signals, were audible in the phones.

Rutherford described his detector as follows:

By using very fine magnetized steel wires surrounded by a fine solenoid, the demagnetizing property proved a very sensitive quantitative method for detecting electrical waves. Using large Hertzian vibrators, the electrical waves emitted were observed by means of the magnetic detector for a distance of about half a mile.

These experiments were made before Marconi began his well-known investigations on signaling by electrical waves. This effect of electric oscillations of altering the magnetism of iron is the basis of the magnetic "detectors" developed by Marconi and others, which have proved one of the most sensitive and reliable receivers in radiotelegraphy.[1]

Marconi further developed and tested the magnetic detector on board the cruiser *Carlo Alberto*; he picked up Poldhu's signals 800 miles away, then 1,600 miles at night, 500 miles in daylight. Marconi's adaptation of the Rutherford detector, built in a cigar box, was exhibited at the New York World's Fair, 1939-40.

As time went on, Rutherford watched with great interest the experiments of E. V. Appleton relative to the electrical properties of the upper atmosphere. In these investigations wireless stations at Cambridge and Oxford were used to prove the reflection of radio waves from an altitude of about sixty miles, thus confirming the Kennelly-Heaviside theory. Rutherford explained that the upper ionized regions must have free electrons present to cause reflection and refraction; otherwise it would be impossible for short waves to travel great distances around the earth.

Rutherford proved in his early experiments that the electromagnetic waves traveled for a half-mile or more from the transmitter to the receiver, and through walls if they intervened. Those who witnessed the results were amazed; Rutherford was interested, but not surprised. To him there were more interesting scientific problems to be solved and he turned away from pursuing the wireless waves. It has since been remarked, "Lucky that he did so, otherwise he might have become an electrical engineer rather than the physicist who was destined to unravel some of the chief mysteries of Nature."

It was not until Rutherford turned his attention to radioactivity that his big triumphs began. His brilliant researches established the existence and nature of radioactive transformation, the electrical

[1] From *The History of the Cavendish Laboratory.*

structure of matter and nuclear nature of the atom. He was one of the founders of the atomic theory of physics, and propounded that atoms are composed of electrons, or negative particles of electricity, and protons, the positive units.

Physicists began to speculate on the possibility of using atomic energy; they looked ahead to the day when a thimbleful of water would light a small community or carry an airplane across the ocean. But creating such energy for practical purposes by bombarding the atom was derided as "mere moonshine" by Sir Ernest. It was said of him that "he plays with atoms as other men play with billiard balls; he was the last of that boldly imaginative dynasty of Cambridge scientists that began with Newton."

Recalling a statement by Niels Bohr that Rutherford's achievements were so great as to provide the background of almost every word that is spoken at a gathering of physicists, Sir James Jeans remarked:

In his flair for the right line of approach to a problem, as well as the simple directness of his methods of attack, he often reminds us of Faraday, but he had two great advantages that Faraday did not possess—first, exuberant bodily health and energy, and second, the opportunity and capacity to direct a band of enthusiastic co-workers. Great though Faraday's output of work was, it seems to me that to match Rutherford's work in quantity as well as in quality, we must go back to Newton.

Voltaire once said that Newton was more fortunate than any other scientists could ever be, since it could fall to only one man to discover the laws which governed the universe. Had he lived in a later age, he might have said something similar of Rutherford and the realm of the infinitely small; for Rutherford was the Newton of atomic physics.[2]

As the autumn of 1937 approached, associates noticed that hard work was drawing heavily on Rutherford's nervous energy; he was a tired man. After a short illness he died at the age of sixty-six, and the world lost one of its outstanding experimental scientists.

Earl Baldwin of Bewdley, Chancellor of the University of Cambridge, said,

[2] At the Jubilee Session Indian Science Congress, January 3, 1938, at Calcutta.

The Cavendish Laboratory under his guidance and through the boundless enthusiasm which radiated from him to inspire even the youngest of those about him, had reached even higher and more sustained levels than ever before. Indeed the Cavendish Laboratory *was* Rutherford, bone of his bone. . . . With a vigor no whit diminished by his scientific labors he devoted much of his time to secure the application in industry of the methods and results of scientific research. . . . His refreshing personality, his dauntless spirit, the merry twinkle of his eye, the exuberance of his ever-youthful, ever-joyful enthusiasm; how can they be recaptured and confined within the limits of mere words![3]

Rutherford's passing was the finale of a great epoch in science. It was recalled that Galileo and Newton opened and closed one such period—the discovery of the mechanism of the universe. Faraday and Maxwell built the foundations of electricity. Einstein and Planck opened the gateways of relativity and of the quantum theory. Rutherford, the Newton of the atom, was king of the microcosm, a man of volcanic energy and immense capacity for work. Appropriately it has been said that he delved with poetic insight and profound imagination into the foundations of Nature.

In the obituary notice written for the Institution of Electrical Engineers, his son-in-law, Professor R. H. Fowler, said:

Seldom can anyone have started his career at a moment more auspicious, for Rutherford entered Cambridge as an advanced student in 1895, within a year or two of the discoveries of x-rays by Roentgen, of radio-activity by Becquerel, and the electron by J. J. Thomson. Seldom can anyone have been better endowed to grasp, or more gloriously successful in exploiting, the opportunities that crowded fast upon him. . . .

He was concerned with unraveling the intricate phenomena of radio-active change and the chemistry of the natural radio-active elements. For this work Rutherford received the Nobel Prize for chemistry in 1908, and it remained to the end a good joke against him, which he thoroughly appreciated, that he was thereby branded for all time as a chemist and no true physicist.

Rutherford's mother, writing to him in 1917, had said: "You cannot fail to know how glad and thankful I feel that God has blessed

[3] From the Foreword of *Rutherford*, by A. S. Eve, 1939.

and crowned your genius and efforts with success. That you may rise
to greater heights of fame and live near to God like Lord Kelvin is
my earnest wish and prayer."

The ashes of Lord Rutherford of Nelson were buried in the nave
of Westminster Abbey, just west of Sir Isaac Newton's tomb, and in
a line with the tomb of Lord Kelvin.

George Washington Pierce

WIRELESS PIONEER, TEACHER AND INVENTOR

BORN: January 11, 1872
Weberville, Tex.

GEORGE WASHINGTON PIERCE, American physicist and pioneer in
electrical communication, particularly radiotelephony, was eminent
in this field as a prolific inventor, a meticulous experimenter and an
inspiring teacher who trained generations of communication engineers. For nearly forty years he taught communication engineering
at Harvard University. His writings on wireless have done much
to shed light on the science for others. Amateur experimenters who
entered the field from 1910 to 1914, when books on the subject were
scarce, found Pierce's *Principles of Wireless Telegraphy* a valuable
text.

A Texan by birth, Professor Pierce received his B.Sc. from the
University of Texas in 1893, M.A. in 1894, M.A. from Harvard in
1899, and Ph.D. from Harvard in 1900. The following year he
attended the University of Leipzig where he studied under Boltz-
mann. Returning to the United States, he was appointed instructor
of physics at Harvard in 1903, assistant professor of physics in 1907
and professor in 1917.

At the time of his retirement in 1940, he held the chairs of Rumford Professor of Physics and the Gordon McKay Professorship of
Communication Engineering. He was also director of the Cruft High-

Tension Electrical Laboratory from 1914 to 1940, and chairman of the Division of Astronomy and the Physical Sciences from 1927 to 1940.

Pierce took to wireless experimenting at Harvard at the time when attempts were being made to establish transatlantic service; hundreds of young Americans with an electrical turn of mind were interested in studying wireless. It was a new branch of electrical engineering, and Pierce, at the Cruft Laboratory, became an educational leader in this new field of science. Under his direction, in Harvard's well-equipped realm of research, pioneer experiments were conducted in wireless, submarine detection and electron tubes.

Harvard's Pierce Hall, named after him, became a center of radio during the First World War when the United States Navy took it over as part of the United States Naval Radio School to train operators; in that building the Navy's "high power watch" was established in which honor students were instructed in electron tubes, and through special receiving sets they kept a record of the long-wave wireless that swept across the Atlantic.

Professor Pierce became a fellow of the American Academy of Arts and Sciences, National Academy of Sciences, American Physical Society, Inventors' Guild and the Institute of Radio Engineers, of which he was president, 1917-18. The Institute awarded him its Medal of Honor in 1928 "for distinguished services in radio communications."

In the field of radio science Professor Pierce's great services as a teacher are recognized as being fully as important as his inventions. Of Pierce it has been said that he probably taught more eminent engineers than anyone in the world. He recognized that the art of communication was neither physics nor engineering but a combination of these disciplines. He also insisted on a liberal grounding in mathematics and physics and usually left the engineering part to be developed by the student himself as he went along. His success as a teacher was largely due to his rational view of electrical communication as an outgrowth of the other sciences. His classes attracted students from all over the world as well as officers of the United States Army and Navy who were sent to him for postgraduate training from year to year. The Navy regularly maintained a special laboratory in Cruft for the use of the officer students. One of the important and unique courses in which the government was interested was "hydrophone engineering," which dealt with the art of communication under water, particularly with supersonic frequencies, a field in which Pierce was a pioneer, having served during the First World War in development of submarine detection equipment.

In recognition of the eminence of Professor Pierce and the importance of his lifework, he was awarded the Franklin Medal in April, 1943, for "his outstanding inventions and contributions in the field of electric communication and his inspiring influence as a great teacher."

The citation which accompanied the Medal revealed the high evaluation of his achievements:

His indirect influence on the art of radio communication through his students is fully as important as his own inventions and contributions. His courses in radio telegraphy and electric oscillations were the first to be given anywhere in this country and were the models upon which similar courses in other universities were later built.

His technical contributions to this art have been many and varied: early work on the rectifying properties of crystal detectors; mathematical calculation of the radiation properties of wireless antennae; invention of a mercury-vapor tube which was the prototype of the thyratron later developed by A. W. Hull, and one of the most important electronic devices; invention of a method of recording sound on film by means of this tube, which was perhaps the first practical method of producing talking motion pictures; work on electric filters and electric compensators for underwater signaling and submarine detection. In this field of signaling by means of so-called supersonic sounds, having frequencies above the range of the human ear, Pierce has been preeminent.

But perhaps his most important and widely used invention is the quartz piezo-electric oscillator. This device is employed in radio transmitters for accurately controlling the emitted frequency to a few parts in ten million. In this way broadcasting stations and other transmitters are kept rigorously in the groove so that they will not encroach upon the frequencies of other stations and cause interference. Millions of these oscillators are now in use.

Pierce also devised another way of doing the same thing by utilizing the magneto-striction effect in nickel and nichrome. This has important application in submarine signaling and submarine detection. He has published about fifty scientific papers, two textbooks on electric oscillations and has been granted over 50 patents.

Once, when Pierce referred to the Cruft Laboratory, he described it as "a private purgatory" of his own, situated midway between the old Jefferson Physical Laboratory and the Pierce Engineering Hall; but it was in that realm that the fire of genius was applied to crucibles of science in which many new ideas and devices of radio were nurtured.

Lee De Forest

INVENTOR OF THE AUDION

BORN: *August 26, 1873*
      Council Bluffs, Ia.

LEE DE FOREST, inventor of the audion, or three-element radio-electron tube, was "cut out in his father's hopes" to be a minister. Henry Swift De Forest was a Congregational minister in Iowa and later became president of Talladega College for Negroes in Alabama. Lee's mother was the daughter of the Rev. Alden B. Robbins, a member of the missionary group that founded Muscatine, Iowa; Lee was born in the parsonage at Council Bluffs. He had a flair for inventing and, aided by his mother, persuaded his father to let him go to a scientific school. Since the Rev. De Forest had attended Yale College (class of 1857), it was natural that Lee should prepare for Sheffield Scientific School at Old Eli and that he did by attending Mt. Hermon Preparatory School in Massachusetts.

At Yale young De Forest heard Professor Henry Bumstead lecture on electromagnetic waves and watched him demonstrate the Hertz experiments. De Forest wouldn't forget that "show." Supplementing it he read a prophetic article by Sir William Crookes on "Some Possibilities in Electricity," which stated: "What remains to be discovered is—first, a simpler and more certain means of generating electric waves of any desired length—second, more delicate receivers —third, means of darting the sheafs of rays in any desired direction."

De Forest began to think about this problem. Tesla's book on electrical phenomena inspired him; he went to New York and talked with Tesla. "Wireless telephoning" became his goal.

Leaving New Haven in 1899, he went to Chicago to work for the Western Electric Company in the dynamo department for $8.00 a week. Dynamos or no dynamos, he couldn't keep away from wireless. He knew that the coherer was a weak link in the wireless circuit, and as such it challenged his inventive mind.

He had read Tesla's account of an electric arc in the flame of a gas light and of the possibility of using it as a source of oscillating current. If properly developed, could it be used in wireless telephony? Instinctively, as the years passed, De Forest felt that in the flame there was magic. One day in 1900 a flickering gas mantle in his Chicago room evoked the idea. He began his search for the genuine response to electrical vibrations in a gas flame. The idea of a hot gas or flame detector fascinated him, but it proved to be far from practical.

As a step in another direction, he developed a self-restoring coherer and called it a "Sponder," or "electrolytic anti-coherer."

Confident that he was on the track of wireless, De Forest in 1901 went to New York with hopes that he might find the necessary financial backing to beat Marconi, who in 1899 had come to America for the first time to wireless bulletins of the America Cup races off the New Jersey coast. He met Abraham White, stock speculator and promoter, and in 1902 White organized the De Forest Wireless Telegraph Company, reported to have been capitalized at $3,000,000, with De Forest as vice president.

Collapse of the company several years later sent De Forest back on the hunt for a new detector. He drew upon the past—the idea of a flame detector. At the same time he recalled "the Edison Effect," which he had learned about at Yale. Further, Fleming had found that although no contact existed between the hot filament of an incandescent lamp and a little metal plate inside the bulb, a current flowed from the cold metal plate to the filament, the electrons, streaming from filament to plate, acting as invisible carriers. That was the basic principle of the Fleming valve detector or rectifier; but it would not relay or amplify.

De Forest sought to make the Fleming device an amplifier, and to achieve this result he connected a battery in circuit with the plate and filament. This addition proved successful, and although the amplification was slight, judged by modern standards, it nevertheless existed.

Why not add a "trigger" device so that the energy of a local battery could be more efficiently controlled by the incoming waves? In 1906 De Forest added the "trigger"—a zigzag piece of platinum wire—between the filament and plate. He called it the grid. With the plate battery still in the circuit, the result was the three-electrode thermionic vacuum tube, a generator of Hertzian waves as well as a detector and amplifier of them. De Forest's assistant, Clifford Babcock, named it the "audion," and it was he, according to the records, who was responsible for enclosing the elements in a glass bulb.

Said De Forest: "Little imagination is required to depict new developments in radio telephone communications, all of which have lain fallow heretofore, waiting for a simple lamp by which one can speak instead of read."

The De Forest Aladdin lamp of electronics revolutionized wireless, and the resulting electronic revolution in radio is unending as new tubes continually serve as keys to new inventions and services. The audion has been classed as one of the twenty great inventions of all time. It made the radiophone practical; it made broadcasting possible. As a forerunner, De Forest took an arc transmitter backstage at the Metropolitan Opera House on January 13, 1910, and broadcast opera arias sung by Caruso and other noted artists.

When the audion was introduced as an oscillator in 1914 it supplanted the arc in radiotelephony. Since that time the electron tube has found no end of use in and out of the field of radio for it has effected radical improvements in telephony, picture transmission, talking films and in various processes of industry.

How is the radio magic performed? First, the filament, or cathode, of the tube is heated by the application of an electric current. As a result, a stream of electrons is driven from the filament. Then, true to electrical tradition—unlike charges attract and like charges repel —the negatively charged electrons flow over to the metal plate, which is positively charged. But between the filament and the plate, suspended in the electron stream, is the meshlike grid. Through it the incoming radio signals are fed into the stream, the flow of which is thus modulated in accordance with dots and dashes, or whatever signal is on the wave. The imposition of the signals upon the filament-to-plate stream produces a corresponding impact on the plate. That impact, in turn, controls the current flowing in the circuit in which the loudspeaker or headphones are located. Thus, the signals passed along in the electron stream are reproduced as sound.

Developed to perform with amazing versatility, the radio-electron tube can talk, hear, see, feel, taste, smell, sort, count, regulate, measure, calculate and even remember. In fact, the engineers who know it best say it lacks only a conscience. That is supplied by man in the use to which he puts the tube.

After the audion was ready for action, the trick remained to find circuits in which the tube would give its best performance as a detector, amplifier and oscillator. Hundreds of wiring diagrams were developed as experimenters everywhere took up the audion and aimed to improve its performance by discovering in what circuit it might work new miracles. Just as De Forest with a little piece of platinum wire and an additional battery had transformed the Fleming valve into a tube with unlimited prospects, so it might fall to the lot of another to revolutionize the tube and its efficiency by merely altering a wire in the hook-up. It was a fascinating challenge and there came a day when radio hook-ups were a national pastime— a "craze" in many an American home.

Naturally, De Forest joined in the search for hook-ups. But he had to fight to defend his claims. After long years of litigation the United States Supreme Court in 1934 upheld him as inventor of the feedback, or regenerative circuit.

His fame is perpetuated in the evacuated glass bulb, millions of which are in use throughout the world; annually more than 200,000,000 radio-electron tubes are manufactured. With the audion amplifier as a telephone repeater, the transcontinental telephone became practical. The delicacy and elegance of the audion was to the old microphonic relay of the telephone as "soap bubbles to a load of coal." De Forest, with "a glass bottle full of nothing," opened wide a whole realm of applied electronics.

For his work in wireless he was recipient of a gold medal at the St. Louis Exposition in 1904; the Elliott Cresson Medal of the Franklin Institute in 1915 for discovery of the audion; and a gold medal at the Panama Pacific Exposition in San Francisco in 1915. Added to his many honors was the presidency of the Institute of Radio Engineers in 1930.

He finally forsook New York for California. One evening an old friend spied him coming out of the subway in Times Square and asked how long he expected to be in the East, and he said, "Don't tell anybody you saw me. I wouldn't take New York if they offered it to me with a fence around it. I'm going back to California just as fast as I can go; that's the place to live."

In 1941 a reporter who went to the coast to interview him came back with the impression that Lee De Forest at sixty-eight should be "a bitter, disillusioned old man.—Actually, he laughs easily and gaily; his eyes dance with new dreams."

William David Coolidge

PHYSICO-CHEMIST IN ELECTRONICS

BORN: October 23, 1873
Hudson, Mass.

WILLIAM D. COOLIDGE, physical chemist, contributed greatly to the advance of electron tubes, incandescent lamps, X-ray tubes, electronic devices and the production of high-voltage cathode rays outside the generating tube.

His father, Albert Edward Coolidge, worked in a local shoe factory; his mother, M. Alice Coolidge, took in dressmaking to eke out the family's modest income. William was a typical farm boy, but from an early age his interest in things mechanical and electrical was keen. Work, to him, was never an ordeal, never a thing to be avoided. Feeling that he should do something to ease the family's financial burden, he left high school during his junior year to work in a rubber factory. But after six months he realized the value of more schooling and rejoined his class.

College was his next goal, but because of lack of money he dared not consider it seriously. Then a friend who was studying at the Massachusetts Institute of Technology suggested that his father might be willing to lend him some money and that, in addition, he might obtain a state scholarship. Coolidge got both—the loan, the scholarship and later a graduate fellowship. In all, his college days left him with a debt of $4,000, the full payment of which took everything he was able to save until he was thirty-one.

Entering M.I.T. in the class of 1895, he majored in electrical engineering. Illness delayed his graduation until 1896. It was in the year following graduation, while he was serving as assistant in physics at M.I.T., that the course of Coolidge's life was again radically changed by the suggestion of a friend: "Why don't you get a fellowship for the study of physics abroad?" As a result, he went to Leipzig, where he received his Ph.D. in 1899.

Returning to the United States, he went back to M.I.T. and for five years did fundamental physicochemical research. At the same time he continued to advance in the teaching profession—from assistant in physics to instructor in physical chemistry and finally to assistant professor of physicochemical research. It was during this time that he worked in a laboratory adjoining that of Dr. Willis R. Whitney, and this association was destined to play an important role in his life, for he had acquired a love for fundamental research—for the study of natural phenomena for its own sake regardless of where it might lead. Whitney became director of the General Electric laboratory, organized for industrial research, and he offered Coolidge a position. After considerable hesitation, the latter arrived to commence work on September 11, 1905.

Coolidge became Whitney's right-hand man, and was appointed assistant director of "the House of Magic" in 1908; associate director in 1928; director in 1932; vice president and director of research in 1940. Through his development of ductile tungsten he made major contributions to the advance of incandescent lamps and electron tubes. Until he gave tungsten all the properties of a wire capable of being drawn down to only one-sixth the diameter of a human hair, it was a delicate, short-lived filament. No longer brittle, it became a practical filament giving longer life to radio tubes and making them much more efficient in millions of receiving sets. Furthermore, since tungsten withstands extremely high temperatures without melting, it is especially useful in the filament construction of high-power water-cooled transmitting tubes.

Coolidge also investigated the applicability of ductile tungsten to X-ray tubes, and this led to his greatest contribution to X-ray science—a radically new tube, accurately controllable and wholly stable. This was accomplished by using an electron "gun." During the First World War he evolved a "C" tube—mechanical sound detector—to help in locating submarines; it was a sort of undersea stethoscope.

Primarily a specialist in X-ray tubes, Coolidge was the recipient of many honors, including the Rumford Medal, Edison Medal, John Scott Award, Faraday Medal, Duddell Medal and a number of others. He has obtained eighty-three patents.

The citation of the National Association of Manufacturers in listing Coolidge among the "National Modern Pioneers" read:

> His invention of a method of producing ductile tungsten permitted the use of this remarkable metal for increasing the efficiency of incandescent lamps and for building a great variety of modern vacuum tubes and electronic devices. His high vacuum x-ray tube is standard equipment wherever x-rays are used in medicine or industry. Electric lighting, electronic arts, and especially x-ray art were significantly advanced by his inventions.

From 1932 on, Coolidge retired largely from direct research work and aimed to guide and encourage his assistants. Described by an associate as "always thorough himself, he is utterly impatient of carelessness or superficiality. . . . His indomitable persistence, broad technical knowledge and keen observation assured his success. But outstanding among his qualities is his resourcefulness in experiment. . . . His is an indefatigable interest in science."

Guglielmo Marconi

INVENTOR OF WIRELESS

BORN: *April 23, 1874*
Bologna, Italy

DIED: *July 20, 1937*
Rome, Italy

GUGLIELMO MARCONI, inventor of wireless, was born "with a silver spoon in his mouth," and his life is a story of the rich man's son who made good—not the usual rags-to-riches tale. His father, Giuseppe Marconi of Bologna, was a dignified gentleman of adequate means; his second marriage in 1864 was with the keen-witted Irish girl, Anna

Jameson, youngest daughter of Andrew Jameson of the well-known whiskey distillers of Dublin. Anna had gone to Bologna to study music and there she fell in love.

The Marconis had two boys, Alfonso and Guglielmo; both were tutored on the parental estate. The teachers noticed Guglielmo's keen interest in science and his surpassing imagination.

In the summer of 1894, while vacationing in the Italian Alps, young Marconi picked up an electrical journal in which he read Hertz's thought-provoking story of electric waves. An idea dawned; something whispered to Marconi that if the radiation could be increased, developed and controlled, it would be possible to signal across space for considerable distances! Obsessed with the thought, Marconi cut short his vacation and rushed home to Pontecchio, near Bologna, to test the "dream."

He brought together the induction coil, the Hertz wave emitter, the Righi gap, the telegraph key, batteries, the Branly coherer, and built them into sending and receiving stations on his father's estate. He sent cricketlike sounds for three-quarters of a mile. That was the birth of wireless; from then on no obstacle on the face of the earth, or distance, could stop wireless.

Marconi's original patent disclosed a two-circuit system (single circuit at both transmitter and receiver) for the transmission and reception of Hertzian waves.[1]

The transmitter comprised an aerial circuit with one end connected to an elevated aerial and the other end to the ground. The circuit contained a spark gap the terminals of which were connected to the secondary of a transformer. The primary of the transformer was connected to a source of current and a telegraph key for signaling. The low-frequency current was caused to discharge through the spark gap, producing high-frequency oscillations which were radiated by the aerial. The receiver similarly contained an antenna circuit be-

---

[1] Marconi applied for his original and basic British patent, No. 12,039, on June 2, 1896. The equivalent American patent, No. 586,193, was granted him on July 13, 1897, and was reissued on June 4, 1901, as No. 11,913.

tween an elevated plate and the ground, in which a coherer (detector) was directly connected. Marconi constructed the transmitter and receiver to be resonant to the same frequency; he accomplished this by careful determination of the size and height of the aerial plates.

His next important step was the invention of tuning—the key to a great advance in wireless.[2] It prevented overlapping of signals, reduced interference, opened the way for a multiplicity of stations and made ethereal communication practical.

Fate brought Marconi upon the stage of science at the time when the world was ready for speedy international communication. Destiny linked his name with wireless, and as wireless spread, so did the name and fame of Marconi. He had the money, courage, patience, initiative, perseverance and intuition to carry his invention to a commercial conclusion. Surrounding himself with experts,[3] he became the perfectionist. He consecrated his life to wireless; to him it became the patient labor of a lifetime.

Wireless in 1896 seemed to hold greater promise for use at sea than on the land, so Marconi, "a serious-minded Italian youth, speaking with grave precision," went to England, there to experiment and promote his invention. Using short waves and reflectors he demonstrated across 100 yards, then miles and miles, but at no time did he claim to be a scientist. He simply explained that he had observed certain facts and developed instruments to meet them. His numerous experiments up and down the English coast put him in the news almost daily. He showed how stations could be separated by the magic of tuning; how ships could communicate with shore.

Marconi returned to Italy as triumphant as a Caesar. Then France called for a test of wireless; on March 27, 1899, he flashed the first

[2] Marconi's famous British patent, No. 7,777, on four-circuit tuning was granted April 26, 1900. It was assigned to the Marconi Company on March 6, 1905. French patent No. 305,060 was issued on November 3, 1900. Marconi filed for an equivalent American patent on November 10, 1900. It was granted June 28, 1904, as No. 763,772 covering "improvements in apparatus for wireless telegraphy by means of Hertzian aerials or electric waves."

[3] Walter William Bradfield, Dr. W. H. Eccles, J. Ambrose Fleming, C. S. Franklin, Andrew Gray, John Erskine Murray, C. E. Rickard, Capt. H. J. Round and Richard Norman Vyvyan.

messages across the English Channel from Wimereux to the cliffs of
Dover. Next America beckoned, and he crossed the ocean for the
first time in the autumn of 1899 on the invitation of the New York
Herald, which arranged for him to transmit bulletins of the America
Cup races off the New Jersey coast.

Then came the grand climax in Marconi's career. Using an
antenna held aloft by a kite at St. John's, Newfoundland, on December
12, 1901, he plucked from space the letter "S" flashed from Poldhu
across 2,000 miles of broad curving ocean. Assisting him were
George S. Kemp[4] and P. W. Paget.

Said Marconi, "Wireless telegraphy is possible anywhere, and it
will, I think, soon be a reality in many places."

He had upset the calculations of mathematicians who warned in
the beginning that wireless would not go beyond the horizon; they
said that the curvature of the earth would stop it. The direct transatlantic link between the hemispheres put the name Marconi alongside those of Morse and Bell. Yet there remained many skeptics.

When the S.S. *Philadelphia* docked in New York March 1, 1902,
Marconi came down the gangplank and handed news reporters yards
of "telegraph" tape, dotted and dashed with hundreds of signals he
had automatically recorded from Poldhu while en route across the
ocean. No one now could say that his ears had been mistaken at
Newfoundland on December 12, 1901.

From that day forth Marconi wireless pushed ahead from triumph
to triumph: The first west-east transatlantic messages were sent from
Glace Bay, Nova Scotia, to England on December 17, 1902, and on
January 19, 1903, station WCC at South Wellfleet, Cape Cod, opened
with an exchange of greetings between President Roosevelt and King
Edward VII. Commercial service began between Glace Bay and
Clifden, Ireland, October 17, 1907. The Nobel prize in physics was
Marconi's in 1909.

That was the year the wreck of the luxury liner S.S. *Republic* off
Sandy Hook put wireless to its first severe test in a major marine

---

[4] Died January 2, 1933, at Southampton, England, at the age of seventy-five.

disaster.[5] It etched the glory of wireless on the dark background of calamity at sea; the CQD saved hundreds of lives and prevented a disaster "darker even than Martinique."

The S.S. *Titanic* disaster—April 15, 1912—put wireless in the news as had no other event; from midocean it taught the world the importance of Marconi's immortal work. He met the rescue ship *Carpathia* in New York with cries of survivors ringing in his ears, *"Ti dobbiano la vita!"* ("We owe our life to you.") And someone remarked, "If I could select a crown for Mr. Marconi, it would be a coronet surmounted by a globe on which would be inlaid in pearls those magnificent, significant letters CQD."

Since that day, because of wireless, many a person has been saved from a watery grave; many a ship afire at sea or battered by wind and wave, wrecked or torpedoed, has called for help through the voice Marconi put on board.

It was not until 1914, however, that Marconi won the title "master of wireless." The United States District Court, Eastern District of New York, in an opinion handed down by Judge Van Vechten Veeder upheld the validity and priority of Marconi's patents. Marconi had discovered the truth in the adage that "a patent is merely a title to a law suit."[6] Many had been aware of Hertzian waves, but the Court in 1914 found no conclusive evidence up to 1896 that anyone had described and demonstrated a system of wireless adapted for the transmission and reception of definite, intelligible signals by such means as revealed by Marconi in his first patent.

Said Judge Veeder, "I find that the evidence establishes Marconi's claim that he was the first to discover and use any practical means

---

[5] January 23, 1909.

[6] Supreme Court of the United States on June 21, 1943, delivered an opinion in the case of the Marconi Wireless Telegraph Company of America vs. the United States invalidating Marconi's American patent No. 763,772 on four-circuit tuning. The Court based its decision largely on finding that John Stone Stone's patent, applied for February 8, 1900, was nine months prior to Marconi's application for his American patent that covered tuning. Stone's patent was allowed February 2, 1902. Marconi's was granted June 28, 1904. It was the equivalent of his famous British patent No. 7,777 on tuning granted April 26, 1900.

for effective telegraphic transmission and intelligible reception of signals produced by artificially formed Hertz oscillations."

The opening of the First World War found Marconi talking prophetically about transoceanic radiotelephony, and he hurried to Italy for wartime duties. At the end of the conflict he resumed short-wave experiments, and the historic observations made on board his floating laboratory, the yacht *Elettra*, became the basis of the beam wireless system. In 1922 he sailed to New York with the *Elettra*, listened to American broadcasting stations for the first time and revealed the results of his short-wave tests. At a joint meeting of the Institute of Radio Engineers and the American Institute of Electrical Engineers on June 20, he urged that attention be directed to the neglected short waves; he induced the engineers to get out of the blind alley they were following in the long-wave spectrum.

As he neared the end of his talk Marconi digressed from his prepared address to say to the engineers that in reference to radio reflectors, he would like to refer to the possible application of reflected radio waves. If successful, he told them, the application would be of great value to navigation. Without using the word "radar," then unknown in the vocabulary of radio, he concluded:

As was first shown by Hertz, electric waves can be completely reflected by conducting bodies. In some of my tests I have noticed the effects of reflection and deflection of these waves by metallic objects miles away.

It seems to me that it should be possible to design apparatus by means of which a ship could radiate or project a divergent beam of these rays in any desired direction, which rays, if coming across a metallic object, such as another steamer or ship, would be reflected back to a receiver screened from the local transmitter on the sending ship, and thereby immediately reveal the presence and bearing of the other ship in fog or thick weather.

One further great advantage of such an arrangement would be that it would be able to give warning of the presence and bearing of ships, even should these ships be unprovided with any kind of radio.

I have brought these results and ideas to your notice as I feel—and perhaps you will agree with me—that the study of short electric waves, although sadly neglected practically all through the history of wireless, is still likely to develop in many unexpected directions, and open up new fields of profit-able research.

When Marconi returned to New York in 1927, he again pointed to short waves, but more so to ultra-short waves as the key to new triumphs in television. Microwaves entranced him from that point on. To him they were the future of radio. He came to America on his last visit in the autumn of 1933, greatly intrigued and enthusiastic over tiny waves measured in centimeters.

"I am known as a man who deals in cold scientific facts and practicalities, not in Utopian fantasies," he said. "As to talk of a saturation point—a limit to radio progress—there is no limit to dis-tance, hence there can be no limit to wireless development."

In the light of the passing years, as his accomplishments were weighed in the scales of history, it was observed that although what Marconi did was simple, it was brilliant and brought big results.

Forty years later schoolboys could perform what Marconi did in 1900. In fact, they surpassed his magic of that time by talking across continents and oceans using no more power than their mothers' electric iron or toaster. Nevertheless, before Marconi, scientists had tried and failed. Marconi the youth entered the race with electrical wizards and men of genius; he worked and won and the ever important element of timeliness was on his side.

Said Justice Rutledge of the United States Supreme Court:

He won by the test of results. . . . The most eminent men of the time were conscious of the problem, were interested in it, had sought for years the exactly right arrangement, always aproaching more nearly but never quite reaching the stage of practical success. The invention was, so to speak, hovering in the general climate of science, momentarily awaiting birth. But just the right releasing touch had not been found. Marconi added it.[7]

What manner of man was he who had drawn "the most distant places and many forgotten lives into the orbit of civilization"? Marconi was an Italian who spoke English as fluently as he spoke

[7] Marconi Wireless Telegraph Company of America vs. United States in United States Supreme Court, Justice Rutledge dissenting in part, June 21, 1943.

his native tongue. His success may be summed up in patience and infinite persistence, plus a great deal of natural ability and an undying devotion to wireless. He was an interpreter of Nature. An instinctive intuition whispered to him what was wanted and how to arrive at the solution. Simplicity was the keynote of his wizardry; the simplicity of his approach to wireless enabled him to succeed where distinguished scientists, mathematicians and theorists had failed.

Always quick to concede that other men of science had contributed much to the development of wireless, Marconi with characteristic modesty said that he had simply observed certain facts and developed instruments to meet them. His restless manner was one of chilly reserve. His features were melancholy in expression; his face impassive, his carriage erect and his bearing confident. Never a voluntary conversationalist, in mood he was quiet and shy. His reticence was the reticence of modesty. Neither was he a laboratory-hugging genius as was Edison. He delighted to be at sea aboard the *Elettra*, tracking down and studying the elusive waves that came in through the air from all parts of the world.

Always cautious in his predictions, Marconi never linked a future possibility with a definite date. He contended that the more a man bends the phenomena of the universe to his will and the more he discovers, the more he will find to discover, and because of this the inventor will realize more and more the infinity of the infinite. He was always punctual; he hated above all things to be kept waiting or to keep others waiting. Never was he the carelessly dressed or traditional inventor, unkempt and unpressed. He looked more like the neatly attired banker or businessman with a handkerchief tucked in the breast pocket of his coat to match the color of his tie. Yet he disliked routine business; he was not a businessman or industrialist.

In a calm, softly pitched voice Marconi talked slowly with no show of egomania. When addressing public gatherings he chose his words carefully. On the radio he was quickly recognized by a characteristic of his speech: He dropped the "g" of words ending in "ing." Revealing a sharp memory he recalled names, dates, events and incidents of thirty years back as if they had been imprinted on his mind only yesterday.

Marconi impressed one as a man possessed of a great idea—an all-absorbing thought from the contemplation of which he could detach himself only with difficulty. When asked about the future he would usually reply that he lived and worked in the present and dreamed only "sometimes" of the future. He liked the past because he was sure of it; it was definite. The present was too fleeting to catch with accuracy, and he cherished accuracy and precision. The future to him was powerfully full of promise. To him youth dreams of the future—the road ahead. Age dreams of the past—the long road back. The one leads on to progress; the other into hazy reveries, into the land of memory.

There was no bluff, no boastfulness in his makeup. He had neither the volatility of the Italian nor the cheery cordiality of the Irishman. He was of an intensely nervous and energetic temperament, easily rattled by trifles when in the stress of work or by miscarriage of plans. Acute observation and a keen ability to concentrate were important parts of his character. It was said that he listened to praise and enjoyed it because he was Italian. He listened to praise and forgot it because he was partly Celtic.

Marconi was not a man easy to meet. Meeting odd people was no happy knack for him. He was no mixer and moved within his own small, intimate circle. He relished only first-rate people around him and only a few at a time. At mass interviews he usually acted bored and restless, nervous and anxious to go on to something else. To some this was evidence of snobbishness until they succeeded in penetrating his reserve. He might be summed up as a fashionable, scientific intellectual possessed of multifarious interests with wireless always omnipotent. He belonged to the intelligentsia of Old Rome, yet nothing could divert him from wireless. Nothing was too simple in wireless for him to devote time and attention to it; it always intrigued his curiosity and tugged at his imagination to the very end of his days.

His vigorous life came to a close in the early morning of July 20, 1937, in Rome. Globe-girdling radio flashed the sad tidings; broadcasting tolled his requiem across the hemispheres as death took Marconi back to Bologna where first he had wirelessed.[8]

Never in all his research had Marconi glimpsed the slightest clue to explain the mystery of humanity's origin and the future. Life was an impenetrable secret, truly frightening to him were it not for faith.

Astounded by the enormous machinery of the universe, Marconi said:

The complexity of the different organs, which all work out in coordinated and determined functions, the constant preoccupation for the conservation of the species, man's marvelous adaptation of his constitution to surroundings, the transmission of instincts, the mechanism of thought and reasoning, and, lastly the spectre of death, place man, who wishes to explain the tormenting mystery, before a book closed with seven seals.[9]

Frank Conrad

PIONEER BROADCASTER

BORN: May 4, 1874   DIED: December 10, 1941
      Pittsburgh, Pa.   Miami, Fla.

FRANK CONRAD, pioneer in public broadcasting, centered world attention on KDKA, Pittsburgh, in the early twenties. The urge to work with tools took him out of seventh grade at the Starrett Grammar School, and he went to work as a bench-hand in the Westinghouse plant at Garrison Alley, Pittsburgh. That was in 1890. Aptitude for mechanics soon advanced him to the testing department. His

[8] Marconi left four children. His first wife, Beatrice O'Brien, daughter of Lord Inchiquin, whom he married in 1905, bore him two daughters, Degna and Gioia, and a son, Guilio. This marriage was annulled in January, 1927, and in June he married Countess Maria Cristina Bezzi-Scali, of an old Roman family. On July 20, 1930, a daughter was born, Maria Elettra Elena.

[9] Lecture before the International Congress of Electro-Radio Biology, September 10, 1934, Venice, Italy.

first important contribution was the circular type watt-hour meter
to measure the consumption of electric current, and it became a
universal home installation. Intrigued with time synchronization and
a desire to have his watch correct to the second, he built a wireless
receiver to pick up the time signals of the Naval Observatory broadcast by station NAA, Arlington, Virginia.

After conducting experimental work for the government during
the First World War, he returned to his amateur wireless station
8XK in Wilkinsburg, Pennsylvania. The radiophone had developed
rapidly during the conflict. Conrad rebuilt his station in his garage
and began to broadcast phonograph music and to chat with other
amateurs. A Pittsburgh department store advertised wireless sets that
would pick up Conrad's broadcasts. The idea clicked and the response
was so encouraging that Westinghouse officials, chiefly H. P. Davis,
vice president, saw the possibilities and applied for a commercial
license. The call assigned was KDKA.[1] As a pioneer station, it broadcast the Harding-Cox election bulletins on November 2, 1920, starting
a "craze" that swept the country to become a vast new industry—
broadcasting! As a result the demand for radio receivers was
tremendous. Building crystal detector sets at home became a national
pastime with tuning coils wound on cereal boxes and condensers
made of tinfoil from the florist shop. Electrical manufacturers, overcome with the demand, expanded plant facilities to fill orders from
every city and hamlet in the land.

The historic "Radio Music Box" plan of development, which would
make radio a household utility, as proposed by David Sarnoff in
1916, had come true.[2] At that time Sarnoff had pointed to the endless
possibilities of utilizing radio for receiving concerts, lectures, events
of national importance and baseball scores in the home. In fact, he

[1] KDKA licensed by Department of Commerce, October 27, 1920.

[2] Sarnoff, then assistant traffic manager of the Marconi Wireless Telegraph Company of
America, embodied the "Radio Music Box" proposal in a letter of recommendation to E.
J. Nally, general manager. Sarnoff's accurate foresight was revealed by the fact that in
three years 1922, 1923, 1924 RCA's sales of home radios amounted to $83,500,000. Sarnoff
became president of the Radio Corporation of America in 1930.

estimated that if his plan materialized, it would seem reasonable to expect the sale of a million "Radio Music Boxes" within a period of three years with actual sales of home instruments totaling $75,000,000.

During the war it had been assumed that radiotelephony should be developed as a confidential means of communication, but Conrad's experience brought a turn in this tide of thought. Suddenly it was realized that the radiophone's field was one of wide publicity, in fact, the only means of instantaneous, direct mass communication ever devised; here was a service of universal application.

There was also a notion in the pre-broadcasting era that frequencies above 1,500 kilocycles would never be of use because the ground loss was so high. Conrad proved that these frequencies were extremely valuable when the sky-wave was used. He also showed that the portion of radiation that went skyward at a low angle could be reflected back to earth at a remote point, from an ionized layer above the surface of the earth. His experiments indicated that a series of reflections between the earth and the ionized layer take place before the signal eventually returns to the earth at the desired receiving station. Radio engineers, therefore, learned to use these frequencies for international communications, although they are of little use for local broadcasting because of the high ground loss.

Attending a London conference in 1924 to discuss establishment of a radio link between Europe and South America, Conrad staged a dramatic demonstration of short waves by picking up signals directly from Pittsburgh. Revealing how the event marked a milestone in international radio communication, Conrad said:

The consensus of opinion was that very long waves should be used. . . . I discussed with David Sarnoff the advisability of proposing a short-wave transmitter. . . . I had taken with me a small short-wave receiver, and found that by using a curtain rod in my hotel room for an aerial, I could receive Pittsburgh on short wave fairly well. . . . So we arranged for Pittsburgh to send extracts from newspapers by code. Mr. Sarnoff played the part of receiving operator, and during the course of an hour or so, in my bedroom he took down an amount of copy, which was practically one day's traffic of the British Marconi Company. At the meeting held next day, he threw a bomb into the group by exhibiting the copy which he had taken.

Incidentally, the success of our little demonstration must have given Mr. Sarnoff some concern as to what to do with several million dollars' worth of long-wave transmitters which had been projected for erection by the Radio Corporation of America on Long Island. Apparently he dissolved his problem because the project as a whole was dropped and short-wave transmitters replaced the proposed long-wave system.[3]

Conrad was appointed general engineer of the Westinghouse Company in 1904 and assistant chief engineer in 1921. He supervised the development of newer transmitting equipment and the design of the WD-11 radio tube operated from a dry cell, which played an important part in making the first domestic electronic tube receivers possible in compact, simplified form.

He received the honorary degree of Doctor of Science from the University of Pittsburgh in 1928. For his work in radio he was awarded the Morris Liebmann Prize by the Institute of Radio Engineers in 1926; the Edison Medal of the American Institute of Electrical Engineers in 1931; the John Scott Medal of the Institute of Philadelphia in 1933; the Lamme Medal of the A.I.E.E. in 1936; the Gold Medal of the American Institute of the City of New York on February 1, 1940.

Oddly enough, radio, the medium in which Conrad flashed the first election returns, was used during the week of his death to broadcast world-wide President Roosevelt's address asking Congress to declare war on the Japanese Empire. Three days later, microphones in the nation's Capitol picked up a second presidential request, and the immediate response of Congress, voting hostilities against Germany and Italy. Radio, since Conrad's pioneering efforts, had become a medium in which history is heard before it is written—a medium in which news is born.

[3] Speech at the American Institute of the City of New York, February 2, 1940.

William Henry Eccles

RADIO PHYSICIST

BORN: *August 23, 1875*
Furness, England

WILLIAM HENRY ECCLES, physicist, studied and interpreted the mathematics of radio and was one of Marconi's right-hand men. He enrolled as a student at the Royal College of Science, South Kensington, in 1894. Three years later he was appointed demonstrator in the physics laboratory at the college, and in 1898 was graduated from London University with first-class honors.

Marconi was in London, surrounding himself with expert electricians, the majority of them English and Scotch. Eccles was one of those chosen; he entered the Marconi laboratory at Chelmsford. Much of his time was spent in the investigation of electrical oscillations. He also devised a laboratory method for testing and classifying coherers, the results of which were presented as his D.Sc. thesis in 1901. Developing the "tuning fork" method of control to maintain the frequency of transmitting stations as nearly constant as possible, he contributed to the minimizing of interference.

Recognized as an authority on radio theory, Eccles was appointed head of the mathematics and physics department of the South-Western Polytechnic, Chelsea, in 1902, and afterwards became professor of applied physics and electrical engineering at the City and Guilds of London Technical College.

Eccles observed, "When electric waves from a high-power sending station pass over the surface of the globe, that portion of their energy which reaches a distant receiving station and operates the receiving apparatus, as far as we know, traveled from the one point to the other along the shortest path—that is, along a great circle drawn on the globe."

Eccles wrote *Handbook of Wireless Telegraphy* in 1915. His second book, *Continuous Wave Wireless Telegraphy*, published in 1921, was a treatise that revealed his grasp of wireless and its mathematics. Indicating his appreciation of the importance of mathematics in the advancement of learning, Eccles quoted from Francis Bacon: "For many parts of Nature can neither be invented with sufficient subtility, nor demonstrated with sufficient perspicuity, nor accommodated unto use with sufficient dexterity, without the aid and intervening of the mathematics."

Through algebra and calculus and through his discussion of the physical properties of wireless as related to mathematics, Dr. Eccles was a pathfinder who contributed much to the understanding of radio science all the way from the Hertz oscillator to the electron, or ionic tube, as he referred to it. His "principal sphere of labour" is summed up as "wireless telegraphy and patents." He was chairman of designers of the Rugby high-power wireless station 1922-24, and served as adviser to the British government on wireless through the Second World War.

The men with whom Marconi surrounded himself in the early days were expert electricians for that was the natural field from which to draw capable men interested in the development of wireless. They were operating engineers more than scientists; they were practical men of engineering skill with a flair for invention. They were "Marconi Pioneers," and as such they helped to blaze new trails in the science of radio. Along with Dr. Eccles they were:

Walter William Bradfield, born in 1879 at London, joined the Wireless Telegraph & Signal Co., Ltd., in 1897, and became electrical assistant to Marconi in his historic tests of wireless at Salisbury Plain. He supervised installation of the first wireless apparatus on British battleships and later assisted in demonstrations to the United States Navy aboard the U.S.S. *Massachusetts*. In 1901 he directed building of the Marconi station at Siasconset, Massachusetts, and Nantucket Lightship. He was appointed chief engineer of the Marconi Wireless Telegraph Company of America in 1902.

When Bradfield died in March, 1925, Marconi said, "He did a great deal of valuable work for me."

Andrew Gray, born at Glasgow in 1873, was educated at Glasgow University, and as an electrician specialized in telegraphy. He entered the employ of the Marconi Company in 1899, and some of the early ship and shore wireless installations were designed by him. He introduced the Marconi system to the Hawaiian Islands, and in 1910 was appointed chief engineer of the Marconi Company.

James Erskine Murray was born October 24, 1868, at Edinburgh and died February 12, 1927. He studied under Lord Kelvin at Glasgow University and enrolled at Trinity College, Cambridge, as a research student. In 1898 Marconi selected him as one of his experimental assistants, and he became chief electrician of the Marconi Company. In 1905, Murray turned to consulting work in radiotelegraphy.

Capt. H. J. Round met Marconi in 1903 and worked with him from 1908 to 1914, conducting numerous experiments for "GM," as Marconi was referred to among his men. In 1911, Round produced a balanced crystal circuit dependent upon the fact that the carborundum crystal required an impressed voltage to bring it to its most sensitive state as a detector. Early in 1913 he introduced a three-electrode gas-filled tube or valve. In 1919 he transmitted speech from Clifden, Ireland, to Newfoundland, and a year later from Chelmsford. He was an outstanding experimentalist and pioneer in the use of Fleming valves, in voice transmission, in the development of circuits and in radio direction finders.

Richard Norman Vyvyan, born in England on December 2, 1876, was educated at Charterhouse and studied electrical engineering at Faraday House, London. Joining the engineering staff of the Marconi Wireless Telegraph Company in 1900, he accompanied Marconi on many historic trips—to the southwest tip of England in July, 1900, to select Poldhu as the site of the first transatlantic station; to Canada in 1901 to build the Glace Bay station; on board the S.S. *Philadelphia* in 1902, when Poldhu's signals were recorded on tape. Vyvyan was engineer in charge at Glace Bay when transatlantic service opened in 1903. He served with the Royal Flying Force in World War I. He became chief engineer of the Marconi Company, and when the Imperial Wireless Chain was established in 1924, he was responsible for construction and engineering of the stations. Vyvyan's book, *Wireless*

Over 30 Years, was published in 1933 as a historic record of wireless pioneering and development.

Of "the Chief," Vyvyan said: "Only those who worked with Marconi throughout the early years of wireless realize the wonderful courage he showed under frequent disappointments, the extraordinary fertility of his mind in inventing new methods to displace others found faulty, and his willingness to work often sixteen hours at a time when any interesting development was being tested. He had an instinctive intuition as to what was wanted and how to arrive at the solution."

Greenleaf Whittier Pickard

INTRODUCED CRYSTAL DETECTORS

BORN: February 14, 1877
Portland, Me.

GREENLEAF WHITTIER PICKARD, electrical engineer and investigator of radio phenomena, was the grand-nephew of the poet John Greenleaf Whittier. Educated at Westbrook Seminary, Lawrence Scientific School, Harvard University and Massachusetts Institute of Technology, he turned to radio in 1898 at Blue Hills Observatory, Milton, Massachusetts, under a grant from the Smithsonian Institution.

Pickard was actively engaged in experiments with crystal detectors, and as a member of the American Telephone and Telegraph engineering staff he assisted in development of a radiophone, demonstrated in the autumn of 1902. After 1906 he was associated with the Wireless Specialty Apparatus Company as consulting engineer until 1931.

He conducted numerous experiments to determine the effect of the sun and sunspots on radio. In his study of the polarization of radio waves, he contributed to development of the direction finder, and noted as early as 1908 that errors in reading radio "compasses" might be caused by buildings, trees and other objects which flip-flopped the waves, or through reflection "fooled" the direction finder. He was elected president of the Institute of Radio Engineers in 1913.

As early as 1903 Pickard became interested in the possibility of using minerals as detectors. He tried iron oxide and then magnetite, but it was not until 1906, when be obtained crystals of silicon—a product of the electric furnace—that he found a good detector. He also introduced the "perikon" detector, two metallic substances pressed against each other, red oxide of zinc and chalcopyrite. Iron pyrites also worked. The hunt for more sensitive detectors led to "detection" tests of all minerals. Galena proved to be the best although it lacked ruggedness and stability for commercial practice. The "cat whisker," a little fine wire which touched lightly the surface of the crystals, was easily jarred off the sensitive spot. The operator used a buzzer test; he occasionally pushed a button with his foot to determine whether or not the detector was still adjusted so he would hear a signal if it came along. Carborundum generally was used aboard ship because a carbon rod, or small brass cup holding a piece of carbon, pressed tightly against the sparkling crystal was not as easily upset by vibration.

Linked with the name Pickard in crystal detector development was that of General H. C. Dunwoody of the United States Army; he observed that carborundum could be used as a detector.

The function of the crystal is to change the incoming high-frequency impulses to low frequency to which the headphones will respond and produce sound within audible range of the ear. The crystal is a rectifier; it permits an electric current to flow through it in only one direction, completely checking the flow in the opposite direction. In fact, the crystal acts in the receiving circuit as a valve in a water pipe does, allowing the water to flow freely in one direction but preventing back-flow. Incidentally, that is why Fleming's first vacuum-tube detector was called a valve. The electron valve or tube, as it was later called, sent the crystal to the archives; but as a simple inexpensive device that boys could make for a few cents, the crystal played a noble role in the forward march of radio.

Recalling his early days in wireless, Pickard said:

My first active interest in communication without wires began in 1894-95 when I conducted experiments with a ground-plate or conduction system in a pond at Deering, Maine. In 1897, I made some short-range—about ¼ of a mile—experiments with a Hertzian oscillator energized from a Wimshurst machine, with a filings coherer for a receiver.

In 1898 I was engaged in taking measurements of atmospheric electricity at Blue Hills Observatory, Milton, Mass. At that time, the Smithsonian Institution became interested in radio and asked our observatory to undertake experiments with long, high aerials. Using kites, very long 'aerials were raised. We soon found that these long, high aerials could not be used with our coherer-receiver. They collected an enormous amount of static. Later we successfully transmitted over three miles from Blue Hills to Mt. Chickatawbut, using a flag-pole aerial for the transmitter and a 100-foot wire held up by a box kite at the receiver.

In the early part of 1899 we transmitted a few coherent messages from Blue Hills to Memorial Hall Tavern in Cambridge, a distance of 10.8 miles, using a carbon-steel microphone detector at Cambridge. Professor A. E. Dolbear of Tufts College became interested in our work and we conducted some experiments between Blue Hills and Tufts College. . . . In 1903-04, in my spare time, while working with the American Telephone and Telegraph Company, I began experimenting with crystals for use as detectors of radio signals. Then, in the early part of 1907, after the introduction of my silicon detector, the Wireless Specialty Apparatus Company was incorporated to develop and sell my various inventions—crystal detectors, loop aerials, novel forms of tuners and an improved Leyden jar condenser.

With more than 100 patents to his credit, Pickard became consulting engineer of the Yankee Network in 1934, specializing in ultra-high frequencies and radio frequency modulation, popularly known as FM.

Ernst F. W. Alexanderson

DEVELOPED THE ALTERNATOR

BORN: January 25, 1878
Upsala, Sweden

ERNST FREDRIK WERNER ALEXANDERSON, electrical engineer, became widely known for his contributions to radio and to television, and especially for development of the alternator which bears his name.

Son of a professor of classical languages at the University of Lund, Alexanderson, as a boy in Sweden, displayed an aptitude for mechanics. After graduating from high school he attended the University of Lund for a year. He then entered the Royal Institute of Technology at Stockholm and carried on with postgraduate studies at Königliche Technische Hochschule in Berlin where he was a student of Professor A. K. H. Slaby, a pioneer in wireless. While there he was so intrigued by a book on alternating current by Steinmetz that he decided to go to America to find work with the electrical wizard at Schenectady. He arrived on these shores in 1901 and as the first step toward his goal he worked as an electrical draftsman in New Jersey. But always there was the burning desire to be with Steinmetz and in 1904 he attained the objective when he became a member of the General Electric engineering staff, designing generators under the direction of Steinmetz.

Alexanderson was not paying much attention to wireless, when in 1904 Reginald Fessenden put the problem to the General Electric Company to build a 100,000-cycle alternator; it would have to revolve 20,000 times a second. Alexanderson was given the assignment and went right to work on it. A machine was completed in the summer of 1906 which was successfully used for one kilowatt at 50,000 cycles, and it was delivered to Fessenden at Brant Rock, Massachusetts, in September of that year. On Christmas Eve it was used to broadcast voice in connection with wireless telephony experiments, which were picked up hundreds of miles away. A water-cooled microphone was employed.

On April 26, 1909, Alexanderson applied for a patent on his alternator, and that same year described the successful operation of a two-kilowatt, 100,000-cycle alternator. It was a powerful machine for the production of smooth continuous waves; it looked like a giant dynamo as used at Niagara to create electricity for lighting and for industry, yet here was a machine that made world-wide communication possible.

Marconi made a pilgrimage to Schenectady in 1915 to see the fifty-kilowatt alternator being tested for installation at the Marconi transatlantic station at New Brunswick, New Jersey. It went into operation in July, 1917, with Marconi present to witness the tests, featuring both wireless and radiophone. Installation of a 200-kilowatt alternator was completed during the winter of 1918, making station NFF, New Brunswick, the most powerful in the world. It gave Uncle Sam a stentorian long-range voice in the international air. Battleships in all parts of the world could hear NFF and so could portable field receivers on the battle front in France. The old arc-and-spark transmitters for long-distance communication were surpassed and doomed—the alternator became the driving force in wireless communication. It accomplished undreamed-of results and was a "voice" in the making of history. From the lofty aerials at New Brunswick President Wilson's "Fourteen Points" were transmitted to Germany and were received at Nauen.[1]

---

[1] Milestones in the development of the alternator also were marked by the work of Dr. Rudolph Goldschmidt and Marius Latour, French physicist (born October, 1875). The Ste. Assise station was equipped with a Latour alternator and his system of balanced multiple leads.

Goldschmidt was born March 19, 1876, at Neu-Buckow, Mecklenburg, Germany. In 1900 he was appointed engineer in the laboratory of Algemeine Electricitäts-Gesellschaft in Berlin; from 1901 to 1902 he served as chief laboratory engineer and designer in Prague. While lecturer at Darmstadt Technical College in 1907, he practiced as consulting engineer and designed a high-frequency alternator which in 1911 was installed at Tuckerton, New Jersey, and Eilvese, Germany. (Sayville, Long Island, and Nauen, Germany, used the Arco alternator.) When the First World War broke out, it was evident that these stentorian transmitters had been built to meet Germany's "needs of the hour," and the stations in the United States were taken over by the government.

After the war the Radio Corporation of America was organized, in 1919, and Alexanderson, while continuing his work at the General Electric Company, became chief engineer of RCA. From 1920 to 1924 in that capacity he superintended construction of powerful stations in Sweden, Poland, England, Hawaii and elsewhere.

His work, however, was not confined to transmitters for he also won recognition for his development of the tuned radio-frequency circuit, which increased signal strength and selectivity of receiving sets. His developments also included magnetic and electronic amplifiers, a multiple tuned antenna, an anti-static receiving antenna, and directional transmitting aerials. He was an active pioneer in television and conducted considerable research in power transmission, electric ship propulsion, electric traction and in the development of industrial control devices. More than 290 patents attest his inventive ability. In recognition of his achievements, he was elected president of the Institute of Radio Engineers for 1921.

In 1924 Alexanderson sent a transatlantic facsimile message, a hand-written greeting, to his father in Sweden.

One of his patents disclosed the principle known as the inverter, by which direct current is changed to alternating current through the mercury vapor arc. In 1935 General Electric installed a DC power transmission line using the mercury arc inverter.

On the "radio reservation," covering many acres in the Mohawk Valley on the outskirts of Schenectady, Alexanderson developed multiple tuned antennas, studied horizontal polarization of waves and erected "panel" aerials to handle high power concentrated in desired directions, so that communication with foreign countries and with the Byrd Antarctic Expedition (1940) was greatly improved.

Television lured Alexanderson in the twenties. He developed novel mechanical scanners.[2] His projector reflected a cluster of seven lights on the screen and when associated mirrors on a drum revolved, the

---

[2] Alexanderson was ably assisted by Ray Davis Kell (born at Kell, Illinois, June 7, 1904) on the General Electric laboratory staff from February, 1927, to July, 1930; he joined RCA Laboratories in 1930 and has made outstanding contributions in development of television equipment.

spots of light gyrated and whirled to cover the entire screen with light that "painted" the picture. He described it as "a multiple light-brush system" and demonstrated it on December 15, 1926, at St. Louis. In Proctor's Theatre at Schenectady May 22, 1930, he projected seven-foot television pictures on a screen, flashed from his laboratory by radio. He used a perforated scanning disc and high-frequency neon lamps.

Shortly before the Second World War Alexanderson and his assistants developed the amplidyne, a sensitive and powerful system of amplification and automatic control which found important military and industrial applications. He has also developed radio echo altimeters, radiant energy guiding systems for aircraft and automatic steering devices for air and water craft.

Alexanderson, a member of the Royal Academy of Science of Sweden, has received the Swedish Order of the North Star, the Medal of Honor of the Institute of Radio Engineers, the Polish Order of Polonia Restituta and the John Ericcson Medal for outstanding radio engineering. He is a fellow of the American Institute of Electrical Engineers and has received honorary degrees from Union College and the Royal University of Upsala, Sweden.

Never a man to publicly prophesy, predict or speculate, Alexanderson, asked in 1930 when television might be ready for the home, replied,

"Well, I don't know. What we wonder is if the public really wants television."

"Scientists do not have many turning points in their lives," he once remarked. "They go straight ahead and one thing leads to the next. But I can safely say that it was Fessenden's demand for something we didn't have that led me to my experiments with radio and television.

"The inventions of tomorrow can be forecast," he went on, "if we know how to interpret what is going on today."

Albert Hoyt Taylor

THE NAVY'S RADAR PIONEER

BORN: *January 1, 1879*
Chicago, Ill.

ALBERT HOYT TAYLOR, radio engineer, investigator of ethereal phenomena and a pioneer in radar, was graduated in 1899 from Northwestern University with a B.S. degree. He opened his career as a teacher and was appointed instructor of physics and electrical engineering at Michigan State College, 1900-03; then instructor at the University of Wisconsin, 1903-05; assistant professor, 1905-08. From the Imperial University at Goettingen, Germany, he obtained a Ph. D. in 1909, and served as professor of physics at the University of North Dakota, 1909-17.

Taylor was a pioneer in the study and development of short waves and concentrated on that phase of radio when he joined the government service in November, 1917, commissioned a lieutenant in the United States Naval Reserve. In 1918, he became a lieutenant commander; in 1919, commander. As superintendent of the Radio Division of the United States Naval Research Laboratory, Anacostia, D.C., he studied polarization of electric waves, 'round-the-earth echoes or multiple signals and the structure of the upper atmosphere. As the result of his experiments in 1925, the "radio deflecting roof" revealed two waves—one "horizontal" traversing the earth's surface, the other rebounding from the sky. The "radio roof" or Heaviside theory was further confirmed.

Taylor, regarded as one of the government's most skilled experts in radio research and engineering, was awarded the Liebmann Memorial Prize by the Institute of Radio Engineers in 1927 for his short-wave work and application of piezo crystals in transmitting circuits. He also designed special radio equipment for aircraft.

World War II found him engaged in important radio research at Anacostia, with all his experience of the First World War and of the intervening years to enhance the value of his work.

Serving as president of the Institute of Radio Engineers in 1929, he once remarked, "I might be classed as 25 per cent physicist, 25 per cent inventor, 25 per cent naval officer and 25 per cent radio engineer."

Taylor's important work in the study of radio echoes and the structure of the upper atmosphere contributed greatly to the development of radar—radio detecting and ranging.

Tracing the United States Navy's early development of radar, the Navy Department on May 23, 1943, called attention to the fact that in mid-September of 1922 Taylor and Leo C. Young, working in the Naval Aircraft Laboratory, Anacostia, observed that certain radio signals were reflected from steel buildings and metal ships. They also noticed that ships passing by a transmitter and receiver attuned to certain frequencies produced a definite interference pattern.

Between 1925 and 1930 the reflection phenomenon was used to measure the height of the Kennelly-Heaviside layer. Taylor and Young performed this work in conjunction with Dr. Gregory Breit and Dr. Merle A. Tuve, of the Carnegie Institute. Their associates during this period included Louis A. Gebhard, M. H. Schrenck, L. A. Hyland and later Robert M. Page and Robert C. Guthrie.

A report prepared by Taylor on "radio-echo signals from moving objects" was submitted on November 5, 1930, to the chief of the Bureau of Engineering, Navy Department. As a result, on January 19, 1931, the Bureau assigned the Naval Research Laboratory the problem of investigating the use of radio to detect the presence of enemy vessels and aircraft. Special emphasis was placed on the confidential nature of the problem.

Many conferences with Army and Navy officers were accompanied by demonstrations during the ensuing years. The importance of having radar tested with the fleet was realized as a result of studies made during the tactical maneuvers of the fleet in the Pacific during the autumn of 1936. As a further step, the Naval Research Laboratory on February 17, 1937, conducted a demonstration for naval officers of radar detection of aircraft. Also in 1937 the first radar equipment was taken to sea. The next year was spent in designing and building a practical shipboard model which was installed on the U.S.S. *New York* late in 1938.

The radio echoes which A. Hoyt Taylor heard coming back to earth from outer space were echoes that challenged scientists to make use of them. Once that was done, radar added a new dimension to the science of radio.

As Chairman of the Medal for Merit Board, Cordell Hull, Secretary of State, presented the Medal of Merit, awarded to civilians for outstanding services in the war, to Taylor with this citation:[1]

> For exceptionally meritorious conduct in the performance of outstanding services in the line of his profession as member of the staff of the Naval Research Laboratory. Undiscouraged by frequent handicaps, Dr. Taylor labored tirelessly in a course of intensive research and experimentation which eventually resulted in the discovery and development of radar. His foresight, technical skill and steadfast perseverance contributed in large measure to the timely introduction of a scientific device which has yielded the United States Navy a definite advantage over her enemies during the present war.

Charles Samuel Franklin

BEAMED THE WIRELESS WAVES

BORN: *March 23, 1879*
    Walthamstow, England

CHARLES SAMUEL FRANKLIN, one of Marconi's outstanding engineers, received his engineering and scientific training at Finsbury Technical School, England. After some time spent in electrical work at Manchester and later with the Norwich Electricity Company, he joined

[1] March 28, 1944.

the Wireless Telegraph and Signal Company (Marconi Company) in 1899. Almost immediately he went to South Africa with a Marconi contingent for duty in connection with the Boer War. In 1902 he was one of the "old guard" of the Marconi Company who sailed on the S.S. *Philadelphia* accompanying Marconi to conduct historic tests. He became Marconi's right hand in experimental research; numerous important patents were credited to him.

Franklin, through intensive research and profound technical knowledge, starred in the short-wave, ultra-short and microwave spectrums. He designed the short-wave beam transmitter and devised the flat-grid aerial which became famous as the beam aerial, giving Britain an imperial, all-empire, globe-girdling system of communication. During the World War—in 1916—when Marconi took up the investigation of directional short-wave beams which he had dropped in the late nineties, he called upon Franklin and in reporting on results of extensive tests, said, "I was valuably assisted by Mr. Franklin."

It was "CSF" who in 1919, while studying the problem of short-wave propagation, succeeded in using electron tubes for the generation of very short waves. Marconi was convinced that given adequate reflectors at both ends, not only would the strength of signals be much greater, but also a reduction of interference by atmospherics or other causes would be obtained. Franklin devoted particular attention to the design of efficient reflectors; he concentrated radiation into a narrow searchlight-like beam, and built a special short-wave transmitter employing tubes of a design which he suggested. Gaston A. Mathieu developed the beam receiver, and assisted Marconi in his short-wave receiving tests aboard the *Elettra*; G. A. Isted specialized in the tubes. Marconi, Franklin, Mathieu and Isted were an unbeatable team.

"After Mr. Franklin, under my direction, had followed up this subject with great thoroughness," said Marconi, "we were quite convinced that short electric waves possessed qualities which up to that time had remained unknown, and that this new line of investigation was opening up a vast field of profitable research full of un-dreamed-of possibilities."

During the spring of 1923, Marconi and Franklin conducted tests between a special station at Poldhu and the yacht *Elettra*, chiefly to ascertain the day and night ranges and reliability of signals trans-mitted on waves less than 100 meters in length, with and without reflectors, and to investigate the angle and spread of the beam. On 97 meters, with 12 kilowatts, daylight signals were heard across 1,250 nautical miles, and night signals were picked up at the Cape Verde Islands 2,320 nautical miles from Poldhu.

The history of radio records that beam wireless is based upon the original work done and the intuition and technical foresight of Mar-coni and Franklin.

At the advent of broadcasting Franklin was called upon to design stations for England, and as a result 2LO became London's first broadcasting station.

Franklin's engineering skill, coupled with Marconi's genius for grasping the essential points on which the future pivoted, enabled the art to reach a new state of perfection of immense practical impor-tance when otherwise it might have become a mere scientific achieve-ment. Marconi's foresight had forged a new implement—the beam reflector system. Franklin, with tenacity in the face of great diffi-culties, helped him carry it to a successful conclusion. The immediate results were called sensational; the prospects brilliant.

On his sixtieth birthday in 1939, Franklin retired from active service with the Marconi Company and went to live near the site of the famous Poldhu station.

Albert Wallace Hull

PROLIFIC INVENTOR OF ELECTRON TUBES

BORN: April 19, 1880
Southington, Conn.

ALBERT WALLACE HULL, research physicist, invented the ultra-high-frequency generator—the magnetron. Originally intended for low-frequency oscillations, or to be used as an electron relay, it proved to be an excellent device for generating microwaves. The theory of the high-frequency behavior of the magnetron is admitted by scientists to be "rather complex, and exact mathematical analysis is difficult."

Hull was a native of Connecticut, the second oldest of eight sons, five of whom went to Yale. Albert was graduated with a B.A. degree in 1905, having majored in Greek and mathematics; his Ph.D. he attained in 1909. From that year to 1911, he was instructor of physics at Worcester Polytechnic Institute, and assistant professor, 1912-14, when he joined the General Electric staff as research physicist. In 1928 he became assistant director of research at the General Electric "House of Magic."

During his first year with GE, Hull invented a vacuum tube having a true negative resistance and named it the dynatron; the pliodynatron soon followed as a controlled dynatron oscillator, useful in radiotelephony. A filter circuit developed in 1917 came into use ten years later in radio receiving sets. This invention resulted from extensive work in X-ray crystal analysis.

In 1920 Hull invented the magnetron, and in co-operation with Dr. F. R. Elder developed oscillators which produced ten kilowatts at fifty kilocycles. It came into renewed prominence in 1928 with the discovery that magnetrons having split anodes could generate very high frequencies.

Since then the magnetron has had many important applications. It depends on the fact that electrons can be altered in their path by a magnet. In ordinary electron tubes, the flow of electrons from the filaments to the plate is regulated by the charge on the grid. In the magnetron there is no grid, but the tube is in a magnetic field. As the intensity of the field increases, there comes a stage at which the electrons are curled back to the filament, and never reach the plate. At this critical point a slight change in the field produces a large change in the current carried by the tube. It is especially valuable for producing high-frequency oscillations used for generating ultra-short waves.

Early in 1923 Hull was given the problem of explaining the "noise" in the newly developed superheterodyne receivers. He thought it might be caused by the "shot effect" of the impact of individual electrons, for such an effect had been predicted but never demonstrated. He found the "shot effect" was to blame as suspected, and obtained an accurate measurement of it. As a by-product of the investigation the screen-grid tube was developed.

My plan for measuring the "shot effect" called for a voltage amplification of 100,000 at a frequency of a million cycles [said Hull]. Since no known method of neutralizing feedback could give this much gain, I decided to make special tubes in which there was no feedback, namely, tubes in which the grid and plate were screened from each other completely. The result was the screen-grid tube.

I was much surprised to find that so simple a solution of the problem was new and broadly patentable. This invention had a profound influence on the radio art. Today nearly all of the tubes used in radio receivers, and many of those in transmitters, are screen-grid tubes.

Present-day radio receivers with their short-wave bands and automatic volume control probably could not be made without screen-grid tubes. In any case, approximately twice as many tubes would be required, and more than twice as many tuning and neutralizing circuits, which would double the cost of receivers. The total sales of radio receivers in 1941 amounted to $416,000,000. If they had been made without screen-grid tubes and the public had bought the same number, it is estimated that the cost would have been $800,000,000. Hence, the screen-grid tube is credited with saving the public approximately $400,000,000 per year in radio receivers. In addition, it has helped to make possible frequency modulation and television which, engineers contend, would be impractical without it.

In 1931 Hull patented a new tube, "the thyratron," essential to electronic industrial control, and in later years, improved the tube by developing more efficient cathodes—for example, the dispenser cathode.

Described as "alert, scholarly, incisive," Hull is said to be the creator of a greater number of electron tubes than any other man, and an important contributor to the fundamentals of physical science. His special alloy glass seals helped to make metal receiving tubes, as well as metal-glass junctions for power tubes, practical.

Many honors have come to Dr. Hull: the Howard N. Potts Medal of the Franklin Institute, presented in 1923 for work on X-ray crystal analysis; the Morris Liebmann Prize of the Institute of Radio Engineers in 1930 for his work on vacuum tubes; and an honorary degree of Doctor of Science the same year from Union University, and in 1931 from Middlebury College. He was elected president of the American Physical Society in 1943.

With eighty-six patents to his credit, he lists work as his hobby.

Irving Langmuir

CHEMIST, PHYSICIST, ELECTRONIST

BORN: January 31, 1881
Brooklyn, N. Y.

IRVING LANGMUIR, American research scientist, has a record of achievement in industrial science which reveals what intuition and hard work can accomplish when a chemist or metallurgist applies his talents to a realm such as radio, although it may seem far afield from test tubes, retorts, metals and mining.

Radio is as fertile a field for the chemist as oil or rubber, and for the metallurgist as steel or the automobile. Those who think of radio as limited to radiomen think of it only in terms of results in communication. So broad is the scope of modern radio and so broad is its development that it calls for far more than electrical engineering; it is all the sciences in one, and its progress evokes the efforts of many scientists. Langmuir's life illustrates the truth of this, and the opportunities that exist when one looks beyond his own profession for new spheres in which his talents may be applied.

Born in Brooklyn, Langmuir lived with his parents for three years in Paris. After a year at Chestnut Hill Academy, Philadelphia, he entered Pratt Institute, then the School of Mines at Columbia University, from which he was graduated in 1903 as a metallurgical engineer. He did postgraduate work at the University of Goettingen, Germany, where he received the degree of Doctor of Philosophy in 1906; from that year to 1909 he was instructor of chemistry at Stevens Institute of Technology.

Langmuir joined the research staff of the General Electric Company in 1909, and under the roof of "the House of Magic" at Schenectady, he turned his attention, in 1911, to radio, concentrating on electron tubes. When first in the "lab," he developed an incandescent lamp which contained argon or nitrogen, providing a type of illumination far superior to any previous form of electric lamp. His next avenue of investigation grew out of his work with the incandescent lamp: He discovered new laws relating to electronic emissions in a vacuum. In 1912 he had already developed the radio tube to a power of several kilowatts. This was a result of his discovery that electrons in a gas-free space built up a space charge which limits the current. Also, he developed the thoriated filament for electron tubes and a process of atomic hydrogen welding.

At Princeton University in 1929, when he was presented the honorary degree of Doctor of Science, the citation said in part:

He has for twenty years attacked fundamental problems with the freedom of the academician, yet with all the powerful resources of the industrial engineer. Langmuir's is the accepted concept of adsorption and orientation of molecules at surfaces; his studies have furnished us a mechanism of gas reactions at the surface of metal tungsten, universally used in electric illumination, long-distance telephony and radio.

Langmuir's medals and honors are many, including the Nobel prize in chemistry in 1932 and the Hughes Medal from the Royal Society of London in recognition of researches in molecular physics. The American Academy of Arts and Sciences presented the Rumford Medal for his thermionic researches, and he was president of the Institute of Radio Engineers in 1923. He was recipient, in 1944, of the Faraday Medal awarded by the Institution of Electrical Engineers in England, for "notable scientific or industrial achievements in electrical engineering, or conspicuous service rendered to the advancement of electrical science." He was the fourth American to receive the honor, a bronze award established in 1921.

Langmuir gave a high place to intuition in human affairs, holding reason to be too slow. In his address as retiring president of the American Association for the Advancement of Science, he said:

It is often thought by the layman and by many of those who are working in so-called social sciences, that the field of science should be unlimited, that reason should take the place of intuition, that realism should replace emotions, and that mortality is of value only so far as it can be justified by analytical reasoning.

In the complicated situations of life we have to solve numerous problems and make many decisions. It is absurd to think that reason should be our guide in all cases. Reason is too slow and too difficult. We often do not have the necessary data. Or we cannot simplify our problem sufficiently to apply the methods of reasoning. What, then, must we do? Why not do what the human race always has done: use the abilities we have, use common sense, judgment and experience. We often underrate the importance of intuition.

In almost every scientific problem which I have succeeded in solving, even those that have involved days or months of work, the final solution has come to my mind in a fraction of a second by a process which is not consciously one of reasoning. Such intuitive ideas are often wrong. The good must be weeded out from the bad, sometimes by common sense or judgment, other times by reasoning.[1]

"Whatever work I've done," Langmuir once remarked, "I've done for the fun of it."

Roy Alexander Weagant

ENGINEERED TO CONQUER STATIC

BORN: *March 29, 1881*
Morrisburg, Ontario

DIED: *August 23, 1942*
Sherbrooke, Quebec

ROY A. WEAGANT, radio engineer, inherited an interest in mechanical and scientific devices from a long line of "ancestors of engineering instinct." One of his father's inventions was a venetian blind. Roy's hobby as a telegraph enthusiast led directly to his career. When he was four years old his parents moved across the Canadian border to Derby Line, Vermont, where he attended the village school.

Dr. M. L. Baxter, a retired physician of the town whose hobby was telegraphy, had set up a circuit between his home and the residences of near-by friends. Roy's stepfather had been a telegrapher and he helped the lad to build a sounder and key to "cut in" on the village line. Young Weagant was fired with the spirit of an amateur telegrapher, and sensing his interest in the apparatus, Dr. Baxter encouraged the boy to learn all he could about telegraphy and electricity.

When he went to preparatory school and college in Stanstead, Quebec, Weagant devoted special attention to physics and electricity. He went to McGill University, Montreal, in 1898, and it was there that Sir Ernest Rutherford taught physics. Because of lack of funds,

---

[1] December 26, 1942.

after one year Weagant dropped out of college and worked for three years. By 1902 he had saved enough money to enable him to resume his studies at McGill, and in 1905 he was graduated with the degree of B.S. He saw Rutherford demonstrate the principle of the magnetic detector and that really gave him his first urge toward radio engineering. He made experiments with Hertzian waves, and by the time he was graduated, his interest in wireless was fast gaining momentum.

For a time he worked with the Montreal Light and Power Company and then joined the Western Electric Company in New York where he worked in the Apparatus Design Department. He left this job in March, 1906; the company record of his work stated, "He had shown considerable originality on subjects of general electrical interest and was particularly adapted for the detailed design of small apparatus."

Weagant then went with the Westinghouse Electric and Manufacturing Company in Pittsburgh as draftsman, remaining there from May 7 until October 31, 1907, when he joined the General Electric Company at West Lynn, Massachusetts. Business conditions caused his dismissal after two months and he found his next position with the DeLaval Steam Turbine Company at Trenton, New Jersey.

It was at this time that Fessenden wanted a steam turbine for his alternator and consulted the DeLaval Company. Weagant worked on the job and was fascinated with Fessenden's idea; it rekindled his interest in telegraphy and linked it with wireless.

As time went on, Weagant noticed in an electrical magazine that Fessenden was advertising for a draftsman—that was Fessenden's way of hiring men. From draftsman, Weagant transferred to engineering, testing and designing. It was not long before he was at Fessenden's National Electric Signaling Company's station at Brant Rock, Massachusetts, working for $112 a month. There he served his "wireless apprenticeship." He worked on the design of the 100-kilowatt spark transmitter to be installed at Arlington, Virginia, the Navy's first high-power station. Elimination of static became

Weagant's "hobby," yet he won a reputation in designing towers, antennas, transmitters and receiving sets.

In March, 1912, he parted company with Fessenden and joined the Marconi Wireless Telegraph Company of America as a designer. He introduced many innovations, among them the panel type of transmitter which became a standard. Within the limits of commercial necessity he replaced the old with the new. Weagant was always a modern; he was also a combination in ability of the engineer and the litigation expert, abetted by a clear method of analysis. He became chief engineer of the American Marconi Company.

One of the first attempts to avoid conflict or infringement of the "third electrode," or grid patent of the audion invented by De Forest, was made by Weagant, who put one of the electrodes outside instead of inside the glass bulb. In 1914, a vacuum-tube detector appeared featuring the Weagant external grid. It was a tubular fountain-pen-shaped affair with the filament and plate inside the glass bulb, but the grid was wound around the exterior. In effect it was a Fleming valve—with filament and plate—and it became an audion in performance when the external grid was applied.

During the First World War, Weagant, as chief engineer of the Marconi Company, designed much equipment used by the United States Navy—and built according to government specifications. The Marconi factory at Aldene, New Jersey, became an arsenal for radio apparatus and was greatly expanded in capacity for manufacture of transmitters, receivers, wavemeters and associated equipment. It was estimated that more than ten million dollars' worth of wireless equipment was made at Aldene during the war, almost all for government use.

As consulting engineer of RCA from 1920 to 1924, Weagant devoted years of intensive research to the problem of eliminating static—Nature's uncontrolled vagaries. He developed directional antennas and other anti-static devices which minimized the effect of atmospherics in transatlantic reception. He predicted that airplanes with direction finders would sail through fog and thick weather with undiminished speed; that wireless would create great ocean lanes of air travel with airships passing to and fro regardless of weather.

At a meeting of the Institute of Radio Engineers and the New York Electrical Society in March, 1919, he explained his method of eliminating static. It dispensed with lofty towers at wireless stations and was credited with effecting a one and one-half reduction in the amount of power required.

He explained that the essence of his anti-static development lay in the discovery of the fact that static moved in a vertical direction, from a source overhead, while the wireless signals traveled in a horizontal direction above the earth's surface. Based on the observation that these two conflicting forces moved at right angles to each other, the next logical step, as Weagant saw it, was to develop a selective device for neutralizing the effect of static, yet at the same time receiving the wireless signals.

As he stated, Weagant believed that static came from above, but it is recorded in the history of wireless that "notwithstanding this misconception, he accomplished genuine advances in antenna construction."[1]

Weagant spent the winter of 1921-22 in Bermuda working on a static eliminator, but with little success. He left RCA in 1924, and shortly after joined forces with Dr. Lee De Forest in research work, finally in 1925 retiring to Lake Memphremagog, Vermont, near his childhood playground.

When the curse of creativeness was on him, Weagant was a man alone [said one of his associates in engineering], and if forced to attend an engineering meeting or routine business conference, he would appear, but in a sullen mood. Now and then, however, between flashes of momentary insight into the unknown, he would become his un-inventive self, and then he was the ideal host indeed. The two natures were as different as black is from white. But is that not the way with all inventors? Weagant's thoughts were with his work; he lived for it, he died thinking of it.

[1] In recognition of his work, the Institute of Radio Engineers presented the Morris Liebmann Memorial Prize to Weagant in 1920.

Ilia Emmanuel Mouromtseff

DELVED INTO MICROWAVES

BORN: December 9, 1881
St. Petersburg, Russia

ILIA EMMANUEL MOUROMTSEFF, electrical engineer, specialized in radio and experimented with wavelengths so short that they fringed the frontier of light; he called the tiny impulses "black light."

Mouromtseff attended Military High School in Orel, Russia, graduating in 1898, after which he entered the Nicholas Engineering School and Academy at St. Petersburg, receiving a degree in military engineering in 1906. To carry on his study of electrical engineering, he enrolled at the Institute of Technology in Darmstadt, Germany, from which he was graduated in 1910.

When the First World War struck Europe, Mouromtseff joined the Signal Corps of the Russian Army with the rank of colonel. For his liaison work with the French, he was awarded the Officer's Cross of the French Legion of Honor. When Germany attacked Russia, Mouromtseff was assigned the important task of getting the word through to the French, and after he and his staff worked all night, the message finally got through, flashed by a station which the Russians had built in four days.

In 1917 Mouromtseff came to the United States as a member of the Russian Purchasing Commission. Like Zworykin and a number of other Russian scientists who came to America during that period, he liked the country and made it his home. In 1923 he joined the Westinghouse Electric and Manufacturing Company at Pittsburgh to take charge of radio transmitter tube developments.

In 1936 Mouromtseff transferred from Pittsburgh to the Bloomfield, New Jersey, works of Westinghouse. He conducted experiments in ultra-high-frequency transmission, and in 1942 was appointed assistant manager of the Electronics Engineering Department.

Mouromtseff is credited as having contributed a number of important achievements to the advance of radio transmission. He helped to develop some of the first water-cooled transmitting tubes and ultra-high-frequency tubes of high output. He worked out a method of calculating transmitting tube characteristics in the positive grid region, which gave radio engineers something they had lacked previously; and in various other investigations, chiefly in the micro-wave spectrum, Mouromtseff added important knowledge to the art.

Long-wave radio gave us sound at a distance; the very short waves now give us vision at a distance [said Mouromtseff discussing postwar possibilities for radio]. Long waves, like those used in standard broadcasting, radiate from a sending antenna like ripples when a pebble is dropped into a pool of water. They travel in all directions and use the earth's surface as a guide, thus following a slightly curved path.

Ultra-short waves, on the other hand, are "channelized" into a narrow path and travel through the air in a straight line. Like light, these short radio waves can be projected in a beam and reflected. Thus they can be harnessed to accomplish many tasks.[1]

Among the feasible applications in industry of this new form of radio Mouromtseff listed such jobs as helping convert chemicals into cloth, aiding in the manufacture of safety glass and treating preserved foods after they already are in the jars or packages.

One of the first industrial experiments with ultra-high-frequency radio which produces ultra-short waves was for the de-infestation of wheat in grain elevators contaminated with rice weevil [he said]. Our laboratory experiments were successful and stirred up a tremendous interest both in this country and abroad. Vacuum packers were interested in the possibility of pre-cooking hams and similar products by high-frequency radio. Restaurants investigated the future of large "radio cookers" which might be installed in dining rooms for grilling steaks, hot dogs or toasting bread in front of the customer. Heat would be generated only in the food itself and the food would be cooked from the inside out giving it a different flavor.

[1] July 7, 1943.

The field of short-wave radio seems almost limitless. In the field of medicine it has been found that various sicknesses can be treated by irradiating the body with radio waves. Very short waves can be focused into narrow beams—narrowcast instead of broadcast—and applied to the body for therapeutic treatment at sharply defined places. Radio, for example, can be used for irradiation of kidneys, lungs, stomach and other areas. It also is the most convenient method of heating the entire body.

Herbert Eugene Ives

APPLIED ELECTRO-OPTICS TO RADIO

BORN: July 31, 1882
Philadelphia, Pa.

HERBERT EUGENE IVES, electro-optical research expert and physicist, did for pictures on wires and the radio what his father, Frederic E. Ives, did for photography on plates, films and the printing press. Frederic Ives, who started as a printer's apprentice, with photography as an overtime activity, invented the first process called halftone in 1878, and in 1885, the halftone engraving process now universally in use, and originated methods of color photography.

Herbert E. Ives was graduated from the University of Pennsylvania in 1905, and received his Ph.D. from Johns Hopkins in 1908. He was appointed assistant physicist of the Bureau of Standards, 1908-09; physicist of the National Electric Lamp Association of Cleveland, 1909-12; worked with the United Gas Improvement Company, 1912-18; and with the Western Electric Company and Bell Telephone Laboratories, 1919 to date.

His earliest scientific work was in photometry and illumination, with special reference to the measurement and specification of color. The generally used trichromatic specification of color follows the lines proposed and elaborated by him. Following this were researches on vision, particularly the phenomena of flicker. The photoelectric effect early attracted his attention and was the subject of numerous investigations. The properties of extremely thin films of alkali metal were the subject of exhaustive study, which subsequently found application in early television pick-up devices.

In 1923 Ives and his collaborators at the Bell Laboratories developed the method and apparatus for the transmission of photographs over telephone lines used at the national political convention in 1924 and at the inauguration of President Coolidge in 1925. This was put into daily operation across the American continent by the Associated Press.

Ives's research in color photography and optics led him into television. He participated in "a triumph of research" on April 7, 1927, when Herbert Hoover, then Secretary of Commerce, speaking over a telephone line from Washington, addressed a group in New York and was seen on a large neon-light screen as he spoke. As another feature "act" in the demonstration, moving images of speakers and entertainers at Whippany, New Jersey, were transmitted by radio to the screen in New York.

Television in color, "a dream of science," was demonstrated by Ives and his staff at the Bell Telephone Laboratories on June 27, 1929, when brilliantly tinted pictures were sent over wires from one end of a room to the other. The pictures, vividly and realistically colored, were about the size of a postage stamp.

It was in 1928 that Ives and his associates demonstrated outdoor television pick-ups, illuminated by the July sun; no artificial lights were used. Ives also played an important part in development of telephoto stations or booths in which speakers saw each other as they conversed over a three-mile telephone line. That was in April, 1930. Mechanical scanners were used in the various Ives demonstrations.

Motion pictures were flashed over a coaxial cable or television "pipe" between New York and Philadelphia in November, 1937, and so successfully that Dr. Ives, in charge of the demonstration, declared there was "no limit to the application of the system, but first we must wait for the development of television."

Other scientific developments of Ives include the production of "parallax panoramagrams," flat pictures which show relief when observed from any direction without the use of any apparatus at the eyes. In the laboratory he also demonstrated three-dimensional motion pictures by application of the same principles. As time went on, he became keenly interested in the more purely scientific field. His experimental verification of the change of rate of a moving atomic clock, by spectroscopic observation of high-speed hydrogren canal rays, furnished direct proof of the system of compensations for motion popularly associated with the Einstein theory of relativity.

Said a radio engineer who knew him well, and as a boy had visited the laboratory of his father:

Herbert Ives is a man with a wide range of interests. His work falls in two domains—advanced optics, largely television, and highly advanced physics, in which he achieved his greatest fame. In television he was a contributor to the art. In physical theory, such as relativity, he became a profound thinker and one of its outstanding critics. In this realm of thoughtful investigation he is brilliant. He inherited family tradition in color photography, and I believe, for this reason he may have been swayed by sentiment into television.

Frederick Augustus Kolster

PERFECTED THE RADIO COMPASS

BORN: *January 13, 1883*
Geneva, Switzerland

FREDERICK A. KOLSTER, radio research engineer, when two years old moved with his parents from Switzerland to Boston, Massachusetts, where his father became violinist in the Boston Symphony Orchestra. Young Kolster entered the Cambridge Manual Training School for he wanted to be a civil engineer. The superintendent of the school called his attention to wireless telegraphy as a new field of opportunity, and he was lucky to find a job in the Cambridge laboratory of John Stone Stone, where he worked from 1902 to 1908. While working he studied physics and engineering at Harvard, completing the course in 1908. Radiotelephony appealed to him and he took up that work with the De Forest Telegraph and Telephone Company, from 1908 to 1911.

From 1912 to 1921 he served as radio specialist at the United States Bureau of Standards and was chief of the Radio Section, which he organized. While at the Bureau he invented the Kolster decremeter, widely used by the Radio Inspection Service and others for determining the wavelength and logarithmic decrement of radio transmission, primarily from ships, as required by government regulations established for the purpose of promoting safety at sea.

In 1913 he prevailed upon the Bureau of Lighthouses to establish radio beacons at all important lighthouses and lightships. As a result the first experimental radio beacons were installed by Kolster on the Ambrose and Fire Island Lightships and at the Sea Girt Lighthouse on the Jersey coast.

Concurrently with this innovation, Kolster invented and developed, for practical applications, the multi-turn rotatable coil direction finder, later known as the Kolster radio compass, which, installed on shipboard, provides means of determining the bearing of any radio beacon or of a radio-equipped ship lost in the fog or in distress. It was widely used during the First World War by the United States Navy under the seal of secrecy. Its commercial application therefore was delayed for several years.

In 1921, Kolster left the Bureau of Standards and joined the Federal Telegraph Company of California to engage in the manufacture of the radio compass for installation on ships, and thus introduced to the maritime world, a simple and effective way of utilizing radio as a navigational aid.

When the Federal Telegraph Company was acquired by the International Telephone and Telegraph Corporation of New York in 1931, Kolster was invited to join the organization as a research engineer and to continue in some early work in the field of ultra-high frequencies which later developed into the application of ultra-high-frequency radio for remote control purposes. In 1938 he left I.T. & T. to engage in consulting work. In the Second World War, as in the First, "DF" (direction finding) was a most important instrumentality with its range and effectiveness greatly extended on land and in the air as well as on the seas.

The radio compass is a loop antenna. In a rugged, weatherproof shield or housing, it is mounted in the open on board ship and its shaft is extended below deck to the face of a compass. When the loop is rotated, the signal becomes loud or faint. That principle applies to the radio compass. Since the point of weakest signal is much sharper and more easily discernible than the point of maximum signal, the lowest volume or complete "fadeout" is used to indicate the direction from which the signal arrives. The weakest signal is obtained when the loop is broadside or at right angles to the incoming wave.

Radio beacon stations dot the coasts, so that bearings may be taken on them much the same as a ship is guided by a lighthouse beam. The compass, of course, can also be employed to detect the location of other radio transmitters whether on a ship in distress or on a submarine, by taking a bearing the same as on a beacon.

Airplanes also fly along beams, guided by radio direction finders of the most modern style—elongated iron-core loop antennas built in streamlined, bullet-shaped housing, usually located atop the aircraft.

Many are mentioned as "inventor" of the radio compass, among them Fessenden, Pickard, John Stone Stone, Capt. H. J. Round, Francis W. Dunmore, Percival D. Lowell, R. L. Smith-Rose and Bellini-Tosi, but generally Kolster is credited with having built a practical device; that others had observed and realized the directional properties of wireless is conceded.

Ettore Bellini, a pioneer in directive wireless, was born April 13, 1876, at Foligno, Italy, and was educated at Naples University. In

1901 he was appointed electrical engineer of the Royal Italian Navy; and in 1906, as chief of the Naval Electrical Laboratory at Venice, he conducted research in the application of wireless telegraphy to naval vessels. Later, in conjunction with Capt. Alessandro Tosi, he invented the radiogoniometer,[1] an early form of radio direction finder, consisting of two triangular loop antennas. Signals set up in the two loops created a resultant field, while the rotating coil produced the loudest signal when it embraced this field to its maximum. Therefore, the movement of the coil, and not of the vessel, indicated the direction of the sending station.

Capt. H. J. Round's careful and accurate work with the radio direction finder during the First World War enabled it to play an important part in the Battle of Jutland by observing the movements of the German battle fleet. Great reliance was placed upon the accuracy of the bearings supplied by Round and his staff, and with excellent results.

Reginald Leslie Smith-Rose, a member of the National Physical Laboratory at Teddington, England, contributed to the knowledge of propagation and directional properties of electric waves, receiving-loop direction finders and radiating beams. He studied the various factors responsible for errors in bearings and sought means of compensating for the deviations by circuit adjustments or chart calibrations. Of Smith-Rose it may be said that he studied every angle of radio direction finding and helped to sharpen the accuracy of the art.

Kolster remedied the faults of older systems by utilizing a multiple loop or coil antenna as the pick-up, and moving it about a vertical axis. In this way, by revolving the loop for maximum or minimum by means of a pointer, the direction from which the signals originated could be determined. This multiple loop had greater pick-up than previous systems, and when used with an electron-tube receiver, its sensitivity as a "bloodhound" was greatly improved.

---

[1] United States patent applied for October 1, 1907; patent No. 943,960 issued December 21, 1909; patent No. 945,440 on January 4, 1910.

Harold DeForest Arnold

DESIGNER OF ELECTRON TUBES

BORN: September 3, 1883
Woodstock, Conn.

DIED: July 10, 1933
Summit, N.J.

HAROLD DEFOREST ARNOLD, physicist and electronist, received his undergraduate training at Wesleyan University, Connecticut, and after graduate work at the University of Chicago under Professor R. A. Millikan, and a year as professor at Mount Allison University, he achieved the degree of Doctor of Philosophy in 1911. Arnold entered the Research Department of the Bell Telephone Laboratories, and later as research director he was a guiding spirit in advancing the telephone art, both wire and radio.

In the field of thermionics he was one of the earliest scientific workers and one of the first to appreciate the necessity for a high vacuum in the three-element thermionic tube. His other contributions to this art were the development and application of methods for obtaining such a vacuum, recognition of the existence and importance of the space charge effect of electrons in such a device, and the calculation of the magnitude of this effect and methods for its adaptation to commercial purposes.

He developed designs for electron tubes and methods for their manufacture so that tubes could be made to meet the telephonic requirements of reliability and ease of maintenance. This work included the development, under his immediate direction and at his suggestion, of an oxide-coated filament as a source of electrons within the tube. He had charge of the adaptation of the tubes to the telephonic problem of long-distance wire telephony and also of radio telephony. In recognition of these achievements, Arnold was awarded the John Scott Medal in 1928.

In addition to his work in electronics, Arnold contributed personally and particularly by stimulating guidance to fundamental researches in speech and hearing and in magnetics. One of the fruits of the magnetic research was permalloy—an invention of G. W. Elmen. This is an iron-nickel alloy of certain compositions which when properly heat-treated, has exceptionally high permeability for weak magnetizing forces. In the form of a continuously applied loading to submarine telegraph cables, permalloy increased their message-carrying capacity more than fivefold, while its application to magnetic structures such as telephone receivers and transformers has been of great value in the undistorted transmission of sound.

One of Arnold's early individual problems was the development of gaseous and electronic amplifiers. In the latter connection his attention was attracted to the De Forest audion. This remarkable device, which had proved so valuable as a detector and amplifier of feeble radio currents, was, however, incapable of meeting the requirements of a power amplifier for the feeble but much larger currents of wire telephony. Arnold, who was fresh from the study of electronic physics in Millikan's laboratory at the University of Chicago, recognized that a pure thermionic effect, free of gas complications, was vitally needed. He set out to produce a higher-vacuum tube, using evacuation methods then only recently available. He succeeded, and thereby helped to take the three-element vacuum tube out of the realm of uncertainty and unreliability; it became a reliable amplifying tube.

At about the same time, in 1912, Langmuir of the General Electric Company arrived at substantially the same result, and that precipitated a patent contest which continued for many years, finally reaching the United States Supreme Court.[1] It was held that Arnold's idea of taking a De Forest audion and, by pumping a better vacuum, extending the range of operation to somewhat higher voltages without modifying the essential nature of that operation, did not constitute invention over the prior art. Neither did Langmuir's patent involve invention; the effect of high vacuum upon voltages above the

[1] Decision May 25, 1931.

point of ionization was known, and the knowledge was thus availed of in practice.

"Research is not in constructing and manipulating," said Arnold; "it is not observing and accumulating data; it is not merely investigating or experimenting. Research is the effect of the mind to comprehend relationships which no one has previously known. . . . To have ideas and to share them—that makes civilization."

Emory Leon Chaffee

SOLVED ELECTRONIC PROBLEMS

BORN: April 15, 1885
Somerville, Mass.

EMORY LEON CHAFFEE, physicist and one of the foremost authorities in the field of thermionic vacuum tubes, received his B.S. degree in 1907, upon completion of the four-year course in electrical engineering at the Massachusetts Institute of Technology. He then attended the Graduate School of Arts and Sciences at Harvard University, studying physics and obtaining an M.A. degree in 1908, and a Ph.D. in 1911.

His doctor's thesis covered a new method of producing continuous oscillations by means of what was known as the Chaffee gap. It was used successfully for radiotelephone transmission over a distance of thirty-five to fifty miles in 1910 and 1911. In the course of this work Chaffee employed the Braun-tube oscillograph using a cold cathode; he was an expert in manipulation of this instrument years ahead of many others.

Chaffee was appointed instructor in the Department of Physics at Harvard University in 1913, and instructor in electrical engineering in 1914. He became assistant professor of physics in 1917, associate professor of physics in 1923 and professor of physics in 1926. In 1935 he was given the title of Gordon McKay Professor of Physics and Communication Engineering, and in 1940 he was also appointed

Rumford Professor of Physics and director of the Cruft Laboratory, the last three titles being held concurrently. He also taught several courses at Radcliffe College.

At the famous Cruft Laboratory, one of the first college buildings to have its roof adorned with wireless towers, Chaffee conducted experiments with electromagnetic waves and delved deeply into the theory of vacuum tubes and associated circuits. His research work in the field of electric oscillations and vacuum tubes resulted in the publication of many papers in the *Proceedings* of the Institute of Radio Engineers and in other periodicals. In 1931 he published a book, *Theory of Thermionic Vacuum Tubes,* which is internationally known.

For several years Chaffee continued research on the eye in which the potentials produced by the nerves in the retina when stimulated by light were recorded by an amplifier system. In collaboration with Charlotte Perry, he completed an accurate direct determination of the physical constant e/m (ratio of the charge to the mass of an electron). From 1915 to 1924, Chaffee was engineer for John Hays Hammond, Jr., in the development of secret radio systems and radio-controlled torpedoes.

Dr. Chaffee is a fellow of the American Academy of Arts and Sciences and of the American Physical Society, and a member of the Executive Committee of the International Scientific Radio Union. He became a member of the Institute of Radio Engineers in 1917, transferring to the grade of fellow in 1921 and becoming vice president in 1922.

A number of patents have been granted to him in the field of radio. As a pioneer, his applied mathematical analysis contributed much to the theoretical development and practical applications of the electron tube. He dispensed with the haphazard trial-and-error methods and applied exact analysis to the operation of power tubes, thereby increasing their efficiency. It has been remarked that through mathematical skill Chaffee triumphed over some of the most complex problems in electrical engineering and electronics.

John Howard Dellinger

INTERPRETED NATURE'S EFFECT ON RADIO

BORN: *July 3, 1886*
Cleveland, O.

JOHN HOWARD DELLINGER, American physicist and investigator of radio phenomena in space, was educated at East High School and Western Reserve University, Cleveland, Ohio, where he received Phi Beta Kappa honors and was instructor in physics, 1906-07. He obtained his B.A. degree from George Washington University in 1908 and his D.Sc. in 1932; from Princeton University a Ph.D. in 1913.

Dellinger joined the National Bureau of Standards in 1907 as physicist, and in 1919 became chief of the Radio Section of the Bureau. His work covered a broad field in radio. As an originator of basic methods of radio measurements, he initiated and supervised experiments to study radio fading, the ionosphere and the influence of cosmic attacks on radio waves. He guided development of the radio-sonde,[1] launching into the upper atmosphere balloons carrying tiny, automatic radio transmitters which provide data for greatly improved weather forecasts. Notable work was done by Dellinger in developing radio and antennas for aircraft, also in directing development of radio-beacon and blind-landing systems for use on the airways.

In his study of radio, Dellinger kept an eye and ear on the sun as well as an ear on interstellar space.

"The sun is in an extremely turbulent state," he said, "and on it occur frequent eruptions from which are emitted radiations having a great range of wavelengths. There is no reason to doubt that some

[1] Radio-sonde, or radio-sounding balloon, is a practical instrument for transmitting information from the stratosphere; it is a lightweight battery-operated transmitter using acorn-type tubes on ultra-short wavelengths. The signals automatically transmitted indicate barometric pressure, temperature and humidity, as recorded by a radio meteorograph which modulates the transmitter.

of the radiations from these eruptions are sudden bursts which cause the sudden disturbance of the ionosphere of this planet."[2]

It has been found that these disturbances have the power to black-out high-frequency radio reception simultaneously over the daylight half of the world. Study of this effect—called "the Dellinger effect" because of its discovery by him in 1935—led to new understanding of the nature of radio-wave transmission, terrestrial magnetism and the sun.

Dellinger wrote many articles, treatises and books on radio and allied scientific subjects which were published by the government in various periodicals. He served at numerous important radio, communication and aeronautical conferences and on committees at home and abroad. He was chairman of the United States delegation at the radio conferences in Portugal in 1934 and in Roumania in 1937. President of the Institute of Radio Engineers in 1925, he was again honored by the Institute in 1938 by presentation of its Medal of Honor for his contribution "to the development of radio measurements and standards, his researches and discoveries of the relation between radio-wave propagation and other natural phenomena, and his leadership in international conferences contributing to worldwide cooperation in telecommunications." First chief engineer of the Federal Radio Commission, 1928-29, is also on Dellinger's record. In 1943-44 his activities included: radio editor of Webster's Dictionary; chief of Radio Section, National Bureau of Standards; chief of Interservice Radio Propagation Laboratory; Joint United States Communications Board; chief of Radio Propagation Section, National Defense Research Committee; vice president of International Scientific Radio Union; chairman of the Radio Technical Commission for Aeronautics.

"Dr. Dellinger is one of our gentlemen scientists," said a pioneer in radio who knew him well. "He is a man of great dignity and noble curiosity, deeply interested in the laws of Nature."

[2] "Sudden Disturbances of the Ionosphere," in *Proceedings* of the I.R.E., October, 1937.

Louis Alan Hazeltine

INVENTOR OF THE NEUTRODYNE

BORN: *August 7, 1886*
Morristown, N.J.

LOUIS A. HAZELTINE, American physicist and teacher, invented the radio neutrodyne circuit. He received the degree of Mechanical Engineer from Stevens Institute of Technology in 1906, and entered the testing laboratory of the General Electric Company at Schenectady. A year later he took a position as assistant in the Electrical Engineering Department at Stevens, serving from 1917 until 1925. He returned in 1933 as professor of physical mathematics, and that year received the honorary degree D.Sc.

The first World War found Hazeltine at the Washington Navy Yard, where he designed an advanced radio receiver (SE 1420) by formulas which he originated. It had wide and extended service in the Navy, and might be called the forerunner of the neutrodyne circuit, for in its original form this receiver embodied neutralization.

It was in 1922 that Hazeltine's attention was called to the great possibilities of a receiver designed to use tuned radio-frequency amplification. Such receivers had failed because of a tendency to oscillate induced by feed-back of energy from the vacuum tube's capacity coupling. As he analyzed the problem he found that his earlier work on the neutralization of capacity coupling held the solution of the problem. He applied it in accordance with algebraic formulas, and it worked.

Hazeltine, a physicist to whom mathematics was amusement, came into radio to invent the neutrodyne at that chaotic time in the twenties when broadcast listeners were beset by howls in the mass of receiving sets. He developed the new circuit from a mathematical point of view. Engineers observed that the theory behind his calculation led

largely to lifting the vacuum-tube amplifier out of the realm of experimentation and into the realm of calculable engineering. In circuits
designed for both tuned radio frequency and audio amplification he
applied "squeal preventers" or stabilizers, known as "neutrodons,"
by means of which he balanced out, or neutralized, the howls; he
described his device as "capacity neutralization." At a meeting of
the Radio Club of America in March, 1923, Hazeltine officially introduced his new set. He named the receiver "the neutrodyne," and in
the winter of 1927 it was estimated that ten million of these sets
were in use.

Someone remarked that Hazeltine took squeaks and howls out of
radio with calculus, but the professor said that there was no calculus
in any of the essential parts of the neutrodyne invention—only
elementary algebra. In fact, he explained, the primary ideas were
physical rather than mathematical.

Hazeltine has been described as an inventor whose main tools were
a pen, notebook and slide rule. Interviewed by the *Scientific American*
in 1927, he was asked for the secret of successful inventing.

That is a hard question [he replied], because I work differently from most
inventors. I believe, however, that the first requisite is a thorough knowledge
of fundamental principles. I never had any intention of being an inventor.
Mathematics was always my favorite subject in school; in mathematics I
used to get my highest marks. When I entered Stevens Institute of Technology,
I thought that eventually I would like to get into teaching.

What I wanted to take up I had no idea, but I was prejudiced against
electrical engineering. Near the end of my course I began to feel that the
performance of electrical apparatus could be predetermined more accurately
than that of mechanical apparatus. Here was plenty of opportunity to work
out mathematical problems, so I took up electrical engineering in spite of
my former prejudices.

In 1915 Hazeltine heard Edwin H. Armstrong read a paper before
the Institute of Radio Engineers pertaining to the radio-electron tube
as a regenerator and oscillator. Here was a new field that offered
opportunity for mathematical study; it fascinated Hazeltine and he

delved into it. As a result, in 1917 he lectured before the I.R.E. on "Oscillating Audion Circuits," which described his analysis.

In recognition of his contribution to radio, Hazeltine was elected president of the Institute of Radio Engineers in 1936, and a year later the Radio Club of America named him for the first award of the Armstrong Medal.

His success as an inventor never dimmed his desire "to get into teaching." In 1938 he transferred to the physics department at Stevens Institute where he developed a new and deeper type of physics course, aimed to present the fundamental observations and to deduce from them logically the important laws. By new methods of presentation, he brought down to the level of the freshman and sophomore various topics often reserved for graduate courses, such as the radiation of sound and electric waves and Fresnel's laws of reflection and refraction. The professor's hope behind this work was that it would have more lasting importance than his well-known radio circuit.

Alfred Norton Goldsmith

ENGINEER, INVENTOR AND TEACHER

BORN: September 15, 1887
New York City

ALFRED NORTON GOLDSMITH, radio and motion-picture engineer, teacher, inventor and native New Yorker, was educated at the College of the City of New York and Columbia University. He became professor of electrical engineering at CCNY and director of research for the Marconi Wireless Telegraph Company of America, consulting engineer of the General Electric Company, and later vice president and general engineer of the Radio Corporation of America. As a pioneer in broadcasting he served as the first chief broadcast engineer of RCA and adviser to the National Broadcasting Company.

Evidence of Goldsmith's versatility and the scope of his active, imaginative mind is found in his inventions. They run the gamut of radio and a wide variety of associated fields. They encompass radio telephony, broadcasting, sound-motion pictures, studio techniques, radio-relay systems, facsimile, optics, phonographs and television, both black-and-white and in color. He contributed many detailed improvements to the art of communication and to sound recording and reproduction. He invented a method, which he called "tele-visibility," to permit an airplane pilot flying by night or in fog to view the terrain below, or, on approaching a landing field he could "see" by radio the exact appearance of the field, in size, perspective and detail, as he would observe it by normal vision in clear weather or daylight.

Recognized as one of radio's outstanding "practical visionaries," Goldsmith mastered the art of being able to explain the science of radio in terms the layman can understand; he has written more than 100 scientific papers and books. As a teacher he has been a guide and inspiration to many radio engineers, industrialists and executives in plotting the advance of wireless to broadcasting and on into television.

To Goldsmith radio has no end; encouraging youth never to think that everything has been invented, he once remarked:

One-third of a century is not much in the life of nations, but it is a long time in the history of radio. At the opening of the Twentieth Century the "ether" was practically undisturbed. . . . Less than ten years later it was possible to put thousands of watts of speech-modulated energy into the air.

Altogether, radio was a rough-and-ready field one-third of a century ago, but it was full of interest, new things happened frequently, and all radio men were enthusiasts. Now radio is respectable and occasionally even stolid. But fortunately, the new arts of radio centering about the ultra-high frequency waves, facsimile and television will provide both headaches and the stimulation which will make radio interesting and worthwhile as a career in the future.

Said Goldsmith to a group of young engineers:

Be strong, thoughtful, tough and vigorous. Let no obstacle discourage you but rather let each problem be an invitation to success and a stepping stone to greater accomplishment. . . . Establish many close contacts with other minds in your field. Let some of them be minds which diverge from yours in their concepts and understandings. It is stimulating and awakening to participate in conflicts of opinion.

Goldsmith listed major engineering virtues as initiative, application, frankness and personal relations.

Life can almost be defined as self-willed motion [he said]. Unless a man is ready to "start something" he will get nowhere. Lethargy, uncertainty, indifference, delay and fear are paralyzing. Enterprise and keen thinking and fast action are the keys to success. Don't be too conservative in trying things out. Remember that a conservative has been humorously defined, with an undertone of indictment, as "a man who doesn't believe anything should be tried the first time." The great rewards of history, as well as inner satisfaction, often spring from trying it the first time. Steady work is an amazing instrument for achieving results. Relatively few people have been ruined by hard work, but many have failed through laziness. . . . Practice imaginative thinking. Never be afraid to discard ideas which seem inappropriate or faulty, or accept new ideas, even though radical, if they seem necessary and practical. . . . One of the worst faults that an engineer can have is vagueness, the concealment of facts, or the lack of courage to face facts. Engineering demands really creative workers with a genuine output.

Elected president of the Institute of Radio Engineers in 1928, Goldsmith was further honored in 1941 when he was awarded the Institute's Medal of Honor. The citation read, "For his contributions to radio research, engineering and commercial development; his leadership in standardization and his increasing devotion to establishment and upbuilding of the Institute and its *Proceedings*." He also served as president of the Society of Motion Picture Engineers. As an inventor, he received the National Pioneer award in 1940.

As an engineer, each of us is a member of a *profession* and not a trade [said Goldsmith]. We are members of an intellectual fellowship. The engineer must develop habits of thought characterized by exactitude, careful reasoning, and willingness to face the facts, no matter how discouraging. A combination of knowledge *and* wisdom is necessary. . . . Science and engineering need the truth, the whole truth, and nothing but the truth.

Hendrik Johannes Van Der Bijl

PIONEER IN ELECTRONICS

BORN: November 23, 1887
Pretoria, South Africa

HENDRIK JOHANNES VAN DER BIJL, noted physicist and electronic specialist, obtained his early education in South Africa; he attended Victoria College after which he took up postgraduate work at Halle University and at the University of Leipzig, where he achieved his doctorate. Intent upon further study and anxious to learn everything he could about electrons, he came to the United States for further work in physics with Professor Albert A. Michelson and Dr. Robert A. Millikan at the University of Chicago. Incidentally, at the time, Millikan was engaged in electronic research for which he was awarded the Nobel prize.

Millikan recommended van der Bijl to Dr. Frank B. Jewett[1] of the Western Electric Company, which in 1912-13 was interested in applying electronic phenomena to the production of a distortionless amplifier to make possible transcontinental telephony. Van der Bijl joined the Research Department and remained a member of the staff continuously until August 3, 1920. Married to an American girl, he had decided to make the United States his home for the remainder of his life when General Jan C. Smuts prevailed upon him to return to his native land to carry on scientific and technological work as technical adviser to the Department of Mines and Industry of the Union of South Africa.

The United States lost a scientist. In the interval from 1913 to 1920, van der Bijl contributed, in the words of Dr. Jewett, "enormously to the advances of the electronic art which made possible, not only transcontinental telephony, but shortly afterward transoceanic

[1] President, Bell Telephone Laboratories, 1925-40; then Chairman of the Board.

227

telephony and the whole art of radio broadcasting." A notable achievement which gained him prominence as an engineer in 1915 was invention of the modulation system used successfully by the American Telephone and Telegraph Company in historic long-distance radiophone tests between the United States naval radio station NAA, at Arlington, Virginia, and Honolulu and Paris.

Van der Bijl, as a leading authority on thermionics, did pioneer work in developing the characteristics of electron tubes, from which curves could be drawn showing the relationship between the various factors in tube operation, both in telephone and radio work. This was followed by an extended study of electron tubes as detectors and modulators. He also made an empirical study of tube geometry, constructing hundreds of tubes of various types, each differing slightly from the others in physical characteristics. This was of great value during the First World War. When it was necessary to make vacuum tubes of specific constants, data was obtained immediately from van der Bijl's records of filament, plate and grid values which would furnish the desired results.

"Dr. van der Bijl put the electron tube on a fundamental mathematical basis," is the way a fellow engineer appraised his achievement.

In two decades—1920 to 1940—it was observed that van der Bijl lifted scientific work in the Union of South Africa "to a high place," and so successfully that in 1942 he was referred to as "the spark plug of South Africa's amazing new war industries."

South Africa was faced with an emergency that called for quick action when the war broke out. One of the first acts of General Smuts on assuming office as Prime Minister and Commander-in-Chief in 1939 was to create the War Supplies Board, a civilian directorate independent of military jurisdiction, to acquire technical military stores and matériel in the shortest possible time and to train rapidly and efficiently a large number of technical workers for war services. Van der Bijl was appointed directorate-general.

Described as "short, blond and dapper," he was further identified as "a powerful personality and an outstanding figure in Empire war production and in the scientific world generally."

The booklet *South Africa at War* commented upon him as follows:

Van der Bijl returned to South Africa some twenty years ago to take charge of the establishment of the South African Iron and Steel Corporation of which he became the Chairman, and also became chairman of South Africa's Electricity Supply Commission. He lost no time in rallying to the service of the nation scores of leaders in mining, engineering, industry, commerce and labor, and the large railway workshops. The framework of a comprehensive production organization was rapidly constructed and South Africa's wartime industrial machine swept into action.

John Hays Hammond, Jr.
CONTROLLED TORPEDOES BY RADIO

BORN: April 13, 1888
San Francisco, Calif.

JOHN HAYS HAMMOND, JR., radio research engineer and inventor, first saw the light of day at the Golden Gate. His father was a famous mining engineer. Jack was a member of the class of 1910 at Yale, from the campus of which he was catapulted into wireless after reading a tale of how Tesla in 1898 had put a model boat in a tank and controlled it fitfully by wireless.

That story put ideas into Hammond's mind; it stirred his imagination. After graduation he established the Hammond Research Corporation, and it was not long before stories were circulating that a young man at Gloucester, Massachusetts, was steering a boat from a lofty lookout tower on the wooded cliff overlooking the harbor. He also had a little box on wheels that moved as he directed. It was called an "electric dog."

Before leaving Yale, Hammond had made a written prediction that some day he would control a moving body at a distance by the sound of his voice. His remotely controlled boat, *Radio*, fulfilled the prediction. It was described as "a boat with not a soul aboard, her lights blazing, her engine pounding, shooting out to sea at night with the speed of a railroad train." From shore he could make it zigzag, stop, go ahead or turn around, full-speed or half-speed.

Hammond then developed the wireless-controlled torpedo—sleek weapons that could be shot into the water and directed by wireless to hit the bull's-eye no matter what the target. He took out hundreds of patents pertaining to radio; on direction finders, circuits, ultrashort waves, frequency modulation, television and secret methods of communication. With the advent of broadcasting he proposed a pay-as-you-listen system utilizing a tuning box for which a coin would serve as the key.

Hammond combined pleasure with scientific research on the 125-foot two-masted auxiliary schooner *Odysseus III*, and also established a radio research laboratory in his "medieval castle" home at Gloucester. He was appointed consultant of the Radio Corporation of America in 1923. Deeply interested in music, he experimented with electric organs and pianos, developing a number of remarkable instruments. At 34, he had 250 inventions to his credit; at 54, more than 700.

Modestly and quietly he worked. There was no fanfare when he discovered something and patented it; he just went on to the next. The very nature of his work with secret radio for aircraft and radio control of torpedoes and warships dropped a curtain of secrecy around his activity. He might be testing a television "eye" for airplanes; he might be flying down the Atlantic coast in a plane which only a certain station could hear or he might be aboard the *Odysseus* in the Caribbean "investigating," but always with secrecy that added to the mystery. Hammond developed a secret radio communications system based on phase modulation that cannot be jammed by a carrier wave of identical frequency.

He always remembered as a vivid incident of his boyhood the day when Alexander Graham Bell, confessing that his invention of the telephone at times might become an instrument of interruption, put his hand on Hammond's shoulder and advised him to get into the habit of staying up all night, because the hours after midnight were the only ones safe from disturbance.

William Dubilier

MASTERCRAFTSMAN IN CONDENSERS

BORN: July 25, 1888
    New York City

WILLIAM DUBILIER, radio engineer, invented the mica condenser. Born on New York's "Lower East Side," he went to school at the New York Technical Institute and Cooper Union. He worked for the American Telephone & Telegraph Company as a repairman; also for the Western Electric Company. One night he heard a lecturer of the Board of Education talk about wireless, and becoming keenly interested, he read everything he could find on the subject. As chief electrician of the Continental Wireless & Telegraph Company he was sent to Seattle during the Alaska-Yukon Exposition in 1909 to conduct demonstrations of an arc system of wireless; he erected a sign "Listen to Wireless for 10 cents."

In 1910, Dubilier formed his own organization, the Commercial Wireless Telegraph and Telephone Company. After demonstration to officials of the Russian government of a new system for generation of quenched, undamped oscillations with the frequency above audibility, he was invited by the Russians to make a number of installations, including one in the palace of Czar Nicholas.

Watching airplane flights in 1911 inspired Dubilier to develop aviation wireless equipment, and after demonstrations before a Parliamentary Committee, he was invited by the British to establish a factory working with Fleming, Eccles and Duddell. The need for compact, lightweight apparatus on aircraft led him to design new condensers to replace the cumbersome and delicate Leyden jars, which were impractical for use in the air. So successful was his achievement in eliminating glass from condensers that the British government encouraged him to establish a factory in England for the manufacture of condensers.

Condensers became Dubilier's specialty. War and the military demand for them intensified his activities. He went to Europe in May, 1915, and demonstrated a portable radio outfit for airplanes in England and France. French authorities requested that he work with Professor Tissot of the University of Paris on experiments with submarine detectors. As a result Dubilier spent considerable time on the anti-submarine problem; a detector was developed and installed along the French coast from Brest to Dunkerque.

Returning to the United States late in 1915, Dubilier resumed experiments with condensers and began manufacturing mica units which were approved and accepted by the United States Navy in 1916. The American Dubilier Condenser Company was organized in 1917. Invention of the mica condenser, which found universal use in the radio and electrical field, linked the name Dubilier with condensers and won him a definite place among the pioneers who blazed new trails in radio.

Introducing a "B" battery eliminator for home radios, enabling the public to use house lighting current to operate radio sets in place of batteries, Dubilier was in the news again in 1926. Having obtained more than 500 patents in the United States, England, Germany, France and other countries on radio developments and parts, in 1933 he organized the Cornell-Dubilier Electric Corporation.

Appraising Dubilier's career, a veteran in wireless who knows him well said:

Bill was one of the earliest radio telephone engineers in the United States; he was ahead of his time in many respects. His career may be divided into three parts—radiotelephony, condensers, and the patent brokerage field, which he entered through the organization of Radio Patents Corporation, in 1917. In radiotelephony he had primitive tools with which to work, for example the arc, and therefore did not achieve as great prominence in this field as he might have, had he had the radio-electron tube. He did an exquisite job in designing mica condensers. He was a fundamental pioneer in these high voltage condensers, and in developing and supplying them he performed a magnificent service to the U.S. Navy in 1916. He developed the real technique of mica condensers that would stand up under extremely high voltages; his condensers were the Rolls Royce of the field, while other attempts to develop mica condensers up to that time might well be classed in comparison as a wheelbarrow.

Outbreak of the European war in 1939 found Dubilier thinking again of submarine detectors, this time suggesting means of ridding the oceans of electromagnetically detonated mines. Friends have called him "the Napoleon of radio," but his sister remembers him as a boy who "was always tinkering with bells and building little steam engines."

Raymond A. Heising

EXTENDED THE USE OF ELECTRON TUBES

BORN: *August 10, 1888*
       Albert Lea, Minn.

RAYMOND ALPHONSUS HEISING, radio engineer, was graduated as electrical engineer from the University of North Dakota in 1912 and obtained an M.S. degree at the University of Wisconsin in 1914. He joined the Engineering Department of the Western Electric Company, later known as Bell Telephone Laboratories.

Heising's important inventions in vacuum-tube technique, in oscillators, modulators and amplifiers as well as in carrier current and radio transmission systems are covered by 117 United States patents and have gone into extensive use throughout the world. Of particular interest are his patents pertaining to multiplex carrier line system, constant current modulation, multiplex radio transmission with plurality of different intermediate frequency carrier waves and the class "C" amplifier widely used at high-power radio stations.

During the First World War he was a member of the Subcommittee on Wireless Communication between Aircraft of the National Research Council. Many of his investigations at that time pertained to radio telephony for airplanes, sub-chasers and other military units. Those radiophone sets were probably the first practical ones ever made. After the war he took part in development of ship-to-shore radiotelephony, and later in development of the long-wave transatlantic radiotelephone circuit.

Multi-channel carrier telephone systems evolved in large part from the early work of Heising. Some of his radio inventions were applied in 1915 in the first long-distance radiophone communication from Arlington to Paris, and helped to lay the basis of radiotelephone development including public broadcasting.[1] For many years the economical and efficient method of constant current modulation which Heising invented was used in practically all high-power broadcasting stations.

In tribute to Heising, his associates said: "His contributions to the radio art are widely recognized and utilized throughout the world. They have been essential to the rapid expansion and commercial utilization of that art in all its forms, whether between fixed or mobile stations, and whether for individual communication or broadcasting."

Heising was president of the Institute of Radio Engineers in 1939. In the late thirties he turned his attention to investigations in ultra-short wave and piezo-electric phenomena. During the Second World War he directed a group assigned to fundamental work in connection with piezo-electric crystals, which had important applications to wartime radio.

[1] It was also during this work that Ralph V. L. Hartley of the Western Electric Company research laboratory invented the Hartley oscillating circuit.

John Logie Baird

SCOTTISH TELEVISION PIONEER

BORN: August 13, 1888
Helensburgh, Scotland

JOHN LOGIE BAIRD, Scottish television experimenter, went to school at Larchfield, Royal Technical College and Glasgow University where he studied engineering. His attention was directed to television in 1923 and three years later he demonstrated a mechanical scanning system before the Royal Institution. Up to that time he had worked as an electrical engineer, and as assistant superintendent of the Clyde Valley Electrical Power Company.

Baird was described as "a self-taught inventor who matched inventive wits against the pooled ability and the vast resources of great laboratory physicists and engineers. . . . He worked in accordance with the best tradition of the 'garret inventor.'" In February, 1927, he showed his televisor to the home folks at Glasgow.

Baird appeared on the front pages in February, 1928, when on the eighth of that month he televised Mrs. Mia Howe in London and her face was reported seen at Hartsdale, New York, as the first to be telecast across the Atlantic—imperfectly, yet the image did appear. He scored again on March 7 when the face of Dora Selvy was telecast from London to the S.S. *Berengaria*, 1,000 miles at sea. In 1930 he televised "abbreviated vaudeville" and coined the term tele-talkies. Again he established a record on June 3, 1931, when at Epsom Downs he telecast the English Derby for the first time; a year later he flashed the race all the way to London where 4,000 spectators sat in a theater and watched the horses on a television screen.

In February, 1935, the Television Committee of the British government decided to establish television as a public service without delay; two systems were tested—Baird's mechanical scanner and the electronic scanning method. The latter was adopted. Baird also developed a system for transmitting pictures by use of infra-red rays. He called it noctovision, and the receiver a noctovisor, since it was "a night seeing eye."

Just as Nipkow, Alexanderson, Jenkins, Ives and other proponents of the mechanical scanners faded from the scene with the advent of electronic scanning, so did Baird's disk which had helped to whirl television into the world.

Lloyd Espenschied

RADIO IMAGINEER

BORN: *April 27, 1889*
St. Louis, Mo.

LLOYD ESPENSCHIED, electrical engineer, moved in his boyhood to Brooklyn, New York. There, in his first year of high school, through contact with the electrical apparatus of the Physics Department and also through the influence of the Children's Museum, he became inspired by things electrical. He built and operated one of the first amateur wireless telegraph stations, 1905-08, training himself for a job as a wireless operator at sea. Realizing the need for more technical training, he entered Pratt Institute and was graduated in 1909.

His first job was in providing the United States Army and Navy with the then new type of wireless telegraph apparatus—the quenched spark built by the Telefunken Company. Seeking to participate in electric communications more broadly, he entered the American Telephone and Telegraph Company. There from 1910 to 1934 he had a long and productive experience in loaded lines, high-frequency transmission on wires and wireless telephony. Transferring to the Bell Telephone Laboratories, he was director of high-frequency transmission, 1934-39, later serving on the staff as a research consultant.

As the electric communications art moved toward the higher frequencies under the influence of radio, the vacuum tube and the wave filter, Espenschied moved with it, in fact, helped it to move by taking an effective part in the early development of radiotelephony and of high-frequency transmission on wires.

He participated in the pioneering radiotelephone experiments of the American Telephone and Telegraph Company in 1915, when the human voice was transmitted overseas for the first time from what was in effect the first vacuum-tube radiotelephone transmitter, installed experimentally in the naval radio station at Arlington, Virginia. Of the various overseas receiving points engaged in this broadcast, and including one at Paris,[1] Espenschied did the receiving in Hawaii with successful results. Following the First World War he took an important part in the development of radiotelephony for ship-to-shore service, for the building of the transoceanic "talk bridge" across the Atlantic and the Pacific and for broadcasting.

He participated in the development of high-frequency transmission over wires by the carrier current multiplex method after its inception about 1916, through the period of the First World War, when carrier current circuits were applied commercially for the provision of much-needed circuits between Washington and Pittsburgh. As a result of his dual activity in radio and high-frequency wire transmission, he was one of those mainly responsible for the development of the so-called wide-band coaxial cable system, whereby it became possible to transmit by wave-guides frequencies of millions of cycles—frequencies which previously had been regarded as the province solely of radio. He invented a quartz crystal band-filter widely used for carving out sharply the communication channels of carrier and radio systems. Another interesting line of development to which Espenschied contributed is the application to useful ends of

[1] Herbert Edward Shreeve of the Bell Telephone Laboratories had charge of reception in Paris.

the phenomenon of electric wave reflection—to railway safety systems; to the airplane altimeter; to airplane distance detection in general and the attaining of a gross form of sight, all by means of reflected short radio waves. Representing his personal contributions, as distinct from administrative participation in a large organization, are more than 100 patents bearing his name.

In the course of his technical work and because of its world-wide character, Espenschied traveled abroad to participate in several international conferences on radio and wire communications as an engineer-member of various United States delegations. He published a number of technical papers and otherwise participated in several engineering societies, being a charter member and a fellow of the Institute of Radio Engineers, which commended him with its Medal of Honor in 1940.

Recognizing the vacuum-tube amplifier as "the greatest advance in electric communications in our time," Espenschied credited it with putting a new face on the whole art.[2]

What makes the vacuum tube such a remarkable instrument [he said] is the fact that the minute electrical carriers—the electrons—are obtained by themselves in free space, free from the encumbrance of the solid matter conductors in which they had been contained heretofore in electrical devices. Electricity is obtained in pure and unadulterated form, as it were, in a bit of vacuous space where it can be operated upon directly by electrical influences, such as those of the received signal waves, without the intervention of mechanical action with its inertia limitations. No wonder then that we find ourselves in the midst of a great new era in electrical communications. . . .

You may have heard the story that "everything has been discovered"—that young men today haven't much chance to be original. It isn't so. New discoveries will be made. For instance, a worker in pure science will find something interesting, curiosity will urge him on, also the challenge to explain it, and before long the world may see a new physical phenomenon. All history is crowded with such evidence.

[2] Meeting of the Institute of Radio Engineers, January 29, 1943.

Richard Howland Ranger

PIONEER IN RADIOPHOTOS

BORN: June 13, 1889
Indianapolis, Ind.

RICHARD HOWLAND RANGER, radio engineer, spent his early days at Indianapolis, Indiana, and was graduated from Massachusetts Institute of Technology in 1911. As a member of the American Expeditionary Force in France during the First World War, he was an officer in the Signal Corps. He returned to Camp Vail, New Jersey, in 1919, and was put in charge of the radio laboratory. His postwar position in civil life was in the Research and Development Department of the Radio Corporation of America, with which he was associated from 1920 to 1930.

Captain Ranger specialized in the development of radiophoto and facsimile equipment. By means of the Ranger system photographs of President Coolidge, the Prince of Wales and others were flashed across the sea from London to New York in twenty minutes on November 30, 1924. Ranger radioed facsimile messages, maps and pictures from New York to Honolulu on May 7, 1925; on April 20, 1926, the picturegram of a check was sent from London to New York, where it was honored and cashed. Ranger became a pioneer in picturizing radio; his machine opened up transatlantic photo service and tossed pictures, weather maps and printed matter to ships at sea.

Basically and briefly, Ranger's original radiophoto system is described as follows: At the transmitter the film was wrapped around a glass cylinder inside of which was a powerful light. The light rays penetrating the film, in accordance with the lights and shades of the picture, struck a photoelectric cell traveling slowly down the length of the cylinder, which advanced slightly with each stroke of the scanner.

This pencil of light did the trick. If the light were strong, it produced a strong current; if feeble, a feeble current. These picture-currents were released through the radio signal which operated a pen that drew the picture at the receiver exactly as the pencil of light varied in intensity as it played across the cylinder at the transmitter.

The film was literally split into hundreds of dashes or marks, the number of which determined the number of radio signals that would make up the ethereal picture. When the photoelectric cell moved over an area of the film that was white, no signal was transmitted and the pen did not make contact at the receiver. But when the photo-cell passed over a solid black portion of the film, the receiving pen was held in contact with a sensitized paper and traced a black line. For gray parts of the film the pen touched the paper at intervals. For dark gray the marks were long; for light gray, short.

At the receiver a pen and cylinder moved at the same rate as the corresponding parts at the transmitter. The receiving cylinder, however, had the sensitized paper wrapped around it, and the pen, traveling the length of it in step with the photoelectric cell at the transmitter, reproduced the radiophoto.

In the late twenties Ranger turned abruptly from radiophotos and organized his own company, Rangertone, Inc., specializing in pipeless organs and other electrical instruments, designed to make music out of electrical howls, "radio squeals" and hums, unfolding, as he described it, "new horizons of power and beauty." In the Second World War he went back to the Army Signal Corps, attaining the rank of lieutenant colonel. His first year was spent in working out the applications of radio in the Air Corps and then in standardizing the components which go to make up radio for the Army, Navy and Air Corps.

Vladimir Kosma Zworykin

INVENTOR OF THE ICONOSCOPE

BORN: July 30, 1889
Mourom, Russia

VLADIMIR KOSMA ZWORYKIN, electronic research engineer, invented the Iconoscope, electronic "eye" of the television camera, and developed the Kinescope, or "eye" of the receiver. After graduation from the Gymnasium in Mourom in 1906, he completed a course in electrical engineering at the Technological Institute in Leningrad in 1912. There he studied under Boris Rosing, professor of physics and a pioneer in realizing the possibilities of the cathode rays as applied to television.

Rosing in Russia and A. A. Campbell-Swinton in England separately and simultaneously in 1907 published methods of electrical image reproduction using electromagnetic means for scanning. The first all-electronic television system, utilizing cathode-ray scanning at both transmitter and receiver, was later proposed by Campbell-Swinton in 1911 in an address before the Roentgen Society. In many respects this proposal visualized the present-day systems, but it lacked one important feature. That "missing link" was storage of the electric charge between successive scannings—the principle that would give the electronic pick-up device, or "eye," the sensitivity necessary to make it practical with high-definition scanning.

Unfortunately, a practical demonstration of these early proposals was impossible at the time, chiefly because the epochal invention of the audion by De Forest needed further development to make available practical video amplification. Much of the task remained for Zworykin. He went to Paris in 1913 and conducted X-ray experiments under Professor Paul Langeven at the Collège de France.

The First World War found Zworykin in the Signal Corps of the

Russian Army working on wireless. After the armistice he decided to circle the globe and after two trips around, concluded that the United States was the land of opportunity. He arrived in America in 1919 and found work as a bookkeeper in the office of the Financial Agent of the Russian Embassy, a position he held for a year, when he went to work in the Westinghouse Electric and Manufacturing Company's research laboratory, "Miracle Hill," at Pittsburgh. While there, he became a naturalized American citizen, and as a result of three years of work at the University of Pittsburgh he achieved his Ph.D. in 1926. His thesis was "The Study of Photoelectric Cells and Their Improvement." Through his research in electronics he perfected the television "eye."

Zworykin named it "Iconoscope"; "Eikon" in Greek meaning image, and "skopon," to watch. Therefore, the Iconoscope observes the scene to be telecast. The receiving tube, shaped like a funnel, was called "Kinescope"; "Kinema" meaning movement in Greek. So the Kinescope observes the motion. On the flat end of this funnel-shaped tube the scene appears as a picture in motion. Both tubes are strikingly like the human eye in performance. There is a "retina" and a controlled electronic beam that performs the same function as the optic nerve which flashes pictures to the brain. In television, the "brain" is the radio receiver. Zworykin first demonstrated the principal invention to Westinghouse officials in 1924, and publicly at a meeting of the Institute of Radio Engineers in Rochester, New York, on November 18, 1929. It had no motor, no moving parts. Scanning was done electronically.

Zworykin's original patent application No. 683,337, filed on December 29, 1923, pertained to an Iconoscope. However, it went through some years of interference proceedings and the important patent No. 2,141,059, based on his fundamental work, was issued on December 20, 1938. His patent No. 1,691,324, issued on November 13, 1928, had to do principally with color television. It had been filed July 13, 1925.

Zworykin joined the RCA Manufacturing Company at Camden,

New Jersey, in 1930 and became a member of the RCA research staff; later, an associate research director of RCA Laboratories at Princeton, New Jersey.

One who saw Zworykin flash television pictures on a miniature screen in 1932 said, "This is not merely a step forward in television. It goes over the wall that has stopped all experimenters. Television is here!"

What I have done in ten years of research is to emulate the human eye electronically [explained Zworykin]. Ten years ago I decided to find a parallel in nature and follow it until I came to television. The new "eye" is so sensitive that it sees the entire picture at once just like man's eye. In fact, it has "electrical memory." For example, look at something and shut the eyes. You imagine you see the scene; that is persistence of vision. The Iconoscope, because of a capacity effect on its "retina" also holds the scene for a second or two.

The electric retina is a mica plate having a metalized back. The mica is covered with millions of globules of light-sensitive material. There is an electron beam or "paint brush" regulated by a "gun" that plays upon the retina or fluorescent screen. That beam is what I call the optic nerve of television. It's all so simple!

What after television? Zworykin undertook the design of a practical electron microscope which he and the research staff of RCA Laboratories developed to permit magnifications up to 100,000 diameters—from 50 to 100 times more powerful than the strongest optical microscope. Appraised by scientists as an epochal development and a potential source of new knowledge, the electron microscope opened hitherto unseen worlds for observation by bacteriologists, chemists, physicists, metallurgists and others.

Using electrons instead of light rays, and magnetic or electrostatic fields to focus the electrons in place of glass lenses used for focusing light rays, the electron microscope enables man to peer deeply into the submicroscope world. For the first time it showed how disease-fighting organisms in the blood, known as anti-bodies, attack disease-producing virus introduced in a living animal. It made possible photographing of the influenza virus. A blood corpuscle on such a scale of magnification would appear as large as a two-foot sofa pillow; a dime thus magnified would look more than a mile wide; a human hair as large as a California redwood tree; and the windpipe of a mosquito, a giant spiral.

From the microscope Zworykin turned to the development of an electron-scanning microscope, to a diffraction camera, an electronic clock and electronic calculating devices. If ever a man opened new worlds of vision, he is Zworykin. In recognition of his research and inventions, in 1934 he was awarded the Morris Liebmann Memorial Prize by the Institute of Radio Engineers; an honorary degree of Doctor of Science by the Brooklyn Polytechnic Institute in 1937; the National Modern Pioneers Award from the National Association of Manufacturers in 1940; the Rumford Award of the American Academy of Arts and Sciences in 1941.

His modesty and good sense of humor, coupled with the simplicity of his approach to greatness, add to his stature and make knowing him a delight to his friends.

During the Second World War, while operating their automobiles on the share-a-ride basis, Zworykin and a group of fellow research workers were driving to work. Delayed en route by a flat tire, they knew they would reach the laboratory late. Zworykin impatiently looked at his watch again and again. Finally when the hands were at 8:30, the usual time to begin work, Zworykin, resigning himself to the predicament, slipped his watch back into his pocket, tilted his head back on the seat, closed his eyes and quietly said, "Well, gentlemen, let's go to work." He didn't have to be at the desk or workbench to work; his laboratory was his brain. Thinking was a major part of his work.

"What do you dream about—electrons and all sorts of new electronic wonders?" he was asked by a reporter who was prodding for a good lead for a story.

"I sleep soundly," replied Zworykin with a broad smile.

John Vincent Lawless Hogan

INVENTED A UNI-CONTROL TUNER

BORN: February 14, 1890
Bayonne, N.J.

JOHN VINCENT LAWLESS HOGAN, electrical and radio engineer, as a boy in 1902 at Bayonne, New Jersey, built one of the early amateur wireless stations using the coherer as a detector. Intensely interested in the new science, he took the opportunity for seven months during 1906 and 1907 to work as a laboratory assistant to Dr. Lee De Forest, experimenting with the audion and radiophone. When De Forest made the first grid audion it fell to Hogan to make the first quantitative study of the plate current characteristic of a grid triode.

Fascinated by wireless, Hogan attended Sheffield Scientific School at Yale University, 1908-10, specializing in physics, mathematics and electric waves. From 1910 to 1914 he served as telegraph engineer of the National Electric Signaling Company, both at Brant Rock, Massachusetts, and in Brooklyn, where he supervised erection of the Bush Terminal station. In 1912 he was instrumental in the formation of the Institute of Radio Engineers (by consolidating the Society of Wireless Telegraph Engineers with the Wireless Institute). In 1913 he had charge of the acceptance tests of the United States Navy's first high-powered station at Arlington, and became chief research engineer, 1914-17, with his work largely confined to development of automatic high-speed recorders for long-distance wireless. In his laboratory at Bush Terminal, he made what were perhaps the first ink tape syphon records of transatlantic radio signals, using an audion amplifier.

Appointed commercial manager of the International Signal Company in 1917, Hogan was put in charge of operations and manufacturing, with emphasis on radio outfits for submarine chasers and aircraft. In 1918 he was made manager of the International Radio Telegraph Company; and in 1920, was elected president of the Institute of Radio Engineers.

As engineer of the National Electric Signaling Company, Hogan had worked under Fessenden at the Brant Rock station, and his first patent, on a crystal detector, was issued in 1910. One of his interesting discoveries during the early days at Brant Rock was the "rectifier heterodyne." His associate, J. W. Lee, had observed some peculiar effects when a special transmitter was being operated while the station was receiving messages. Referring back to some of his work at Yale, Hogan analyzed the phenomena with the result that he succeeded in multiplying the sensitiveness of the radio receivers literally a hundred or more times. His work in this connection was described before the Institute of Radio Engineers in 1913.

In 1912 he patented a single-dial tuning system for radio receivers, an invention worked out to simplify and co-ordinate the handling of ship-and-shore messages. It was his good fate to capitalize upon it when home-broadcast reception called for a simple, one-control tuner. The advent of broadcasting and its development inspired Hogan to write many scientific articles for the technical press as well as a book, *The Outline of Radio,* published in 1923.

Establishing his own consulting practice in 1921, he specialized in broadcasting apparatus and "problems of radio regulation"; in 1928 he added facsimile and television to his laboratory work. As a crusader for tonal quality and realism in broadcasting, he built station WQXR as New York's first high-fidelity station, and was among the first to operate an FM station in New York.

Hogan discovered by accident the existence of a public demand for quality music, while experimenting with a high-fidelity transmitter licensed in 1934 as W2XR. Aiming to reproduce radio at the receiver as faithful to the original as possible, his tests featured classical and semi-classical music, mostly played from recordings. To his surprise, the mail revealed thousands of listeners in the New York area applauding not only the station's wide range of tone but the musical programs. As a result, the 250-watt W2XR, key station of the Interstate Broadcasting Company organized by Hogan in 1936, became a commercial station under the call WQXR, with 10,000 watts of power and a reputation based upon Beethoven, Brahms and Bach.

George Clark Southworth

GUIDED WAVES THROUGH PIPES

BORN: August 24, 1890
  Little Cooley, Pa.

GEORGE C. SOUTHWORTH, a research engineer, is best known for his early work on the transmission of electromagnetic waves through hollow metal pipes and dielectric wires. Particularly important is the new technique for dealing with microwaves based on the principles which he and his associates evolved.

He received his grammar-school education in a local country school and high school in a near-by village in accordance with the usual rural pattern. He became interested in wireless in 1915, while at Grove City College where Dr. H. W. Harmon, professor of physics, had set up a station with an audion as a new and distinctive feature of the receiving set. As one of his first papers on the subject of radio, Southworth prepared a thesis on the construction of the station. His degrees of B.S. and M.S. from Grove City College in 1914 and 1916, and Sc.D. from his alma mater in 1931, are symbols of his interest in science. From Yale he received a Ph.D. in 1923.

After a year or more at the Bureau of Standards, Southworth went to Yale in 1918 as instructor in physics. There he did some of the earliest work directed at the practical utilization of ultra-short waves. Both speech and telegraph signals were transmitted on waves between one and two meters in length, using a parabola as the antenna. This was demonstrated at Camp Alfred Vail (Fort Monmouth) in January, 1921. He entered the Bell system in 1923. His first job was on the newly established *Bell System Technical Journal*. Later he was assigned to various problems relating to transoceanic radiotelephony followed by microwave researches. His activities were not always confined to microwaves, as indicated by various papers he published on skip-distances and other peculiarities of short waves, the best proportions for antenna arrays, and the nature of earth currents. He was a member of the International Radio Telegraph Conference held in Washington in 1927, and on a number of occasions lectured at various universities.

Southworth's ultra-short-wave researches at Yale were the forerunners of his guided-wave experiments for which the Institute of Radio Engineers in 1938 awarded him the Morris Liebmann Memorial Prize. The citation read: "For his theoretical and experimental investigation of the propagation of ultra-high frequency waves through confined dielectric channels and the development of a technique for the generation and measurement of such waves."[1]

Previously there had been two common methods by which ultra-high-frequency power might be propagated from one point to another. One was by its projection as ordinary radio waves, and the other by the usual wire-line, one form of which was the coaxial cable. Radio, as ordinarily used, wasted energy because of the lack of directivity. The coaxial cable entailed substantial line attenuations, caused chiefly by losses in the central conductor and in the insulators supporting the conductors, especially when the highest frequencies were attempted. Southworth's contribution was the use of a little-understood wave, so that the central conductor and its associated insulators could, in effect, be removed. It then became possible to reduce by a factor of five, or even more, the power that might otherwise be dissipated. The resulting structure, which often takes the form of a hollow metal pipe, is generally known as a wave-guide.

In 1938 and again in 1939 Southworth delivered several interest-

---

[1] W. L. Barrow was awarded the 1943 Morris Liebmann Memorial Prize by the Institute of Radio Engineers "for his theoretical and experimental investigations of ultra-high frequency propagation in wave guides and radiation from horns, and the application of these principles to engineering practices."

ing lectures before the Institute of Radio Engineers consisting of a series of experiments each of which revealed, in a very concrete way, some important principles of wave-guide transmission. As a result of these experiments, it became apparent that he had evolved a radically new transmitting medium different from ordinary radiation from an aerial and from the ordinary transmission line. What was even more important, he had developed a new technique for dealing with microwaves which could be applied either to the transmission of program material through pipes or to its projection cross-country by radio.

Commenting on the progress made by radio and also its trend toward higher and higher frequencies, Southworth said:

It also happens that as we pass to the higher frequencies (shorter waves) it becomes feasible to build radio antennas of increasingly higher directivity, thereby conserving a very substantial amount of the power that is ordinarily wasted. Although these very short waves have definite limitations as regards transmission to points far beyond the horizon, it is not impossible that for point-to-point work these limitations can be overcome, at least in part, by transmitting cross-country from one tower top to another.

As contrasted with this still speculative use of radio there is another equally good prospect that a very special kind of line can be devised that will guide these same waves, rather efficiently, from one point to another, possibly over the horizon, and do this with relative immunity from interference and atmospheric noise. It is still too early to appraise completely the merits of these two schemes but it is probable that here, as elsewhere in the frequency spectrum, radio and the transmission line will each have its own peculiar field of usefulness and the two together will be mutually complimentary in accomplishing a useful result.

Somewhere along the frequency scale in the neighborhood of a billion cycles per second—wavelength about one foot—microwave technic undergoes a marked change. Methods using the conventional go-and-return-conductor type of circuit give way to the somewhat simpler hollow pipe, or wave-guide circuit. These newer methods seem to be at their best in the centimeter wavelength range. At the longer wavelengths, the component parts become inconveniently large. For shorter waves, it would appear that ability to manufacture small parts would become an important limitation. What the technic will be beyond this point, is a matter for the future.

Pointing to "somewhere above 1,000 megacycles as an indefinite but nevertheless real frontier," toward which the engineer has been gradually working since becoming interested in radio, Southworth pictured him as a kind of homesteader recently arrived in a new and strange region.

Although thoroughly explored by physicists many years ago this new territory, beyond the ultra-short waves, has been as yet only crudely charted and but partially surveyed as to natural resources. The engineer-homesteader is plowing primeval sod to plant new seeds that he hopes will place the air over countryside on a more productive basis. It would appear, that in this region *beyond the ultra-short waves* there will be interesting variety both in the principles and methods of engineering toward which the homesteader as usual will look with high hopes.[2]

Edwin Howard Armstrong

INVENTOR OF REVOLUTIONARY RADIO CIRCUITS

BORN: December 18, 1890
  New York City

EDWIN HOWARD ARMSTRONG, American electrical and radio engineer, specialized in development of radio circuits, which made for revolutionary advances in the art.

As a boy, Armstrong first attracted attention with his pioneer amateur wireless station at Yonkers, New York, and became widely known in amateur circles as early as 1906. He was graduated from Columbia University in 1913 with the degree of E.E.; the honorary degree Doctor of Science was conferred upon him by C 'umbia in 1929, and the same degree was awarded him from Muhlenberg College in 1941. At Columbia he had studied under Dr. Michael I. Pupin, who encouraged his activities in wireless and became a lifelong friend. After Pupin's death in 1935, Armstrong became professor of electrical engineering at Columbia.

[2] At a joint meeting of the Institute of Radio Engineers and the American Institute of Electrical Engineers, January 28, 1943.

Recounting the story of Armstrong's achievements, Professor Alan Hazeltine[1] first called attention to the fact that the one development in electrical technology which stood out from all others during the past twenty-five years was electronics, and specifically the application of the three-electrode vacuum tube.

Said Professor Hazeltine:

> The real foundation for the unlimited development which we have witnessed was laid by the Edison Medal recipient, Dr. Edwin Howard Armstrong, in an article published in the *Electrical World* in December, 1914. Here the common engineering tool, the characteristic curve, was employed for the first time to show how the tube amplifies; and the theory was substantiated by oscillograms which Armstrong had taken. The previously mysterious action of the tube as a rectifying detector with a good capacitator was illustrated in the same way.

Hazeltine said that he well remembered the impression this article made upon him, and the conviction that it contained some great possibilities. He recalled the excitement produced a few months later by Armstrong's first paper before the Institute of Radio Engineers, on his feed-back circuit, which employed this theory to give undreamed-of amplification of weak radio signals and promoted the general use of heterodyne reception by proving for the first time a source of continuous oscillation of frequencies as high as any then used for radio transmission.

> It is rather hard now to take ourselves back to conditions in radio prior to Armstrong [continued Hazeltine]. Attempts were being made at transoceanic telegraph communication, but with only very restricted success, even with enormous receiving antennas and elaborate commercial apparatus. The radio amateurs, who shortly were to be the mainstay of Signal Corps and Navy radio in World War I and were later to supply the radio engineering talent called out by broadcasting, could receive only local signals. Armstrong's work removed the barrier to regular long-distance radio telegraphy. By increases in power of the vacuum tubes, it also provided an easily modulated high-frequency source for radiotelephone transmitting, so that long-distance radiotelephony soon followed. And then came the great broadcasting development with its far-reaching social consequences.

[1] Speaking at the presentation to Armstrong of the Edison Medal (1942) of the American Institute of Electrical Engineers, January 27, 1943.

The early work of Armstrong, the experimental part of which was done while he was still an undergraduate at Columbia University, soon received recognition. Its importance was appreciated by Professor Pupin, who took Armstrong under his wing. Together they carried on several researches in radio. In 1917 the Institute of Radio Engineers awarded its Medal of Honor to Armstrong for the feed-back circuit, the presentation being made by Professor Pupin, then president of that society. I recall a remark of Professor Pupin on that occasion: that inventions are sometimes ascribed to luck, but that the best luck is to have a good head on one's shoulders! The correctness of Pupin's appraisal has been demonstrated amply by Armstrong's subsequent career.

Hazeltine recalled how Armstrong paved the way for his next important invention—the superheterodyne receiver—by clarifying the matter of heterodyne reception in a paper presented to the I.R.E. in 1916. Armstrong, using the vacuum-tube oscillator, changed the incoming wave frequency to a lower intermediate frequency by heterodyne action. That is, he made use of the fact that when two high frequency waves interact, they produce a lower frequency wave. This wave has a frequency equal to the difference of the frequencies of its parent waves. He then carried out further amplification at this intermediate frequency, thereby gaining additional receiver sensitivity and signal strength. He developed this method for military purposes during World War I while he was an officer in the Signal Corps in France. Now the superheterodyne is employed almost universally in radio reception.

Armstrong never abandoned his first love, radio [said Hazeltine]. After the war, he returned to his laboratory researches at Columbia; and here, in an experimental set-up for another purpose, he happened to notice an extraordinary amplification of a locally generated signal. Ninety-nine out of one hundred experimenters would have failed either to notice the effect or to find its cause. But Armstrong's characteristic persistence and ability to analyze physical phenomena tracked down the demon; and super-regeneration was added to the radio art. Although it was not of such wide utility as Dr. Armstrong's other fundamental inventions, it was found essential in pioneer work at ultra-high frequencies and now is applied to certain military purposes.

By this time, we were in the era of broadcasting. Some of the best analytical brains had been directed to the theory of radio. It seemed that all the foundations had been laid, that no new fundamental methods were to be anticipated. Frequency modulation had been considered, used to some extent, and then discarded. The fallacy of using it to narrow the band of transmitted frequencies had been exposed. It was rejected as useless and even harmful. But Armstrong had other ideas. By going contrary to accepted notions and greatly widening the range of frequency variation, he developed a system of frequency modulation ideally suited to broadcasting, which was announced in 1936. Although facing the tremendous handicap of an established broadcasting system, with thousands of transmitting stations and many millions of receivers in use, none of which could employ it, it already seems destined largely to supplant the conventional amplitude modulation.

Armstrong's contributions to the advance of the radio art are reflected in the honors and medals bestowed upon him: the first Medal of Honor of the Institute of Radio Engineers, 1917; Chevalier de la Légion d'Honneur, 1919; the Egleston Medal of Columbia University School of Engineering, 1939; the Holley Medal of the American Society of Mechanical Engineers, 1940; the Franklin Medal of Franklin Institute, 1941; the John Scott Medal of the City of Philadelphia, 1942; the Edison Medal of the American Institute of Electrical Engineers, 1942. The citation of the National Association of Manufacturers in selecting Armstrong as one of the National Modern Pioneers in 1940 read:

First to make use of the 3-electrode tube for generating continuous electric waves which made radio broadcasting feasible, inventor of the long and widely used superheterodyne receiving circuit, and inventor of the new broadcasting by frequency modulation that so well avoids static as almost to defy the lightning. He is one of the leaders in accomplishing the miracle of radio communication, a reality so inconceivably novel that the imagination of no poet, no author of tales or fables, had ever anticipated it.

Armstrong was among the first recipients of the Chief Signal Officer's Certificate of Appreciation, announced by Major General H. C. Ingles, Chief Signal Officer, on June 1, 1944. The citation read:

For loyal and patriotic services rendered the Signal Corps of the Army of the United States in the accomplishment of its vital mission during a period of national emergency.

Ralph Bown

SPECIALIST IN OVERSEAS RADIOTELEPHONY

BORN: February 22, 1891
Fairport, New York

RALPH BOWN, physicist and electrical engineer, was graduated from Cornell University with an M.E. degree in 1913. Following this, he spent four years in the Department of Physics at Cornell as instructor and graduate student, receiving his M.M.E. in 1915 and his Ph.D. in 1917. It was during this period that he became interested in radio and conducted investigations on vacuum-tube detectors. At the outbreak of the First World War he joined the United States Army Signal Corps, Radio Division, as a lieutenant, and later became a captain in charge of the radio development work at the Signal Corps Radio Laboratories at Camp Alfred Vail, New Jersey. While there, he participated in early experiments in communication between aircraft and ground by radiotelephone.

Upon discharge from the Army, he joined the Department of Development and Research of the American Telephone and Telegraph Company, and engaged in the radio development activities of that company from 1919 to 1934. His work in these years covered the fields of broadcasting and ship-to-shore and overseas radiotelephony.

In 1927 Bown was elected president of the Institute of Radio Engineers, and that year received the Liebmann Memorial Prize "for his researches in wave transmission phenomena." In 1934 he was appointed associate director of radio research of the Bell Telephone

Laboratóries, and in 1937 became director of radio and television research.

Throughout the period of his radio work in the Bell System, one of Bown's main interests centered on the development of the transmission side of radio engineering in a quantitative way. In the earlier phases of this work he took an active personal part, and in collaboration with associates published a number of papers describing their pioneering studies in this field.

Bown directed the engineering group at the Bell Telephone Laboratories which developed the overseas long- and short-wave radiotelephone services of the Bell System, single side-band radiotelephony, the rhombic antenna, wave-guides, ultra-high-frequency apparatus and "Musa," synthesized from the initial letters of the descriptive words, "multiple unit steerable antenna." Ten years had passed since the opening for public use of the transatlantic radiophone circuit in January, 1927, when Bown, in reviewing a decade of progress, went before the Institute of Radio Engineers in June, 1937, to describe the "Musa" system as used in transoceanic radiotelephony. Designed to remedy fading and distortion in short-wave reception, the "Musa" was described as providing extremely sharp directivity in the vertical plane.

"It consists of a number of rhombic antennas stretched out in a line toward the transmitter and connected by individual coaxial lines to the receiving apparatus," Bown explained. "The apparatus is adjustable so that the vertical angle of reception can be aimed or 'steered' to select any desired component from the others, as a telescope is elevated to pick out a star. The antennas remain mechanically fixed. The steering is done electrically with phase shifters in the receiving set."

During the Second World War Dr. Bown served as a division member and consultant of the National Defense Research Committee, and in the summer of 1942, he served as expert consultant to the Secretary of War.

Robert Alexander Watson-Watt

BRITAIN'S HERO IN RADIO-LOCATION

BORN: April 13, 1892
Brechin, Scotland

ROBERT A. WATSON-WATT was knighted on King George VI's birthday in 1942 identified merely as "a pioneer in radio location." Later, as war restrictions were lifted slightly, he was credited as "the British scientist who had the leading scientific part" in England's development of the aerial watchdog, known in the United States as radar, and credited equally with RAF in winning the Battle of Britain.

Sir Robert was a lecturer in physics at University College, Dundee, Scotland. He attended University College and the University of St. Andrews before embarking on a career in meteorology and electrical engineering. These two forces—weather and electricity—led him in 1933 to announce a system of determining location of thunderstorms hundreds of miles away by analyzing atmospheric disturbances. Then he took up radio echo experiments. This work culminated in development of radio-location, or spotting of objects in the air.

He was meteorologist in charge of the Royal Aircraft Establishment from 1917 to 1921; superintendent of the radio research stations of the Department of Scientific and Industrial Research from 1921 to 1933; and superintendent of the radio department of the National Physical Laboratory from 1933 to 1936. During the war he was scientific adviser to the Air Ministry on Telecommunications and vice-controller of communications equipment for the Ministry of Aircraft Production.

Beginning in 1919, he received a series of patents on mechanical radio direction finders, and in 1935 he began his major research in airplane radio-location. With his wife, Lady Margaret Robertson Watt, as his principal assistant, he established his laboratory in a

256

hut and on a truck along a lonely road near the Daventry overseas short-wave transmitting headquarters of the British Broadcasting Corporation. He worked seven days a week, as is his habit when tackling an important problem.

Little was written and less was spoken about radar until the spring of 1943, when it was revealed in dispatches from London that this key device of offense and defense had played a mighty role during 1940-41 in saving the British Isles from a knockout by the Luftwaffe.

The Germans, continually encountering concentrated RAF fighter opposition, gained the false impression that Great Britain had a tremendous number of fighting planes. The British actually were woefully weak compared to their later aircraft strength. Had they been forced to keep fighting patrols in the sky, spreading planes over a wide area, observers said that they never would have been able to counter the German bomber thrusts so successfully. Through radio-location, the fighter command was able to conserve its power and throw what limited strength was available into a hard-smashing defense that eventually knocked the Nazis out of British skies.

Harold Henry Beverage

EXPLORER OF THE WAVELENGTHS

BORN: *October 14, 1893*
North Haven, Maine

HAROLD HENRY BEVERAGE, radio engineer, through the introduction of new antenna designs and investigations of the behavior of electromagnetic waves contributed much to the advance and dependability of world-wide radio communication. He explored in space and helped to conquer forces of Nature such as static and fading that hindered radio reception.

As a boy in Maine, Beverage became interested in wireless and with his home-made set picked up signals from the S.S. *Carpathia*, rescue ship that rushed to the scene of the *Titanic* disaster. Wireless led him to study electrical engineering, and he graduated in 1915 from the University of Maine with a B.S. degree. His first job was that of testman for the General Electric Company at Schenectady, New York, but in 1916 he was transferred to the radio laboratory of Dr. E. F. W. Alexanderson, who was busy trying to improve reception to and from the AEF in France. As a result, Alexanderson developed the "barrage receiver," on which Beverage had been assigned to assist. It was tested at the transatlantic station at New Brunswick, New Jersey, and at the naval radio station NBD, Otter Cliffs, Bar Harbor, Maine, where Beverage installed two of the receivers and laid the long antenna wires through the woods on Mount Desert Island.

While at New Brunswick during the First World War, Beverage assisted in development of a modulator so that the Alexanderson alternator could be used for voice broadcasting. Later, when it was decided to put a radiophone on the U.S.S. *George Washington*, the presidential ship to the Peace Conference, Beverage was one of the engineers assigned to install the equipment.

He was on board the *Washington* on July 4, 1919, when President Wilson addressed the crew, and it was decided to attempt to send his speech ashore to be intercepted at Otter Cliffs for relay over a telephone line to the White House. When the idea was suggested to Dr. Cary T. Grayson, the President's physician, he said the microphone would disturb the President, so it was hidden behind a flag. But when the President came out on the deck to speak he was about twenty feet from the microphone and stood with his back to it, so the pick-up was weak. Only near-by ships heard a word now and then. The experiment is remembered as "the voice that failed," although it marked the first attempt to broadcast the voice of a President of the United States.

In the fall of 1919, Beverage was sent to Long Island to study methods of receiving signals from South America utilizing long wires similar to those used on the "barrage receiver." He noticed that with the longer wires, directivity was very pronounced. By use of a receiver along the wire, he discovered that the signals built up stronger and stronger. To explore the effect, a wire was stretched alongside a road running from Riverhead to Eastport, which was almost straight in a northeast-southwest direction, for a distance of about nine miles. Using this antenna, Beverage found that the signals from Europe increased over a distance of four or five miles and then began to decrease. It was also found that static would decrease under certain conditions when the northeast end of the wire was grounded. From a study of the results of these experiments, Beverage developed the theory of how the antenna worked and Philip S. Carter[1] made a complete mathematical analysis to confirm the theory. In 1920 a full-size antenna on poles was erected for further studies. From this work evolved the "wave antenna," destined to become the standard for long-wave receiving not only in the United States but also in other countries. For this invention Beverage received his first patent on June 7, 1921.

At the end of 1921, as a member of the engineering staff of the Radio Corporation of America, Beverage, accompanied by Noel Rust of the Marconi Wireless Telegraph Company, Ltd., went to Brazil to study reception conditions. One night he was making measurements on signals from Cavite in the Philippine Islands when he discovered by means of a direction finder that the signals were coming from both the west and the east—they were arriving around the world from both directions simultaneously.

During 1923 Beverage and his associates concentrated on exploration of the short-wave spectrum—100 meters and below. Marconi at the time was conducting extensive tests from his floating laboratory, the yacht *Elettra*, and in 1925 Beverage checked the reception on this side of the Atlantic.

[1] Born July 22, 1896, Glastonbury, Conn., graduated from Stanford University, A.B. in Mechanical Engineering, 1918, Carter joined the GE staff in 1919 after service in the Signal Corps, and in 1920 transferred to RCA. In 1927 he joined the Transmitter Laboratory group at Rocky Point specializing in directive antenna and transmission-line problems. He has been issued more than fifty United States patents.

One day he and his associate, H. O. Peterson, by comparing signals over a town telephone line noticed that signals received at Peterson's home faded differently from those intercepted at the radio station, although the two points were only a half-mile apart. To learn the cause, they experimented and found that even receivers working with antennas separated by only a few hundred feet also faded differently. The same was true with antennas located at the same place but with different polarization. As a result of these observations, the RCA diversity receiving system was developed.

During the period of this pioneering work, that is, from 1920, when Beverage was first employed by the Radio Corporation of America, to 1929, he was in charge of development of RCA's transoceanic receiving systems. In 1929, when RCA Communications, Inc. was formed, Beverage became chief research engineer. Laboratories were established at Riverhead, Long Island, on reception; Rocky Point, Long Island, on transmitters; and 66 Broad Street, New York City, for terminal facilities equipment. Beverage continued in this position until December, 1940, when he was made vice president in charge of research and development. The Research Department of RCA Communications was expanded and in addition to developing complete commercial transmitting and receiving equipment, automatic printers and multiplex, a great deal of work was done on radio relaying for communications and for television, including special antennas for television. Also an ultra-short-wave system was developed for the Mutual Telephone Company of Hawaii to connect the islands of Oahu, Hawaii, Maui and Kauai.

The Institute of Radio Engineers presented the Morris Liebmann Memorial Prize to Beverage in 1923 and elected him president for 1937. From the University of Maine he received the honorary degree of Doctor of Engineering in 1938. Appointed director of communications research of RCA Laboratories on January 1, 1941, he had thirty-eight issued United States patents to his credit. In this position he directed the work of some of the most able communication research men and engineers in the radio field.[2] Many of them were inventors who contributed to the advance of the art on the domestic as well as the international wavelengths as related to all branches of radio, including facsimile, frequency modulation and television.

In World War II, Beverage was on the job, handling work that fell within the realm of military secrecy. As temporary consultant for the War Department on radio communications, he received high commendation from Major General H. C. Ingles, chief signal officer of the Army: "Please accept my sincere appreciation for this and the many other outstanding services you have rendered the Army in the communications field."

Since the First World War Beverage had learned much about "the ether" and about antennas, wavelengths long and ultra-short; he would be the last one to say that there was nothing more to learn after such a long and useful career in radio.

Beverage was awarded the United States Army Signal Corps Certificate of Appreciation with this citation:[3]

Your tireless effort and valuable advice during the installation of a radio-teletype circuit in the North Atlantic Route constituted a great contribution to the Signal Corps in its gigantic task of furnishing the United States Army the world's greatest military communications system.

Irving Wolff

A PIONEER IN RADAR

BORN: *July 6, 1894*
New York City

IRVING WOLFF, research specialist in ultra-high frequencies, attended the Ethical Culture School in New York and then went to Dartmouth

[2] H. O. Peterson, C. W. Hansell, Nils E. Lindenblad, George L. Usselman, Murray G. Crosby, Philip S. Carter, J. L. Finch, J. L. Callahan, O. E. Dow, H. E. Goldstine, G. S. Wickizer, R. E. Mathes, B. A. Trevor, R. W. George, A. M. Braaten, J. Ernest Smith and Alfred Kahn.
[3] June 19, 1944.

to major in physics. He was graduated with the degree B.S. in 1916. During the winter of 1919-20 he was physics instructor at Iowa State College, but he left in 1920 to take graduate work at Cornell University where he was also physics instructor until 1923, when he attained his Ph.D. For the next year he conducted research under a Heckscher Research Fellowship at Cornell University.

Shortly after joining RCA Laboratories in 1928, Wolff developed the first beat-frequency audio signal generator, and with Abraham Ringel evolved new methods of loud-speaker testing. He co-operated in the development of what turned out to be the most widely used magnetic loud-speaker of the twenties. Engineers under his direction developed some of the first loud-speaker units installed in sound-motion-picture studios, the velocity microphone and the volume-compensated gain control used in many radio sets.

In the early 1930's, Wolff's interest shifted to the development of fundamental equipment for producing microwaves. As one application he began radio reflection work in 1934, and shortly after that his own activities and those of the group associated with him were almost entirely concentrated in this field of communication.

The military applications of radio detecting and ranging prevented publication of the results in technical literature. While many research workers and engineers participated in the development of radar by contributing integral parts, it may be stated that much of the apparatus developed by the group associated with Wolff found important military use, and that many of the possibilities of radar were first demonstrated by him and his associates in RCA Laboratories.

During 1937 operating equipment was completed and tested, indicating the distance and position of reflecting objects. These developments had grown to such importance to the military services during 1937 that RCA was requested to put all of this work on a secret basis.

It is part of the historic record that probably the first application of radar principles to aviation was achieved by RCA through equipment built and installed in its own plane in 1937, in connection with research on collision-prevention apparatus. Many flights were made testing this apparatus during 1938 and 1939, showing the effectiveness in warning of collision between aircraft, or between planes and mountains, or other obstacles. This equipment not only determined the altitude with accuracy but was found able to detect objects ahead at a sufficient distance to warn of an impending crash.

Under the direct supervision of Wolff, the radar work in RCA Laboratories continued and expanded. The research men knew that it would help to win the war and save many lives in peacetime through applications to marine and aerial navigation and possibly on railroads and highways.

Nils Erik Lindenblad

DESIGNER OF ANTENNAS

BORN: *October 30, 1895*
      Norrköping, Sweden

NILS E. LINDENBLAD, as specialist in radio-transmitting antennas, helped radio hit its stride in communication on both long and short waves. When Marconi won the Nobel prize in 1909, he became Lindenblad's hero; twenty-two years later the two men met and compared notes at RCA's "Radio Central" at Rocky Point, Long Island.

After four years in public schools and five years in high school, young Lindenblad worked a year at the Norrköping Public Service, 1911-12, while attending evening school at Norrköping Polytechnic Institute. He continued in the day school and was graduated as mechanical engineer in 1915. Complying with the compulsory military service program of that time, he spent a year in the Swedish Signal Corps, after which he attended the Royal Institute of Technology in Stockholm, 1916-19, studying electrical engineering.

Being fatherless from a tender age, he found that student years were not smooth, and obtained a part-time job in the laboratory of the Swedish Gasaccumulator Company during 1918. Beginning with 1919, he joined as a co-inventor in the formation of a marine radio manufacturing venture. All radio activity in Sweden at that time was controlled and supervised by the Government Telegraph Administration. Thus, while the equipment was approved as an engineering success, the commercial doors were closed for the next five years owing to legislation and airtight contracts between the Telegraph Administration and foreign radio manufacturers. Subsisting on the manufacture of equipment for locating iron ore deposits, the company was eventually dissolved and its members scattered.

Lindenblad arrived in the United States in October, 1919, with two inventions and a poor vocabulary; one invention concerned projection of three-dimensional pictures, and the other was a water-cooled vacuum tube, but nobody seemed interested. Procuring a job as a draftsman with the General Electric Company at Schenectady in February, 1920, was, as he described it, "really the beginning anew of existence." In September of the same year he was transferred to Alexanderson's staff of the newly formed Radio Corporation of America. Transmitting aerials, one of radio's most neglected items in those days, became his specialty. Foundations of engineering calculation and design methods had to be laid.

As early as 1923, Lindenblad had proved the practicability of placing transmitter and aerial far apart and connecting them by means of ordinary two-wire transmission lines, which became a necessity in the new short-wave art.

Assigned to the task of developing short-wave beam aerials, he produced the multiple-point loaded transmission line in 1926 by means of which the aerial elements in an array could be fed in phase through a common line. This method resulted in great reductions of cost. By 1928 Lindenblad had made one of his major contributions to the art by demonstrating that wires, each having a length of several waves, could be combined in extremely simple and inexpensive arrays to form excellent beam patterns. This work resulted in a universally accepted technique in beam aerial design.

In 1929 Lindenblad began a study of methods for generating ultra-short waves. In 1931 he found that lower frequencies could be multiplied efficiently in triodes subjected to axial magnetic fields. In this way he was able to generate 115 watts between 400 and 500 megacycles. This was a world's record. With this power he signaled to an airplane up to a distance of 172 miles. Signals to fixed points were well received at distances over 100 miles. Duplex telephony across 15 miles was established with a 10-watt transmitter. This work showed what could be done with very short waves and stimulated efforts to produce suitable circuits. By 1936 the American radio industry had reached a point where the possibilities shown by the early pioneering work could begin to be utilized.

In the meantime, television had made great strides. With increased picture definition it was necessary to operate television in the ultra-short wave spectrum. Conventional transmitting aerials could not be used; new types were needed to avoid shadow or "ghost" effects caused by optical radiation.

Lindenblad found in 1936 that a triangular array in which the dipoles were fed at their ends would give a band width just enough to pass a 348-line picture. Such an aerial was erected by RCA atop the Empire State Building. The television crew, encouraged by initial success, decided to go one better and aim for a 441-line picture. This time the aerial problem became serious. After considerable experimentation, Lindenblad came upon the idea that solved the problem. Following his specifications, an aerial was built and installed on top of the Empire State Building in 1938. Its band width was 50 per cent, or about fifteen times that of what previously had been considered possible.

With 167 inventions to his credit and 88 patents, Nils Lindenblad has proved himself to be a modern pioneer in exploration of the "ether," and one of radio's outstanding Norsemen.

"I am a Maxwellian," said Lindenblad, "and as such behold the electric, magnetic and gravitational fields as the original manifestations of creation. The 'particles of matter' are to me simply oddities at the converging points of the infinite fields of which they have become the center. Only the transverse aspects can be observed and utilized by man. The longitudinal aspects of the fundamental fields remain God's secret forever."

Stuart Ballantine

RADIO PHYSICIST AND INVENTOR

BORN: September 22, 1897 *DIED: May 7, 1944*
Germantown, Pa. *Morristown, N. J.*

STUART BALLANTINE, physicist specializing in radio, became interested in wireless in 1908 while attending public school in Philadelphia. During the summers of 1913 to 1916 he served as radio operator with the Marconi Company. Other features of his career were: consultant to the Radio Apparatus Company, Pottstown, Pennsylvania; research worker in the laboratory of H. K. Mulfurd Company, bacteriologists, 1916; engineer with the Bell Telephone Company of Pennsylvania, 1917. He studied mathematics at Drexel Institute in 1917 and took up mathematical physics in the Graduate School, Harvard University, 1920-21, 1923-24. He was elected John Tyndall Fellow in Physics, Harvard, 1923.

During the First World War, Ballantine served as expert radio aide, United States Navy, from 1917 to 1920 at the Philadelphia Navy Yard, in charge of development of the Navy coil-type radio compass. During this period he made several important contributions to the direction-finding art, among which was a "compensator" to control the "antenna effect" which resulted in a considerable increase in the sharpness and accuracy of observation. This device is still in extensive use. For his work in radio-direction finding he received a special award and citation in 1921 from the Secretary of the Navy.

In 1922 Ballantine joined L. M. Hull in the newly established Radio Frequency Laboratories at Boonton, New Jersey. Several of his inventions were incorporated in broadcast receiver designs which were licensed by the Laboratories to a number of radio manufacturers. Among them was a method of neutralizing radio-frequency amplifiers which employed the Wheatstone bridge principle. He was granted about fifteen patents on these circuits as well as on the "crossed condenser" method of neutralization universally used in push-pull transmitter circuits employing triodes. Among other developments of his origination during this period were linear detection and delayed automatic volume control incorporated in most radio receivers. In 1923 he developed the principle of negative feed-back to stabilize and reduce distortion in transmission circuits, modulators, amplifiers and detectors, described in United States Patent No. 18,835. This patent also described automatic volume control.

From 1924 to 1927 Ballantine engaged in private research, collaborating with E. H. Funk, M.D., and H. R. M. Landis, M.D., of Jefferson Medical College and Phipps Institute, in the study of auscultation, recording of body temperatures and other physico-medical problems. This resulted in the development of a new type of electro-stethoscope. He also investigated, in collaboration with F. M. Huntoon, M.D., the effect of high hydrostatic pressures on micro-organisms and devised a new method of manufacturing vaccines based upon these results.

Ballantine formulated the theory of the vertical radio aerial operated above its fundamental frequency, and showed that the effective power could be doubled and a better vertical distribution obtained by operating at about 2.5 times the fundamental frequency. The majority of broadcasting stations adopted this method with "vertical radiators," and in recognition of his work, the Elliott Cresson Gold Medal of the Franklin Institute was awarded to him in 1934.

In 1929, in collaboration with H. A. Snow, Ballantine devised the "variable-mu" (or "remote cut-off") principle of vacuum-tube construction in which the grid is given a variable pitch. This eliminated to a large extent cross-talk and modulation distortion in radio broadcast receivers and prevented overloading the first tube in the set.

Used in millions of tubes since then, this principle has been universally applied.

Also active in the field of electro-acoustics, Ballantine in 1928 announced the discovery of large errors in the calibration of condenser microphones due to diffraction (obstacle effect) and cavity resonance. He proposed the "free field" method of calibration, which supplanted the older methods; also a new technique of calibration called the "method of three electrophones," based on the reciprocity principle, which is replacing the older thermophone method. For this and other developments the Institute of Radio Engineers in 1931 presented him with the Liebmann Memorial Prize for "outstanding theoretical and experimental investigations of numerous acoustical and electrical devices." He was elected president of the Institute for 1935.

Working again in the acoustical field, he developed for the Army Air Corps a throat-type microphone which was the first to be tested and standardized for use in United States military airplanes. This microphone picks up the voice sounds directly from the larynx and replaces the conventional hand-held aerial type; in this way it frees the pilot's or bombardier's hands for more important duties, permits the use of oxygen masks and excludes engine and propeller noises. Seven patents were granted him on this device. Developed long before Pearl Harbor, thousands of these throat-type microphones performed useful service in World War II.

Indicating his wartime activity, Ballantine reported: "During the past ten years I have been independently engaged in the invention and development of a method of detecting distant objects by radio wave reflection, especially as applied to an absolute altimeter for aircraft."

Ballantine was a fellow of the Institute of Radio Engineers, American Physical Society, Acoustical Society of America, a member of the American Institute of Electrical Engineers, American Association for the Advancement of Science, Radio Club of America and the Franklin Institute. His publications included one book and more than fifty papers on scientific subjects. About thirty patents were issued to him. Technically and electrically with engineering skill, he contributed much to the refinement and efficiency of radio without fanfare and dramatic strokes. When Ballantine passed away at the age of forty-six, a fellow engineer remarked, "Radio has lost a brilliant, mathematical physicist, a superb engineer, capable, original, as keen and analytical as they come."

Clarence Weston Hansell

RADIO TRANSMITTER DESIGNER

BORN: January 20, 1898
Medaryville, Ind.

CLARENCE W. HANSELL has more than 400 inventions which attest his great activity as a radio engineer—a total of 260 United States patent applications, 640 foreign patent applications, 190 United States patents issued, of which at least 42 relate to inventions which have gone into commercial use, while others have additional promise of commercial usefulness.

Graduating from high school in Medaryville, Indiana, in 1915, Hansell enrolled at Purdue University and completed the course in 1919 with a B.S. degree. At Union College he took postgraduate work in electrical engineering while employed in the test-training course of the General Electric Company at Schenectady. It was with GE that his career in radio engineering had its start.

On September 1, 1920, Hansell became a member of the RCA Engineering Department, specializing in long-distance communication on both long and short waves. His work encompassed radio relaying, directive transmitting aerials, methods of frequency control, radiotelephony and numerous phases of development which greatly enhanced the efficiency of world-wide communication, broadcasting and television.

For a time he was in charge of the commercial factory tests of the Alexanderson alternator equipment with which RCA established its world-wide radiotelegraph service in 1920. He directed the placing of some of this equipment in operation at the New Brunswick, New Jersey, transoceanic station.

A year later he designed the aerial-ground system for the RCA Rocky Point station, saving the station from threatened failure caused by high-ground resistivity. He managed the acceptance tests on the equipment, made the initial adjustments and placed the two original installations of alternators and aerials in operation at that station. In co-operation with other engineers, Hansell in 1922 developed and installed at Rocky Point the first vacuum-tube transmitter ever used to handle transoceanic radiotelegraph commercial service. Soon after, he assisted engineers of the Western Electric Company in developing, at Rocky Point, the first commercial transoceanic telephone transmitter.

In 1923-24, Hansell developed a single side-band radio relay station at Belfast, Maine, for receiving long-wave signals from Europe and for relaying by radio to Riverhead, Long Island, and New York. He then began short-wave transmitter and directive transmitting aerial development for RCA and in 1923-24 with S. W. Dean he set up and operated one of the first transmitters to utilize piezo-electric quartz-crystal frequency control.

Hansell moved to the RCA transoceanic transmitting station on Long Island in 1925 and established the Rocky Point Laboratory of RCA Laboratories, on the staff of which were many well-known radio engineers.

In the first year of the Rocky Point Laboratory, Hansell with George L. Usselman,[1] developed a 15-meter vacuum-tube transmitter and established the first short-wave circuit to handle commercial

[1] Born November 27, 1888, at Sylvania, Indiana; graduated with a B.S. degree in electrical engineering from Kansas State College, 1916, Usselman became a student engineer for General Electric in 1916-19 and joined the Radio Department of GE in 1919. He joined RCA in 1920 as transmitter research engineer. He has more than 150 inventions disclosed; 78 United States patents issued.

traffic over very long distances in daylight. For about two years this installation handled nearly all the daytime traffic from Europe and the United States to South America. The transmitter, costing about $15,000, employing 7 kilowatts at 20 megacycles and a 20-foot aerial, gave commercial service to South America, whereas the 200-kilowatt Alexanderson alternators with aerials 400 feet high and 1.5 miles long, costing about $1,500,000, found it difficult to provide a commercial service to South America, chiefly because of static on the long wavelengths.

Hansell and Usselman added frequency modulation to a short-wave transmitter in 1925 and used it in commercial service to reduce the effects of fading. In 1927 frequency modulation was applied to the chain of successively higher-power amplifiers of short-wave transmitters, thereby eliminating tremendous difficulties with instability and parasitic oscillations which had been characteristic of short-wave transmitters up to that time. Additional frequency modulators were developed in 1929 and in following years. On July 31, 1931, "FM" was used to transmit a ringside account of the Sharkey-Schmelling fight to Manila after amplitude modulation failed because of noise.

Throughout the thirties Hansell with his associates continued radio propagation investigations, development work on short-wave systems, directive aerials, magnetrons and the application of water-cooled tubes as well as a radio relay system to handle communications, including television and facsimile.

In looking forward to the future it seems clear that we have only just begun the era of radio-frequency power [said Hansell]. It is only a matter of time until not only industry, but every housewife will use radio-frequency power as freely as 60-cycle power is used today.

Not only are there limitless new applications to be anticipated, but services already in existence are due for a thorough technical overhauling. By the end of the war it will have been nearly 20 years since there have been any startling changes in the technical features of equipment now used both for radiotelegraphy and standard frequency broadcasting. From the research engineer's point of view these businesses have gone to seed and are due to be replanted.[2]

Russell Harrison Varian

ONE OF THE KLYSTRON BOYS

BORN: April 24, 1898
Washington, D.C.

RUSSELL H. VARIAN was awarded the honorary degree of Doctor of Engineering from Brooklyn Polytechnic Institute in 1943 "for his work on the development and leadership in the expansion and improvement of the klystron," an electron tube which produces extremely short wavelengths.

Klystron is from the Greek word for the "breaking of waves on a beach." That is what the electrons do in the klystron; they break up traveling at the rate of 25,000 miles a second!

To Russell's younger brother Sigurd Fergus[1] goes the credit for anticipating the need for a reliable blind-landing or radio-guiding beam, which he foresaw when he was a flight captain for Pan-American Airways on the Mexican and Central American air lanes.

This, therefore, is the story of two men in one, in fact, "three men and a tube," for to the Varian team is added Dr. William Webster Hansen,[2] associate professor of physics at Leland Stanford University, who collaborated with the "Klystron Boys" on the project; he made electrons dance the rhumba inside a "copper apple" which is the nucleus of the klystron.

Russell is described as deliberate and patient; Sigurd as nervous and dynamic. Their father, John Osborne Varian, a masseur born in Dublin, was married in Ireland to Agnes Dixon. They migrated to California.

---

[2] Statement prepared for presentation at RCA Laboratories April 21, 1943.
[1] Born May 4, 1901, Syracuse, N.Y.
[2] Born May 27, 1909, Fresno, Calif.

Russell obtained a scientific background at Stanford where he worked his way through the School of Physics by doing odd jobs in the laboratories and by helping professors with their lawns and gardens. He was graduated with a B.A. degree in 1925 and after obtaining his master's degree in 1927, he worked on geophysical surveys for the Humboldt Oil Company in Texas and later joined the Farnsworth Radio and Television Corporation, 1930-32. Sigurd did not go to college, for he was too anxious to learn to fly after finishing at a polytechnic school in San Luis Obispo, California.

Back in California to dream up their big idea for generating and projecting an invisible beam along which planes might fly with safety, the Varian brothers took up residence in the little village of Halcyon, their old home town. Once the idea began to take practical form their need for a physics laboratory, tools and machine shop became apparent. They decided to go to Palo Alto with hopes of making arrangements to use Stanford's physics laboratory. There they contacted Dr. David L. Webster, head of the Physics Department, who let them use the laboratory and model shop as research associates without pay. Numerous experiments followed, which finally led Russell Varian and Dr. Hansen to develop a design based upon "the velocity grouping principle." Sigurd built the apparatus —a neat little five-pound machine—and it worked! It oscillated!

By mere chance, H. Hugh Willis, chief research engineer of the Sperry Gyroscope Company, accompanied by two officials of the Civil Aeronautics Authority, arrived at the Oakland Airport when the magic "beam maker" was ready for demonstration and were invited to see the new gadget. No longer was finance a problem— the "three men and a tube" became connected with Sperry Gyroscope and were established in a small laboratory in San Carlos under the direction of William Cooke.[3] This laboratory was subsequently moved east and was consolidated in another Sperry laboratory.

When the Varians' discovery was announced late in 1939, the klystron was front-page news. The M.I.T. *Technological Review*

[3] Later research director in charge of radio in Sperry's Garden City (L.I.) Laboratory.

acclaimed it as "the most important advance in radio since the invention of the audion tube in 1906 by Lee De Forest." It was described as an ultra-high-frequency resonator, nicknamed "the rhumbatron" because it made electrons dance at terrific speed yet with a rhythmic motion. The invisible beam it projects is "as straight as a sunbeam" and as such was quickly recognized as possessing untold possibilities for use in aviation, in electric power transmission by radio, telephony, television and other branches of communication. News stories told how the klystron would enable airplanes to take off and land automatically. With radio beams projected ahead, the pilot would be warned of mountains or other obstructions in the path of the plane; shot downward they would tell him how far above the ground he was flying. War came, and the klystron became an instrument of war. Military secrecy shrouded its activity.

Charles Jacob Young
PRINTED BY RADIO

BORN: December 17, 1899
    Cambridge, Mass.

CHARLES J. YOUNG as a wireless amateur in 1913 was inspired by his father, Owen D. Young, who posed the problem of using a radio machine to print a radio-facsimile newspaper in the home. Specifically this is what he proposed:

"I want a great camera arranged with a lens in London and a plate in New York, so that when the London *Times* goes on the streets five hours earlier than the morning papers here, the 20 sheets may be held up singly in front of the lens and, with a click for each sheet, be transmitted to New York, so that I may find a copy of the London *Times* waiting with the New York papers on my breakfast table."

Laconically, Dr. Alfred N. Goldsmith, who was sitting next to

Mr. Young at dinner when he first flung this challenge at the engineers, remarked, "It's a fine thing to have an imagination wholly unrestrained by any knowledge of fundamental facts."

Charles Young tackled the problem and became an expert in the field. From Hackley School at Tarrytown, New York, he enrolled at Harvard where he followed the radio trail by specializing in physics and taking all of the radio courses then being given by Professor George W. Pierce and Professor Emory L. Chaffee. Graduating with a B.A. degree in 1921, he took postgraduate work in electrical engineering at the Harvard Engineering School.

With this training as a springboard, Young joined the radio engineering staff of the General Electric Company in 1922, where he became interested in studio acoustics, microphone development, the application of super-regeneration and power-line "broadcasting." But at this point his father's challenge to flash a page of the *Times* of London to New York shifted his career to radio facsimile.

When Young joined the RCA staff in 1930, he clung to radio facsimile as his specialty and continued to study and to develop it from many angles. In 1942 he was appointed a research supervisor of RCA Laboratories at Princeton, New Jersey. Whenever he was seen in the Laboratories, always there was a facsimile machine not far from his elbow, rolling off a printed message, diagram or picture.

Facsimile had a difficult time getting started and in winning a following; it lacked the mass appeal and usefulness of broadcasting and television in the home. Further, it always seemed to have some "bugs" to be ironed out. But in 1943 Young, who must be admired for his perseverance, remarked, "My later work on high-speed facsimile recording by chemical methods may be particularly important because it gets nearer to the speed needed to 'zip' a newspaper."

Allen Balcom DuMont

SKILLED IN ELECTRONICS

BORN: January 29, 1901
Brooklyn, N.Y.

ALLEN B. DUMONT, development engineer specializing in radio and cathode-ray tubes and oscilloscopes, naturally found his way into television. From 1920 to 1924, he was a student at Rensselaer Polytechnic Institute and received the degree of Electrical Engineer, after which he was employed by the Westinghouse Lamp Company at Bloomfield, New Jersey, and later was in charge of production of radio receiving tubes. He applied for a number of patents on improvements in tubes and in manufacturing equipment.

Employed from 1928 to 1931 by the De Forest Radio Company at Passaic, New Jersey, as chief engineer, DuMont designed and had built under his supervision factory equipment to greatly increase production, exceeding 30,000 tubes a day. In 1931 he organized the DuMont Laboratories in New Jersey, and turned his attention to development of cathode-ray tubes for use in oscillographs and other electrical instruments, including television. He is credited with invention of the radio receiver's cathode-ray visual-tuning indicator, or "magic eye," which is wide open when a station is out of tune, but narrows to a thin slit when the point of exact tuning is reached.

With a "passion for accuracy and a transcendent belief in the future," DuMont described his work in 1943 as "precision electronics." For use in World War II, he reported development of a cyclograph—"a precision electronic device that can locate, analyze and sort metals according to their physical properties, revealing previously unattainable information with lightning speed and without damage to precision metal parts."

276

Harry Ferdinand Olson

AN AUTHORITY ON SOUND

BORN: *December 28, 1902*
Mt. Pleasant, Iowa

HARRY F. OLSON took up sound as his stock in trade and became an authority on acoustics, particularly as applied to radio. He had his early schooling at Olds, Iowa, and then went to the University of Iowa where he majored in physics and was graduated in 1924; a year later he achieved his M.S. degree; in 1928 his Ph.D.; and in 1932 his E.E. He joined RCA Laboratories in 1928. His numerous articles on sound, including three textbooks, *Applied Acoustics*, *Elements of Acoustical Engineering* and *Dynamical Analogies*, rank high in the literature on the subject. He has lectured on sound engineering at Columbia University.

Olson won fame in radio for his invention of the velocity-type microphone, widely used by broadcasting stations and in public-address systems. He pioneered in development of directional microphones, including the most commonly used uni-directional and the varacoustic microphones. He also developed the long-pointed, ultra-directional microphone designed to pick up sound from a particular direction, or to focus on certain sections of orchestras or parades without picking up extraneous sounds.

Olson also developed various types of loud-speakers, ranging from the shoulder-strap personal radio set's loud-speaker, which is the size of a silver dollar, to huge systems weighing hundreds of pounds and capable of handling kilowatts of input. He pioneered in the development of wide-range and high fidelity loud-speakers.

In addition, he carried out many developments in other fields of acoustics and vibrating systems—for example: the reverberation time bridge, phonograph pick-ups, supersonics, mechanical filters and acoustic networks. His acoustic stethoscope covers a wide range of frequencies enabling doctors to hear many sounds they never heard before.

The Second World War put new demands upon Olson's time, and he concentrated on acoustical systems as applied to warfare on land, sea and in the air.

Olson's sanctum sanctorum in the RCA Laboratories at Princeton is known as the "free field sound room." As such, it is one of the most unique ever built—a room three stories high with the suspended floor a lattice-steel grated platform resting on rubber pads; the walls are lined with heavy baffles, or curtains, of ozite, so that absolutely no extraneous sounds of any kind are heard. Spoken words in that odd and eerie room sound as if you are going under ether, as a visitor described the sensation—no echoes, no reflections, no resonance, no sounds of any kind, except those exactly as uttered. This uncanny realm of Olson's does for sound what a dark room does for light, and in it he has been able to develop new microphones and loud-speakers. So true is the room to sound that a measurement made in it one day can be made exactly the same a year later.

Browder Julian Thompson

EXCELLED IN ELECTRON TUBES

BORN: *August 14, 1904*
 Roanoke, La.

B. J. THOMPSON, radio research specialist in vacuum tubes, has contributed much to shaping keys that open gateways into the future of radio. He attended elementary school at Lake Charles, Louisiana, and public schools in Minot, North Dakota. From the University of Washington (Seattle) he was graduated in 1925 with the degree of B.S. in Electrical Engineering, in which he did postgraduate work.

"When I was six years old," said Thompson, "electrical toys

made me decide to become an electrical engineer. Later I had another ambition—I wanted to work in the General Electric Research Laboratory. While I was at the University of Washington a GE man scouting for young engineers opened the way for me."

Joining the Research Laboratory of General Electric at Schenectady in 1926, he remained until 1931, the last two years in charge of a group conducting research and development on radio receiving tube problems. In June, 1931, he was placed in charge of the research section of the Research and Engineering Department of the Radiotron Division of RCA at the Harrison, New Jersey, plant. In 1940 he was associate director of the research laboratory, and when RCA Laboratories were opened at Princeton, New Jersey, in 1942, Thompson moved there as associate director of general research.

Throughout the period from 1926 into the forties, "BJ" did research and development on broadcast receiving tubes, ultra-high-frequency receiving and transmitting tubes, as well as electron tubes for industrial applications. He directed work in the field of television tubes, and contributed much to original studies of amplifiers and radio-electron tube theory and design.

Thompson was awarded the Morris Liebmann Memorial Prize by the I.R.E. in 1936, for "contributions to development of ultra-high-frequency tubes." From his analysis of the fundamental frequency limitations of the conventional type of tube, he worked out a new conception of mechanical and electrical design which would permit the operation of tubes at ultra-high frequencies. The "acorn" tube was the result of this research. It extended the useful radio frequency range far beyond previous practical possibilities.

"In the ultra-short wave field we have no time to sit and think," said Thompson. "The demands for new tubes are ever so great. And this is evidenced by the fact that the monthly demand for acorn-size tubes has reached magnitudes which we never thought would be reached in a year."

As he moved around a table covered with an assortment of electron tubes, he picked up an Iconoscope and said, "We can look forward to much more sensitive tubes of this type—so sensitive as television 'eyes' that it will be possible to pick up the last quarter of a football game even on a dark rainy day. We may also expect quite a change in television receivers and at moderate costs."

With that statement Thompson turned to a television receiver, pulled up a retractable screen on the front and showed a clear picture eighteen by twenty-four inches, as broadcast from the NBC transmitter atop the Empire State Building. Then he explained, "This is a prewar model that uses a small projection tube. The picture on its face is projected by lenses to the mirror and on to the translucent screen. It employs the techniques and a system of optics of 1941 . . . prior to Pearl Harbor. But it reveals what may be expected based upon wartime developments which will make it so much better and economically reasonable."

Then modestly, as if he had caught himself talking outside of his field, he added, "I'm just a tube man."

Brilliant in his analysis of phenomena related to the control of electrons, Thompson won high esteem in the realm of science as one of the country's most capable young men in research related to electron tubes. The war made great demands upon his time, and in 1944, he became associated with the War Department as a civilian consultant. While on a flight in a plane over occupied territory in Italy on July 8, 1944, he was reported missing.

Philo Taylor Farnsworth

LINKED HIS NAME WITH TELEVISION

BORN: *August 19, 1906*
Beaver, Utah

PHILO TAYLOR FARNSWORTH, specialist in cathode-ray tubes as applied to television, first became interested in electricity through a farm lighting system and its electric motors. Popular magazines told him of "such a thing called television," and he linked his life work to it.

Farnsworth was described by a friend as "an omnivorous reader of scientific literature." While at Rigby (Idaho) High School, 1921-22, he delved into the molecular theory of matter, electrons, the Einstein theory, automobile engines, model airplanes and chemistry. He went to Glens Falls, Idaho, in 1923 as electrician on a railroad; then to Provo, Idaho, to work in a machine shop. He attended high school at Provo in the fall of 1923 and devoted spare time to study in the library maintained by Brigham Young University. In 1924 he enrolled in the University, but at the end of the second year his father died and young Farnsworth left college to help support the family. He entered the radio business at Salt Lake City as a serviceman, but the shop failed and he went to work in the railroad yards.

To Farnsworth, television was still "a day-dream, a day-dream only." He had no laboratory or facilities for research or money to buy equipment. One day in applying for a job in connection with the Salt Lake City Community Chest campaign, he met Leslie Gorrell and George Everson of San Francisco, who were conducting the drive. Farnsworth was hired. As the men became acquainted it was natural that they should learn about television from the young man. That was a turning point. Everson agreed to finance the idea.

A laboratory was set up in Los Angeles. In October, 1926, with additional financial assistance, they established the Crocker Research Laboratories in San Francisco "to take all the moving parts out of television." The idea conceived in 1922 was brought to a practical result in 1927 when a sixty-line image of a dollar sign was the first image Farnsworth transmitted. The company was reorganized as Television Laboratories, Inc.; and later, in May, 1929, was renamed Farnsworth Television, Inc., of California.

Farnsworth's first application for a television patent covering a complete electronic system, including a dissector tube, was made

January 7, 1927. The dissector was used to scan the image for transmission. At the receiver an oscillite tube reproduced the picture. An electron multiplier tube, which Farnsworth called a "multipactor," increased the sensitivity of the dissector. In 1931 he moved his experiments to Wyndmoor, near Philadelphia.

The Farnsworth Radio and Television Corporation was organized in 1938 with headquarters at Fort Wayne, Indiana, with E. A. Nicholas as president, and Farnsworth as director of research. His numerous patents, associated with the idea of converting an optical image into an electrical image, deal with cathode-ray tubes, electrical scanners, amplifier tubes, photoelectric materials and electron multipliers.

"It is an intriguing art," remarked Farnsworth. "Why, it is difficult for me to make an accurate guess as to what originally got me started. I believe I had decided before I was twelve that I could be an inventor."

Joseph Lyman

APPLIED RADIO TO AIR NAVIGATION

BORN: *August 26, 1906*
Northampton, Mass.

JOSEPH LYMAN was a licensed radio amateur at the age of 12, entering the field at a time when short waves and ultra-short waves were beckoning experimenters to follow these lines of development. Aviation rapidly coming to the fore was more in need of radio which was prepared to accept the challenges because of new electron-tube developments. Opening of the high-frequency spectrum cleared the way to give aviation the services it needed—communications, guiding beams, direction finders, radio altimeters, collision-prevention apparatus and navigational aids. Here, in the dovetailing of these two great industries, radio and aviation, was opportunity aplenty for a young man with an aptitude for radio science.

Joseph Lyman and his brother had one of the earliest high-frequency amateur radio stations in the country. They were among the pioneers along the 100-meter, 40-meter and 20-meter waves. Their station 1-KC at Northampton was credited with establishing several distance records in those early days of high radio frequencies. The results of their pioneering were reported in *QST* in 1926.

Lyman continued to explore the ultra-short waves and this led him in 1932 to conduct a series of radio tests with aircraft on the five-meter channel. Assisted by the American Radio Relay League, he organized New England radio amateurs for a series of tests between Boston and New York, in which he talked from the plane with various amateur stations.

Lyman, with many others, realized that one of the great problems in aviation was the avoidance of collision under poor flying conditions. His work as a radio amateur led him to think how radio might be applied to solve the problem. After graduation from Williston Academy in 1926 he attended the University of Michigan and Massachusetts Institute of Technology, and then applied his knowledge to make radio more useful to aviation.

Just as important as his radio work, however, in demonstrating to him the importance of radio in aviation, was his twelve years' flying experience with the United States Marines, two years of which were spent on active duty. He holds a commission as captain in the USMCR. This experience led him directly into his first position with the Sperry Gyroscope Company in February, 1936, as an assistant engineer testing aviation instruments.

Five years later, in February, 1941, a patent (No. 2,231,929) was granted to him for a "novel indicator" described in his specifications as "adapted for use on aircraft either for indicating the direction of approach of other aircraft, thereby to prevent collisions under conditions of poor or zero visibility, or for use on the ground as when locating aircraft for purposes of gun fire control, or for controlling aircraft landings from the ground, and for other purposes."

Lyman, appointed director of aircraft radio navigation research at the Sperry Gyroscope Company in 1943, was put in charge of developing radio aids to navigation and instrument landing equipment.

George Harold Brown

PIONEER IN RADIOTHERMICS

BORN: October 14, 1908
Milwaukee, Wisc.

GEORGE H. BROWN, specialist in radiothermics, helped to kindle the art of radio-frequency heating, including development of the radio-electronic "sewing machine," radio rivet "hammer" and many other appliances. Under his supervision these devices were developed in RCA Laboratories.

Schooled at Green Bay and Portage, Wisconsin, he matriculated at the University of Wisconsin, majored in electrical engineering and was graduated B.S. in 1930. He achieved his M.S. degree in 1931, Ph.D. in 1933 and E.E. in 1942, all at his alma mater.

From 1933 to 1937, Brown was a research engineer on the RCA staff; for a year he operated as a consulting radio engineer, but rejoined RCA Laboratories in 1938. Considered an authority on antennas, he developed many new structures, as well as related equipment. Turning to the television field, he designed the vestigial sideband filter put into use in the NBC television transmitter atop the Empire State Building.

Among Brown's antenna developments was the "Top Hat," a structure added to the upper end of a number of existing broadcast antenna radiators to decrease fading of the signals. He also originated a turnstile antenna for use with frequency modulation transmitters and a short-wave antenna, widely used with police transmitters.

Brown was very active as a pioneer in the field of "radiothermics."

He directed the work of applying radio-frequency power to the case-hardening of steel, annealing of brass, thermosetting of glue, bonding of thermoplastic materials and drying problems.

A few of the many possible fields in which radiothermic equipment can be used are: heating, drying, gluing, case-hardening, annealing, riveting, welding, melting of rare metals and deactivating enzymes in foods to be dehydrated. In the processing of laminated wooden propellers for aircraft, heat is required to set the adhesive. Radio-frequency heating accomplishes this in minutes instead of the hours required by ordinary steam and pressure processes.

The use of radio high-frequency "furnaces" or "ovens" is being extended to speed and improve hundreds of drying operations. In them railroad ties may be seasoned and "cakes" of textiles dried quickly and uniformly. Rubber may be "radio-cemented" to wood or plastic; thermoplastic "cloth" seamed by radio heat; plastics "cooked" to molded perfection; plywood "tacked"; and fresh vegetables deactivated without loss of food value, flavor or color.

Inspired by a newspaper story reporting urgent wartime need for speeding the process of penicillin production, Brown and his associates, Cyril N. Hoyler and R. A. Bierwirth at RCA Laboratories, applied radiothermics to the problem. Since radio frequency-drying provides a continuous process in the manufacturing procedure, their efforts were remarkably successful. The method of dehydration which they developed is lower in cost than the conventional freeze-drying.

Radiothermics is one of the new fields of radio which possess great promise. Application of radio-frequency heating to accelerate and improve industrial processes, reduce costs and create better results is rapidly coming into use. Many industrial products of the future will be cooked, and baked, tempered, welded, dried, melted, seamed and laminated by means of radio heat.

Of radio's 100 men of science forty-six were born in the United States. Eighteen others came from foreign lands to seek freedom and opportunity under the Stars and Stripes; the majority, including Tesla, Pupin, Steinmetz, Alexanderson and Zworykin, became naturalized American citizens. In America they found encouragement, recognition of their talents and reward for their achievements. As pioneers and creators they contributed to the advance of civilization.

There must remain in the United States the opportunity for an Edison, the opportunity for any youth with initiative, resourcefulness, practicality, and vision, to create in his own name and by his own efforts new things that will tend to make this country vigorous and strong and safe. . . . We seek in the United States something beyond mere mechanical efficiency; we seek a society in which initiative and talent may have an outlet, and in which the individual may have opportunity. . . . In particular, opportunity for the individual creator, for the industrial pioneer, for the inventor with vision and practicality should not be lost; and the atmosphere of our industrial life should be favorable for his efforts in our behalf. . . .

If we are wise there will be, in the future, many Edisons in the United States. They may not shine with his peculiar brilliance, but they will add to the well-being of the nation a necessary element which can be added in no other way. Their opportunity must be preserved open before them.[1]

Today the shadows of early wireless and its pioneers are lengthening. Since Marconi's first signal the evolution of radio has covered almost half a century. The world of radio is swinging back to the very short waves which Hertz and Marconi used in the beginning. They and their predecessors, with the equipment and knowledge then at hand, had but one choice if they were to gain quick results and prove the practicability of wireless—that one choice was to harness the long waves.

Scientists who followed them have turned the tide back to the high-frequency spectrum. With development of new electron tubes, the tiny waves measured in centimeters have come into their own again, far surpassing in achievements the dreams of the pioneers.

Out of the Second World War, scientists march into the boundless realm of microwaves in which radio is used not only for signaling

[1] Dr. Vannevar Bush, president of Carnegie Institute and director of the Office of Scientific Research and Development, speaking before the American Institute of Electrical Engineers when awarded the Edison Medal for 1943.

but for new applications of communication, including television, facsimile, collision prevention, navigation, radiothermics and various other industrial services.

The Columbuses, Marco Polos, Cabots and Daniel Boones of radio have long since passed in the procession of shadows. New explorers are pioneering; they are charting new trails—microwave trails—into the future across the wondrous horizon of radio. Theirs is the heritage to keep alive the spirit of the pioneers—to continue onward, to achieve new triumphs that will serve the world and thereby unfold the saga of Radio's Second 100 Pioneers in Science.

> The barriers are not yet erected which can say to aspiring genius: "Thus far and no further."
>
> —Beethoven

INDEX

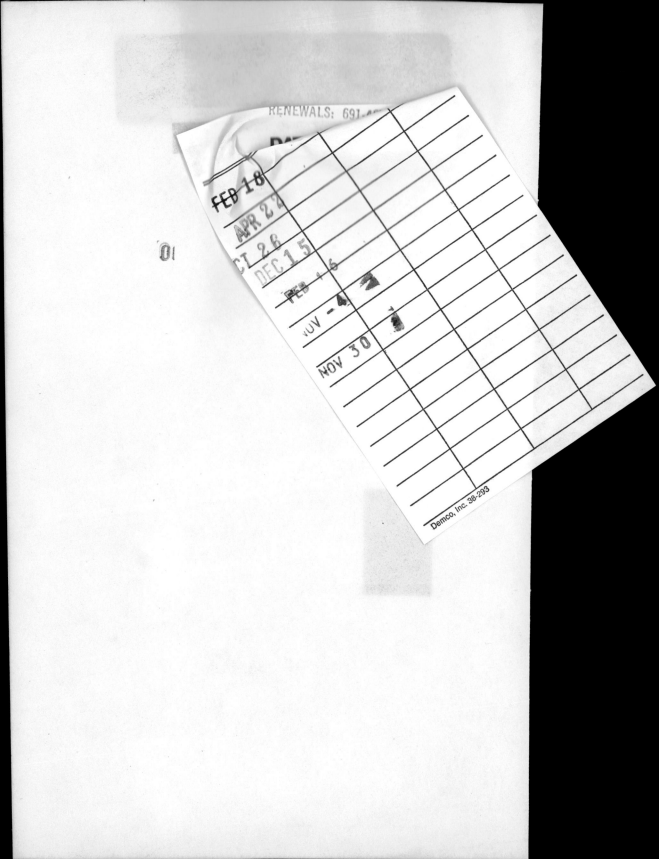